# MARKED FOR DEATH

**James Hamilton-Paterson** is the author of the bestselling *Empire of the Clouds,* a classic account of the golden age of British aviation. He won a Whitbread Prize for his first novel, *Gerontius.* He lives in Austria.

# JAMES HAMILTON-PATERSON

# MARKED FOR DEATH

## THE FIRST WAR IN THE AIR

HEAD
of ZEUS

First published in Great Britain in 2015 by Head of Zeus Ltd

A catalogue record for this book is available from the British Library.

1 3 5 7 9 10 8 6 4 2

ISBN (hb) 9781784970390
ISBN (e) 9781784970383

Typeset by e-type, Aintree, Liverpool

Printed and bound in Germany
by GGP Media GmbH, Pössneck

Head of Zeus Ltd
Clerkenwell House
45–47 Clerkenwell Green
London EC1R 0HT

WWW.HEADOFZEUS.COM

'Every man who went aloft was marked for death, sooner or later, once his wheels had left the ground.'

—Anthony Fokker

# CONTENTS

—— •—— ——

To Chris Royle, with grateful thanks

# AUTHOR'S NOTE

There are several scholarly histories of the Royal Flying Corps and the first war in the air, all of which treat the subject chronologically. I have chosen a less exhaustive approach by means of chapters dealing with aspects that particularly interest me – such as the medical issues of flying, how aircrew were chosen and behaved, and the relationship between the design of early aircraft and the tasks the military increasingly demanded of them. I hope by this means to give a vivid overall sense of the air war, together with its consequences for the aviation age that followed it.

In each of the chapters I have tried to preserve a rough sort of chronology. However, from time to time readers may find it helpful to refer to the Chronology on p.311 that puts some of the aviation milestones into a timeline of events on the wider battlefield in Europe and beyond.

This book does not pretend to be any sort of comprehensive survey of the hundreds of different aircraft types the various combatants flew during the war. This has already been admirably done in the specialist literature.

# INTRODUCTION

———

Scarcely ten years after powered aircraft had first left the ground they were pressed into service in the First World War, which consequently also became the world's first-ever air war. Seen from a purely military point of view, aviation in that vast conflict was little more than a highly visible sideshow. Historians generally agree that it had limited influence on the war's outcome, even though by the end it was clearly going to change the nature of warfare and ensure its own future. Air power developed to have a decisive strategic function in the Second World War and thereafter was destined to reign supreme down to the present day, when air dominance above a conflict is considered essential.

Out of the 65 million men mobilised between 1914 and 1918 by the Allies and the Central Powers combined, it is now generally estimated that some 9 million were killed outright and 21 million wounded. Even allowing for the first-ever air war's restricted dimensions, the toll it took of flying men was minuscule compared to that of the trenches. Nearly lost in the overall statistics are the 6,994 British and Empire aircrew who were casualties on the Western Front between 1914 and 1918 – a figure that includes those killed, wounded, or missing in action.[1] Such statistics are contentious and often vary wildly from source to source, but comparable figures would presumably be true for France and Germany. In all, it is estimated that some 50,000 aircrew died in all the various nations' fledgling air forces – a total that includes many thousands killed in training and accidents. Assuming this to be roughly accurate, it still represents little more than a half of 1 per cent of the war's total combatant deaths. Nevertheless, airmen shared with the infantry an identical 70 per cent chance of injury or death.[2] Flying was an extremely hazardous affair in the First World War.

The grip aviation held on the public's imagination at the time was remarkable. This was partly because flying itself was still a novelty and widely seen as daring and glamorous, and partly because most people understood – and still understand – so little about it and how it was used in the war. Newspaper coverage at the time did much to promote this ignorance by tending to concentrate on the air 'aces', whereby a handful of particularly successful combat pilots were singled out for propaganda purposes to become bemedalled national heroes. This system was clearly an instinctive response to the wholesale slaughter of the infantry battles. It promoted publicly visible examples of individual heroism, gallantry and self-sacrifice. But it also promoted a myth that has endured to the present day. The impression took hold that pilots in the air above the trenches were conducting a throwback to a 'cleaner' sort of war: gladiatorial, personal, even romantic. This careful skewing of reality has made it easy for later generations to retain a very limited and trivialised version of the first war in the air and, indeed, to misunderstand its significance ever since.

The example of Manfred von Richthofen, the war's top-scoring fighter ace (with a tally of eighty victims of whom fifty-four were downed in flames), offers a case in point. Until the last months before the Armistice no airman other than observation balloon crews wore a parachute in the First World War, and fire was the chief nightmare that haunted them awake and asleep. During his pre-eminence Richthofen became known as 'The Red Baron' partly because he actually was a baron and partly from his later affectation of flying an all-red aircraft. In recent decades this nickname has been appropriated for films, a pizza chain and a motorbike franchise, as well as for arcade and video games (one internet advertisement reads 'Fly your biplane in air battles of the First World War and defeat the Red Baron...!'). The jokey title of Britain's early seventies TV comedy series *Monty Python's Flying Circus* was also a direct reference to the nickname given to the 'Jasta' formations in which Richthofen flew. Probably the most extreme example of this stone-cold killer being tamed into a cuddly fantasy is afforded by the comic-strip dog Snoopy, who now and then sits atop his kennel pretending to fight the Red Baron, wearing a leather flying helmet and goggles with a scarf blowing behind him in an imaginary slipstream. There are even stuffed toys of Snoopy in this guise. This is surely one of the strangest trajectories in all contemporary myth, stretching as it does directly from a modern child's bedroom back to a war in which many a nineteen-year-old victim of Richthofen, his flying gear soaked in petrol, fell wrapped in flame from 8,000 feet, trailing smoke and screaming for the thirty-odd seconds it took him to hit the ground. Richthofen once observed: 'When I have shot down an Englishman my passion for the hunt is satisfied for fifteen minutes.'

A similar conversion of the horror and agony of aerial warfare into near-jocularity can be followed in what happened in Britain to the fictional character of 'Biggles' or Major James Bigglesworth, RFC, the creation of W. E. Johns. Having served in the trenches on two fronts, Gallipoli and Salonika, Johns retrained as a pilot with the Royal Flying Corps and by 1918 was in France flying two-seater Airco (de Havilland) 4 bombers with 55 Squadron out of Azelot, near Nancy. In D.H.4s the main fuel tank was between the two cockpits and very likely to be hit by an attacker aiming for either the pilot or the observer. On 16th September 2nd Lieutenant Johns and his observer, 2nd Lieutenant A. E. Amey, were shot down over the German lines. By some miracle the machine did not catch fire even though, as Johns described it later, it was trailing a grey plume of petrol vapour and 'my cockpit was swimming in the stuff'.[3] Amey was killed in the attack. Johns crash-landed in a belt of trees and was knocked unconscious. On coming round he was told by his captors he was to be executed: his aircraft had been mis-identified as one that had bombed a village Sunday School some days earlier, killing many children. He was saved from death only by the timely intervention of the pilots who had shot him down and he was harshly interned for the remaining months of the war.

In early 1932 Johns became the editor of a new monthly magazine, *Popular Flying*. For its April edition he published his first story featuring the fictional Biggles in order to tell British readers what war flying was really like, drawing on his own experiences in the Army, the RFC and the RAF. He did this partly to offset the absurdly US-centric accounts of the air war in imported American pulp magazines, and partly as a corrective to what he saw as Europe's gradual slide towards another war facilitated by mythologised memories of the previous one. Johns's hard-hitting editorials warning the government of Britain's unpreparedness for air war and Nazi Germany's ever-expanding Luftwaffe were eagerly and widely read, although little welcomed in Whitehall.

From the start *Popular Flying* was a great success and Johns wrote sundry more stories about Biggles that became a feature in themselves. Almost from the first they attracted the attention of a children's editor who spotted Biggles's potential as a pilot hero of boys' adventure fiction, and Johns duly became a children's author even as he went on writing editorials and technical articles about aviation for his magazine. Given the period, Johns's hero was remarkably un-jingoistic. Biggles consistently condemned war, was often cynical about authority and officialdom, and was not chauvinistic about the enemy pilots he flew against unless they had first earned his moral condemnation. This was probably a fair rendering of attitudes that prevailed among airmen, who by 1918 were frequently nihilistic and sometimes downright mutinous. One early story for *Popular Flying* had Biggles suffering from burnout and combat fatigue, often close to tears and hitting the whisky bottle before flying on early morning patrols. The description fits exactly with many

non-fiction accounts (including those by squadron medical officers), and the spectacle would have been all too familiar to
Johns and his contemporaries in a front-line squadron. When
the story was republished in book form the publisher wanted
the whisky removed. Heroes in boys' stories were not allowed to
have a drink problem, no matter how shattered their nerves.
Johns refused, although he did judiciously suppress some of the
other details of life on the front such as airmen's swearing,
whoring and gruesome injuries. Even so, this is hardly a description of a conventional storybook role model:

> a slight, fair-haired, good-looking lad still in his teens but an
> acting flight commander. His deep-set hazel eyes were never
> still and held a glint of yellow fire that somehow seemed out
> of place in a pale face upon which the strain of war, and sight
> of sudden death, had already graven little lines. His hands,
> small and delicate as a girl's, fidgeted continually with the
> tunic fastening at his throat. He had killed a man not six
> hours before. He had killed six men during the past month
> – or was it a year? – he had forgotten. Time had become curi-
> ously telescoped lately. What did it matter, anyway? He knew
> he had to die some time and had long ago ceased to worry
> about it. His careless attitude suggested complete indiffer-
> ence, but the irritating little falsetto laugh which continually
> punctuated his tale betrayed the frayed condition of his
> nerves.[4]

Johns's realistic flying sequences – especially those of combat –
were left as they were and remained the stories' centerpiece. To
judge from other ex-pilots' accounts and reminiscences, they
were entirely accurate. Years later, several pilots who flew in the
Second World War wrote gratefully to him claiming they were
still alive because they had read his stories and had survived by
using some of the tricks of air combat their author had himself
learned the hard way and had passed on to Biggles.[5] Even so,

Johns must inevitably stand accused of having played his part in romanticising the first war in the air: Biggles and his pals did manage to down an awful lot of Huns with remarkably little damage to themselves. Such are the conventions of juvenile fiction. But there is a difference between romanticising and blithe falsification, of which Johns was never guilty, except perhaps in harmlessly affecting for himself as an author the army rank of captain, whereas at the war's end he had actually left the RAF as Pilot Officer Johns (the rank given those who had been 2nd lieutenants in the RFC). Otherwise, in matters that were all-important to him such as war and flying, Johns was firmly on the side of truth.

At the polar opposite, it is difficult to imagine a less accurate rendering of the First World War generally than that portrayed in *Blackadder Goes Forth* (1989), the final six episodes of the BBC's hugely popular TV comedy series. In particular, the fourth episode with Rik Mayall as Lord Flashheart and Adrian Edmondson as Baron von Richthoven [*sic*] is grotesque in its caricature of the airmen of the RFC and the Luftstreitkräfte. Apart from the fatuous antics of all concerned, Captain Blackadder is seen already sporting his RFC 'wings' on his uniform even before his first day of training; and immediately afterwards he is shown impossibly piloting his 'observer', Private Baldrick, in a single-seat S.E.5a fighter. Maybe this pantomime version of war would scarcely matter were it not now apparently taken as having some historical accuracy by those paid to know better. In October 2013 the BBC presenter Jeremy Paxman told the Cheltenham Literary Festival that some schoolteachers were showing their pupils episodes of *Blackadder Goes Forth* as an aid to teaching the First World War. If true, it does explain how some young Britons are encouraged to fall giggling ever further down the international rankings of the uneducated.

Maybe where flying is concerned the more recent Second World War, with its own heavily mythologised aerial warfare (the Battle of Britain, the 'Dam Busters', the Blitz, Pearl Harbor and the Allies' saturation bombing campaign in Germany) has supplanted the previous war by retaining a degree of seriousness. Certainly at the level of popular culture Biggles and his comrades have long since acquired a faintly risible aura, a shorthand for outdated public school chaps indulging in derring-do in antiquated biplanes. If the aircraft themselves earn indulgent smiles it is perhaps because people conflate them to some extent with their earlier counterparts in the 1965 film *Those Magnificent Men in their Flying Machines*. Although this internationally popular British comedy was supposedly set in 1910 and concerned a wholly fictitious air race from London to Paris to prove Britain was 'number one in the air' (very far from the truth, as we shall see), it probably did much to embed an association in the popular imagination between early aviation and comedy. To that extent it was the airborne counterpart to the 1953 film *Genevieve*, an equally farcical story about the London to Brighton veteran car run. To audiences in the new supersonic Jet Age, machines from the dawn of the internal combustion era were deemed funny in themselves. Those spruce, wire and fabric flying contraptions were 'wonderful' but a joke, too, as they puttered about the sky; and so by extension were 'the intrepid bird-men' who flew them. The film's jaunty Ron Goodwin title song and Ronald Searle posters merely set the seal on this image. There is even a brief cross-reference in the script of the *Blackadder* episode to the 1965 film's song. For ever after, this merry fantasy has somehow preserved itself untouched by the grim daily realities of early and wartime flying: of men falling to their deaths through a mile of air because their aircraft had without warning shed a wing at 5,000 feet, or of a pilot blinded by the entrails of his front seat observer who'd been cut in half by shrapnel.

★

The first use of aircraft in war arguably represented the steepest learning curve of any innovation in the history of warfare because it was constantly accelerated by technological advances.

In 1914 little of aerodynamics was well understood. Engines were generally so weak and weight so crucial that a pilot could reduce his chances of getting off the ground in time to clear the trees at the edge of the field simply by donning a heavy sheepskin flying coat. Maximum speeds of fifty or sixty miles an hour were the norm, and in a strong enough headwind it was quite common for an aircraft to fly *backwards* relative to the ground. A mere four years later many fighters could reach more than 200 mph in a dive and altitudes of well over 20,000 feet. They could also be thrown about the sky with g-forces that would have reduced earlier models to instant matchwood. Indeed, the chief strain was increasingly on the humans who flew them, and medical understanding lagged behind the technology, particularly where the effects of altitude, disorientation and g-forces were concerned.

It is perhaps not so strange that when war broke out across Europe in the summer of 1914 none of the armies involved had given much thought to aerial combat as such, although it was widely recognised that aeroplanes had potential for observation. It was, of course, hardly news to the military anywhere that an army's ability to 'see over the hill' could be decisive. In fact the history of airborne observation already stretched back well over a century. In 1794 the newly formed French Compagnie d'Aérostiers had used a balloon for observation at the Battle of Fleurus, when two officers remained aloft in their basket with a telescope for nine hours, dropping notes about the Austrian Army's movements that greatly aided a French victory. Seventy years later balloons were similarly used in the American Civil War; and towards the end of the nineteenth century the British Army in South Africa employed them extensively during the Boer War. But it was generally agreed by the military everywhere that tethered balloons were bulky and inconvenient to deploy in a mobile campaign, dependent on large supplies of hydrogen gas as well as highly vulnerable to wind and weather.

It was therefore possible to see the far more manoeuvrable and independent aeroplane as being potentially useful for spying on enemy movements and maybe even for helping an artillery battery to get its shells on target. But despite H. G. Wells's prophetic 1908 novel *The War in the Air*, the idea of aircraft actually fighting each other remained for a while the stuff of fiction. Most existing aircraft could scarcely lift the extra deadweight of a gun and ammunition, and still less could they safely perform much in the way of evasive manoeuvres. But it was not only their physical limitations in the air that needed to be overcome. Resistance on the ground was also considerable. In 1914 there was no independent air force anywhere. Whatever military air arm did exist was part of a country's army or navy and very firmly under its control. Since armies everywhere tend to be conservative in outlook, high commands mostly viewed the new airborne machines with the deepest scepticism and even disgust.

In 1911 Field Marshal Sir William Nicholson, the Chief of Imperial General Staff, who had taken a few cautious steps to reorganise the British Army after the humiliations of the Boer War, delivered a withering verdict on the subject: 'Aviation is a useless and expensive fad advocated by a few individuals whose ideas are unworthy of attention.' That same year Sir Douglas Haig confidently asserted that 'Flying can never be of any use to the Army.' He may have regretted this dictum the following year when he was soundly beaten in manoeuvres on Salisbury Plain by Lieutenant-General Sir James Grierson, who had made extensive and intelligent use of reconnaissance aircraft. If so, there was little sign of repentance when Haig addressed his officers in 1914: 'I hope none of you gentlemen is so foolish as to think that aeroplanes will be able to be usefully employed for reconnaissance purposes in the air. There is only one way for a commander to get information by reconnaissance, and that is by the use of cavalry.'[6] Four years later he was relying heavily on air support as he began the Battle of Amiens.

Similar dismissive opinions were initially also common in the French and German armies – especially among cavalry officers, an elite caste who bitterly resented the very idea that these noisy, smelly and unreliable new contraptions might usurp their beautiful horses and centuries of glorious tradition. However, as will be seen, the French had already established a clear lead in aeronautics and could field better aircraft backed up by better organisation than anybody else at the time, and there were influential factions in the French Army with an imaginative grasp of aviation's potential in war. Although by September 1914 German aircraft outnumbered French, the German General Staff was for the moment less forward-looking. 'Experience has shown that a real combat in the air such as journalists and romancers have described should be considered a myth. The duty of the aviator is to see, not to fight,' as one of their reports put it.[7]

\*

The ensuing four years of war were to produce as profound a change in military attitudes and strategy as the aircraft themselves were to show in development. By the Armistice in November 1918 cavalry had gone the way of bowmen and it had become an article of faith that domination of the air above the battlefield was henceforth crucial to success. Only fifteen months after the war in Europe had ended Britain's new RAF would intervene decisively in what was then British Somaliland to overthrow the rebellious Dervish leader known as the 'Mad Mullah'. In early 1925 bombing and strafing alone enabled the RAF, without the loss of a single airman, to quell a revolt by tribesmen in Waziristan, today's still-restive borderland between Pakistan and Afghanistan. From that moment on, such policing of the British Empire using aeronautical terrorism (under the bland title of 'air control') was to maintain an unbroken lineage up to and beyond enforcing the 'no-fly zones' in Saddam Hussein's Iraq from 1991.

The extraordinary thing is the speed with which this new order came into being. A mere eleven years after a British Army general had rated aircraft as less useful than horses, the future of air power with global reach was assured and Britain had the world's biggest air force. Exactly how war had driven technology, and then technology war, is worth examining in some detail.

CHAPTER 1

# AIR WAR AND THE STATE

———————

THE DESIGN, MANUFACTURE and supply of aircraft in Britain during the First World War were from time to time critically affected by social and industrial upheaval, as also from the first by political indecision and military rivalries. This needs explaining.

In 1960 Philip Larkin wrote 'MCMXIV': a poem both sentimental and disingenuous, which no doubt explains its popularity. Like a black-and-white period photograph it is full of the tokens of a supposedly immemorial time: old coinage (farthings and sovereigns), enamelled tin advertisements, dusty unmetalled roads, a pre-industrial countryside. Together with its refrain of 'Never such innocence,/Never before or since ... Never such innocence again' it plays to a trope so popular among the English middle classes it has become an article of faith. This is that the high summer of British Imperialism (Durbars, *Pomp and Circumstance* and all) coincided with a secure world of Edwardian certainties that war was about to sweep away abruptly and for ever: the 'watershed' theory of social history. Countless documentary films have pandered to this version by emphasising the exceptionally beautiful summer of 1914, with plenty of grainy old black and white footage showing people swimming and boating beneath skies in which not even a metaphorical cloud was to be seen. The voice-over assures us that prosperity was on the up-and-up in Europe generally and that war was the very last thing on anybody's mind.

The facts are rather different, above all in Britain. By the closing years of Queen Victoria's reign German industrial output had overtaken British and was seen in London as a clear strategic threat. At the turn of the twentieth century both countries embarked on huge naval programmes of submarine- and warship-building, each warily eyeing the other, which doesn't look much like Larkin's 'innocence'. That a national fantasy of Edwardian tranquillity is historical nonsense has never dented its appeal, sedulously reinforced as it has been by popular TV series like *Upstairs, Downstairs* and *Downton Abbey,* complete with butlers, wing collars, parasols and Rolls-Royce landaus drawn up in Mayfair or on scrunchy gravel drives. Larkin explained that for his poem's title he had copied the style adopted on war memorials, so there is no doubting its valedictory intent. It is hard to tell from his poem that he is talking about a largely urban and industrialised country with severe social problems where a third of the population was living in wretched poverty. His version is part of a literary myth fervently believed by the British middle class to this day. Modern students of the period might instead do better to take their cue from Kipling's short poem 'Recessional', which in 1897 caused a stir with its intimation of national weakness and undercurrent of profound unease.

For in reality the years preceding the First World War were a period of increasing social turmoil in Britain. Crucial British industries like steel and shipbuilding had already been overtaken by their counterparts in Germany and the United States. In particular, shipbuilding in Britain had become seriously dysfunctional, where a mass of different craft unions dating from the days of wooden ships led to constant quarrels over demarcation in building the Royal Navy's all-steel dreadnoughts. On Tyneside alone between 1890 and 1893 there was an average of one major strike every month. From then on, strikes throughout industry became increasingly frequent. In 1901, the year of Edward VII's accession, the notorious Taff Vale Judgement (over a strike by a railway union in South Wales) made the government's draconian anti-union stance very clear. It ushered in years of labour unrest until in 1911, the year after the king's death, nearly a million workers nationally were involved in stoppages, totalling a loss of 10,319,591 working days.[8] That year troops had to be sent to quell riots. The passions aroused shocked even a seasoned industrial arbitrator like George Askwith. When the dockers struck in Goole and Hull there was an outbreak of looting and rioting. He later wrote: 'I heard one town councillor remark that he had been in Paris during the [1871] Commune and had never seen anything like this, and he had not known that there were such people in Hull – women with hair streaming and half nude, reeling through the streets, smashing and destroying.'[9]

Nor was the unrest restricted to labour issues. Studies written at the end of the nineteenth century, such as Charles Booth's *Life and Labour in London* (1889), the sociologist Seebohm Rowntree's *Poverty* (1901) and Wilson and Hawarth's *West Ham* (1907), did not shock the enlightened middle classes alone with their detailed descriptions of the disgusting conditions of life in the London slums. They were also read by some of the slum-dwellers themselves, who increasingly decided that their squalid warrens of grimy brick, reeking of urine and excrement, had not after all been ordained by God but were the logical outcome of their inhabitants being treated as expendable coolie labour. Union membership grew and by the summer of 1911 London's East End was restless with discontent. This was the area where the docklands workers lived, and it finally became clear to Westminster that if ever the dockers became organised enough to withdraw their labour all at once, the great Empire's capital city would be crippled. Within four years this was to become a serious threat when East Enders felt themselves completely undefended against German air raids targeting the docks.

In addition there were politically divisive struggles with Irish nationalism and the militant women's suffrage movement that polarised opinion throughout the land. The savage reaction to this last issue by government, police and prison officers culminated in the infamous 'Cat and Mouse Act' in 1913 that further exacerbated ill feelings. In early 1914 the Curragh Mutiny over Irish Home Rule forced the resignation of the Secretary for War, J. E. B. Seely (who as General Jack Seely would lead what was probably history's last great cavalry charge in 1918). On the labour front, between January and July of 1914 there were 937 strikes, including industrial action by the munitions workers at Woolwich Arsenal. Worse still, in addition to the civil war looming in Ireland a General Strike was called for September that was only pre-empted by the timely outbreak of war in August. In short, far from Larkin's roseate innocence prevailing in the land, by the year MCMXIV there was a strong sense of calamity in the air and people up and down Britain were talking nervously of revolutionary fervour in sections of the working class. The fervour may not yet have been truly revolutionary, but it was certainly highly rebellious.

In the context of aviation this increasing social unrest and the questioning of class and political relationships might seem like a mere historical footnote. Quite the reverse, however, since the processes already begun were to have a direct bearing on industrial attitudes, practices and the production of aircraft. Among these were the strikes by women munitions factory workers and popular reaction to the night raids by German Zeppelins and the later Gotha bombers, especially in London. It was public demonstrations of panic and anger at these seemingly unopposed air raids that eventually obliged the government, in the teeth of strenuous opposition from the Army, to withdraw experienced pilots from the battlefront in France in order for them to set up a credible Home Defence force in squadrons based around London. Strikes and go-slows were also to have crippling consequences for the industries supplying the RFC, in particular with its aero engines and armaments. There were times when chronic alcoholism among factory workers as well as widespread drug-taking (chiefly opium and cocaine) had seriously deleterious effects on both the quantity and quality of their output.

*

Well before the war British officialdom had struggled to decide what attitude to take toward the new-fangled flying machines. Nowhere was this more evident than at Farnborough, the home of the Army's Balloon School. In October 1908 the American showman and pioneer aviator, Sam Cody, achieved Britain's first powered flight at Farnborough in an aircraft of his own design. Whitehall's instinctive response to this historic landmark was to order the immediate abandonment of all further work there on aircraft in favour of airships and balloons. Nevertheless, a small section of pioneer aircraft enthusiasts like the Irishman J. W. Dunne continued their work at Farnborough despite the mockery of the favoured 'gasbag aeronauts'. In April 1911 the War Office formed an Air Battalion of Royal Engineers to continue Farnborough's work on observation balloons and man-carrying kites. But by now, two years after Blériot had flown the Channel, glacial shifts in army thinking were at last taking place and the military possibilities offered by aircraft were grudgingly recognised. In May 1912 the Air Battalion became the Royal Flying Corps and any further experimental work with airships and floatplanes was hived off to the Navy. From that moment the Royal Aircraft Factory at Farnborough (confusingly abbreviated at the time as the R.A.F.) became the official government aircraft establishment. The military wing of Britain's air services now comprised the RFC, a Central Flying School for training instructors, a Reserve and the Royal Aircraft Factory, while the naval wing became the Royal Naval Air Service. Traditional inter-service demarcations meant that the RFC and its adjuncts were controlled by the War Office, while the RNAS and its facilities came under the aegis of the Admiralty: an administrative formula that was to prove disastrous.

The new Royal Aircraft Factory was told it would become the sole supplier of aircraft for the Army, whereas the Navy was to be supplied by the private sector. Since late 1909 the Superintendent of the Balloon Factory at Farnborough had been Mervyn O'Gorman, himself an accomplished engineer of considerable

charm and even artistic talent. Given that his employers at the
War Office were still thinking in terms of balloons and cavalry,
he was also remarkably far-sighted. He believed in aircraft; and
in 1910 he set up departments specialising in physics, chemistry
and fabrics, engines and instruments, as well as a main drawing
office. Over the next seven years he staffed these and later
departments with some of the country's ablest technicians and
scientists. He also forged close links with the National Physical
Laboratory at Teddington. From the start he saw that despite its
name, the new Royal Aircraft Factory's most valuable function
was as a centre of aeronautical research and design rather than
as a factory in the conventional sense of mass-producing aircraft.
At the most it would build experimental types and tinker with
them, while any real production would be contracted out to the
private sector. Unlike his bosses O'Gorman had recognised from
the first that the future lay with aircraft rather than balloons and
kites, and accordingly he nurtured and encouraged young pioneers like Geoffrey de Havilland. He was thus in the odd position,
as a War Office appointee, of working to subvert what the Army
believed it wanted in favour of what he knew it needed.

Geoffrey de Havilland had taught himself to fly and had
already built two aircraft to his own designs. With a young
family to support he was now badly strapped for cash and
hoped to impress O'Gorman enough that Farnborough might
buy his latest design and even perhaps give him a permanent
job. On a freezing winter day in 1910 he successfully flew his
brainchild for an hour in front of O'Gorman who duly took
him on and, because the aircraft was a 'pusher' type, O'Gorman
awarded it the classification F.E.1. This was according to an
idiosyncratic system that he had himself devised and referred
to an aircraft's layout, everything being named after established foreign designs.* De Havilland's F.E.1 was followed in
early 1911 by the B.E.1, the first in a long series of B.E.

* For an explanation of this classification system see the Note on p.319

machines, most of which looked fairly similar to the casual eye. They were two-seater tractor biplanes with the engine at the front and a slender-hipped, rather elegant fuselage. The B.E.1 was designed expressly as the observation and photographic machine the Army had by then ordered. Even though the pilot in the rear cockpit had a much better view than the observer in the front, it had the advantage for aerial photography of being so stable it could be flown 'hands off' for extended periods. This was demonstrated by Major Sefton Brancker in June 1914 when he claimed to have flown the prototype B.E.2c most of the way from Farnborough to Netheravon without touching the controls. Once he had reached 2,000 feet and set his course Brancker spent his time writing notes about the countryside he was overflying at a stately 65 mph. The aircraft's stability was ideally suited to photo-reconnaissance. The pilot could almost forget about flying the aircraft while he leaned over the cockpit's edge trying to steady his heavy wood-boxed aerial camera with its gelatin-coated glass plates. However, this same stability was about to become notoriously less valuable in war flying when the pilot needed to defend himself against attack in the air.

For suddenly, barely two months after Sefton Brancker's flight, Britain was at war. At Farnborough the leisurely pace of experimentation and scholarly research was banished by urgent demands for new aircraft capable of matching whatever the Germans could put into the air. The RFC's demands for new and better aircraft had to percolate through official bureaucratic channels staffed by senior Army officers, many of whom were old cavalry types still unconvinced that aircraft had any military role: men whose priorities lay far more insistently with the early disasters even then befalling the infantry in France. O'Gorman quickly found himself enmeshed in the politics of wartime aircraft production. He was dealing directly with the Director-General of Military Aeronautics, General Henderson, who was then also commanding the RFC in France.

Henderson was sympathetic to aviation, having learned to fly in 1911 aged forty-nine (at that time he was the world's oldest pilot). Indeed, many people think he has better claims to be considered as the father of Britain's air force than his successor in France, Hugh Trenchard, who took over as commander in August 1915. O'Gorman's unenviable task was to interpret Henderson's requirements as relayed by the Army, and then to ensure that Farnborough's designs not only met them but were built by competent factories. It hardly helped that two of Britain's most able and effective private aircraft companies, Short and Sopwith, were by now designing and building orders exclusively for the Navy's RNAS. Nor did it help that the Royal Aircraft Factory itself had meanwhile fallen victim to the popular 'white feather' hysteria that had Farnborough's ribald tram conductors stopping at its gates to shout: 'Alight here for the Home of Rest with Army Exemption thrown in.'[10] Members of O'Gorman's large work force were hastily given a military rank and he himself was made a lieutenant-colonel.

Farnborough's B.E. aircraft, and in particular the B.E.2c, fell victim to a political debate that was tragically to dog O'Gorman until his death in 1958. The B.E. series as a whole was destined to be built in quantity – some 3,500 machines – by several factories up and down Britain, and over time the different aircraft were fitted with a variety of engines and modifications; but in all versions the aircraft retained the characteristic stability for which it had been purposely designed. The B.E.2c was never intended to be agile, and certainly not for air combat. The pilot was hard pushed to take quick evasive action, while even with a machine gun the observer in the front seat between the wings was virtually unable to use it, surrounded as he was by the most vulnerable parts of his own aircraft. The result was that for the first eighteen months of the war in the skies above France this most ubiquitous of Britain's home-grown aircraft grew ever more vulnerable to attack until in the autumn of 1915 it became a sitting duck for the Germans' new Fokker *Eindecker* (the E.1 monoplane) with its synchronised machine gun able to fire through its propeller arc. Yet at the same time aircraft capable of observation and artillery spotting were more and more in demand by the respective armies, now sightlessly bogged down in the trenches. Consequently that autumn Trenchard's RFC Headquarters in France sent to the War Office in London a list of urgent basic requirements for a next-generation observation aircraft to replace the B.E.2c. They demanded an aircraft that was well able to defend itself. Ideally it should even be manoeuvrable enough to be capable of attack as well.

Alas, Farnborough's response betrayed a very British attitude that combined ingenuity with foot-dragging conservatism. Instead of designing a brand new aircraft from scratch that could meet the Fokker menace with some hope of survival, the Royal Aircraft Factory's designers clung to their basic B.E. shape and produced variants in swift and exuberant succession. The fundamental problem for all British aircraft designers at the time was the lack of any home-grown interrupter or synchronising gear for a forward-firing machine gun to match the Germans'. In a move that now looks either like a boffin's solution or a gesture of despair, Farnborough came up with the extraordinary B.E.9. Their solution was to stick the gunner right at the front of the aircraft in a box *ahead* of the propeller, the engine being moved back a few feet to occupy the former position of the B.E.'s front cockpit. In this little nacelle, which was hardly more than a rickety plywood tea-chest, the gunner perched with the propeller whirling lethally only inches behind his back. The box was supported in front by struts attached to the undercarriage and in its rear wall by the lengthened propeller shaft that slotted into a ball-race bearing. This type, which immediately became known sardonically as the 'Pulpit', went to France in the autumn of 1915 for evaluation by 16 Squadron. By any standards it was an abortion of an aircraft but Farnborough must have thought it a viable solution because draughtsmen went on to sketch a single-seat fighter version for 1916, the F.E.10. Those who flew the B.E.9, however, had very different views. 16 Squadron's Duncan Grinnell-Milne was one:

> There was no communication possible between front and back seat; if anything happened, if the pilot were wounded, or even if nothing more serious occurred than a bad landing in which the machine tipped over on its nose, the man in the box could but say his prayers: he would inevitably be crushed by the engine behind him.
>
> One of these machines was attached to the Squadron in which I served; but by the merciful dispensation of Providence it never succeeded in defeating an enemy craft. Had it done so I have no doubt that the brains of the Farnborough Factory would have rejoiced in their war-winning discovery, hundreds of 'Pulpits' would have been produced and in a short while we should not have had a living observer left in France to tell the experts what it was like in that little box – for I feel sure no civilian expert ever risked his own life in it. However, even in 1915 when almost every new machine was looked at with delighted wonder, it was recognized that in the B.E.9 unsuitability of design had reached its acme. The 'Pulpit' was soon returned to the depot.[11]

This damning assessment from a pilot who finished the war with six confirmed 'kills' and who was himself shot down and escaped from Germany to fight again, does reveal the deep scepticism RFC aircrew often felt about what looked to them like an unbridgeable chasm in understanding between those 'brains' back home in Farnborough who had bright ideas about design, and the men who had to fly the resulting aircraft each day against deadly opponents with superior machines. The question of how much consistent feedback there was between front-line airmen in France and the designers with their drawing boards back in England remains perennially moot. It is also likely that what airmen wanted for themselves did not necessarily coincide with Hugh Trenchard's demand for machines to wage an ever-more aggressive air war. There is reason to think that privately owned aero companies like Sopwith and Bristol were more speedily responsive. Certainly Farnborough's apparent stubbornness in clinging to a basic design that was obsolete – particularly by keeping the observer in the front seat for so long – docs seem wilful.

Yet at the same time Farnborough was well on the way to producing possibly Britain's best fighting aircraft of the war, the S.E.5. As proof that O'Gorman and his designers had indeed foreseen the possibility of air combat even before war broke out, in 1914 the S.E.4 prototype had flown at an astonishing 131 mph – then an unofficial world speed record. Was Mervyn O'Gorman to blame for the Royal Aircraft Factory's failure to come up with the sort of aircraft the RFC so desperately needed in the first two years of the war? Or was the organisational chaos and indecision caused by the Army having a separate air service from the Navy and both having to compete for the same funds and supplies simply too much for one man to deal with? The question is still debated in air historians' circles to this day, all of a century later.

O'Gorman also managed to make an influential enemy. This was Charles G. Grey, who in 1911 had founded the magazine *The Aeroplane* and was to remain its able if idiosyncratic editor until the outbreak of the Second World War. Some time before 1914 Grey had paid a visit to Farnborough and O'Gorman, refusing to see him, had had him turned away at the main gate. The reason for this snub can only be guessed at now, although it may be worth noting that both men had been born and schooled in Dublin, and the enmity was possibly of boyhood standing even though O'Gorman was four years older. Far more likely, though, the feud grew from Grey's criticisms in *The Aeroplane* of Farnborough and O'Gorman personally. At any rate, from that moment Charles Grey seldom lost an opportunity to denigrate Farnborough in speech and print. The main burden of his frequent barbed editorial remarks was that as a government institution the Royal Aircraft Factory enjoyed unfair patronage and public funding at the expense of the private aero companies. Once war had been declared Grey pointed out that the place with its 'official' imprimatur now had a near-monopoly of aircraft production and, like all monopolies, this led inevitably to gross inefficiency in getting new and improved designs of aircraft into service; and if anybody doubted this they had only to look at the awful example of the B.E.2c.

Charles Grey soon acquired a powerful ally in the extraordinary figure of Noel Pemberton Billing, whose name was sometimes hyphenated and sometimes not. He bears scrutiny since, for better or worse, he became a critic of political significance in Britain's first air war which had got off to a poor start. Born in 1881, he was an imposing man of six feet four with a monocle that he needed after injuring an eye in a fight in South Africa. PB, as he was conveniently known, was an eccentric of amazing energy and considerable charm, as his many female admirers could attest. He was also a remarkably fertile inventor of some originality and imagination, as witnessed by his own pioneering efforts in aviation as well as in many other fields where he had numerous patents to his name. Many of his inventions were frankly daft, like his idea for what in a modern aircraft is known as the ground proximity warning system. This involved the pilot lowering a rod below the aircraft 'which, when the machine was fifteen feet above the ground or water, operated a gong and electric bulb simultaneously – the former to attract the attention of the pilot and the latter to project a beam of light to aid his vision for landing.'[12] *Flight* magazine thought this 'decidedly simple and ingenious' while apparently ignoring the difficulty and consequences of a pilot lowering a rod to touch the ground while trying to land an aircraft at night.

Well before the war PB had designed and built several floatplanes. These either refused to fly or did so without much promise, which is small wonder given that he had had no formal training whatever as an aircraft designer. But he was not a man who was easily discouraged and in June 1914 he began trading as an aero company, Pemberton-Billing Ltd., whose confident tele-graphic address was 'Supermarin' (he coined the word as the antonym of 'submarine', knocking off the final 'e'). Under the pressure of his many other activities PB was to sell the company barely two years later to its works manager, Hubert Scott-Paine, who renamed it Supermarine Aviation Works Ltd.: the same company that in due course went on to produce the S.6B float-plane that in 1931 won the Schneider Trophy outright for Britain, then the Spitfire, the Swift jet fighter of the early 1950s and finally the Scimitar Fleet Air Arm fighter of the same decade.

On the outbreak of war Pemberton Billing joined the Royal Naval Volunteer Reserve. In November 1914, wearing civilian clothes that would have got him shot as a spy had he been caught, he personally reconnoitered the German Zeppelin sheds at Friedrichshafen on Lake Constance and planned a daring raid there by three Avro 504s. Owing to the distance involved the aircraft were crated and secretly transported by ferry and road from Britain to Belfort in France. Once reas-sembled, and each carrying four twenty-pound bombs, they managed to find their way to the target without maps, the French having banned these from the cockpits for security reasons since their airfield at Belfort was supposed to be secret. The raid was a partial success and a new hydrogen plant the Germans had just built disappeared in a huge fireball easily visible across the lake from Switzerland.

Such exploits gave Pemberton Billing public visibility as some sort of authority on aviation matters. He began making noisy denunciations of Farnborough even before the RFC began taking heavy casualties in the 'Fokker Scourge' in the autumn of 1915 – indeed, it was he who duly coined that phrase, perfectly contrived as it was to be taken up by the newspapers. When in 1916 he resigned his commission in the RNVR and became the MP for East Herts he was able to use the House of Commons as a soap-box for his increasingly vehement views about the Royal Aircraft Factory's supposed incompetence and the way Britain was bungling its air war. In his maiden speech in March he went straight to the point, referring to the RFC as 'a subject of almost tragic mirth in its efforts to defend this country', a piece of rhetoric nicely calculated to shock its hearers. Having got their attention he went on to challenge A. J. Balfour's statement (as First Lord of the Admiralty) that 'the lack of material is responsible for our present policy of masterly inactivity and deplorable delay in answering the challenge of the enemy in the air,' saying:

> For the first six months of this war our Air Service was rich in leadership and poor in material. During the last six months we have been somewhat richer in material, but infinitely poorer in leadership. The six months gap between these two definite periods was devoted to internal intrigue and consequent service bitterness. This deplorable condition of affairs is directly responsible for the present impotence and inefficiency of the service.[13]

In the charged emotional atmosphere of the time, when the appalling casualties of the infantry in France were a daily topic, any allegation of poor leadership, intrigue and impotence inevitably struck home. There was already talk that the centuries-old rivalry between the Army and the Navy – and now that between Farnborough and the private sector – were a perfect formula for inefficiency and chaos in the RFC and RNAS. Such things were taken up by the press and especially by Lord Northcliffe's *Daily Mail.* PB guaranteed the widest coverage by quoting an intemperate accusation made by Lieutenant-Colonel Walter Faber, the MP for Andover, that RFC airmen were being 'murdered rather than killed' by not being given good enough aircraft. This was very shocking to the House of Commons even though by then the phrase had become a near-cliché among squadron commanders in France who daily and reluctantly sent out undertrained boys still in their teens, many of whom never returned. Those were the aircrew PB described as 'Fokker fodder'. And how could it be otherwise? he demanded. Their commanding officers were constantly sending urgent requests back home for better aircraft, and all they got was more of the same or even worse. Farnborough was hidebound and sclerotic. Mervyn O'Gorman and General David Henderson should both be held to account for their blunder in clinging to the B.E.2c and the rest of their outmoded aircraft. Farnborough's near-monopoly of supplying the RFC should at once be broken and the inventiveness and energy of the private aircraft companies properly exploited. More heads were better than one and (PB managed to imply) almost any head was better than one wearing an Army hat... There was a good deal more in the same vein, and for many months to come.

As he had calculated, such remarks caused frequent uproar in Parliament as well as in the press. In the ensuing official enquiry both Mervyn O'Gorman and Sir David Henderson defended Farnborough in the most spirited fashion. Far from having a monopoly that excluded the private sector, O'Gorman said, half his establishment's work came from dealing with the aerodynamic and design problems the private companies encountered and which, by nature of the place's remit as Britain's main centre for aeronautical research, he was both obliged and happy to try and solve. A good deal of Farnborough's time and effort was being taken up by having to design the various gadgets and accessories requested by aero companies up and down the country. Although the enquiry exonerated him, O'Gorman's contract was not renewed and he duly left Farnborough in October 1916, simultaneously vilified and lamented, while remaining behind the scenes as an adviser to both the War Office and the government.

From that moment dates a strand in the writings of aviation historians that sides with Pemberton Billing and Charles Grey in lambasting O'Gorman for Farnborough's shortcomings, and singles out the B.E.2c as a hopeless and even disgraceful aeroplane. An example of this taken at random would be Alan Clark's denunciation of the B.E.2c as 'a bad and dangerous aircraft' (neither of which it was) in his 1973 book *Aces High*. His description of O'Gorman as an 'empire-builder ... at pains to ensure by the placing of contracts and other means that no other aspirant manufacturer could produce a design – still less an aeroplane – whose merits might rival or eclipse those of the Royal Aircraft Factory'[14] ignored the reality of the various aero companies such as Sopwith, de Havilland, Bristol and Short doing exactly that, especially for the Royal Navy. Clark was, of course, merely extending to the war in the air his popular if overstated thesis that the British Army in the First World War had been 'lions led by donkeys', in General Ludendorff's alleged phrase.

It is all good emotive stuff; but as usual the truth was very much more complicated. For one thing, Pemberton Billing's accusation about Farnborough existing at the expense of the private aero companies was specious. At the very least he could be accused of sour grapes, given that he himself had until recently run just such a company, scarcely a single one of whose aircraft designs had yet managed to fly, still less had gone into production. Secondly, his diatribes conveniently ignored the fact that companies in the private sector were not only doing their own original design work but were also building Farnborough's machines by the hundred, and being well paid by the government for doing so. And thirdly PB, with firm loyalties to his late service the Royal Navy, was only too happy to see the rival War Office get any blame that was going.

There was also a good deal that PB could have told the House that he did not, such as that British losses in the air at the time were not so very different from those of the French, who were always cracked up to be so much more advanced in aviation. He also failed to mention that it was not so much the wrong aircraft as the lack of a British version of synchroniser gear that was giving the Germans such a huge advantage, and anyway that was for the professional armaments companies like Vickers to produce and not Farnborough. He might also have pointed out that a high proportion of the British casualties during the six months of the 'Fokker Scourge' had little to do with German air supremacy and a great deal with the RFC's inadequate training for its pilots and poor maintenance by its ground crews which led to unnecessary accidents.* Furthermore, although the RNAS was getting all its aircraft from private companies there was no reason to suppose it was getting superior machines. As of March 1916, the month of PB's maiden speech, the first truly effective fighters from stables such as Sopwith and Bristol were not yet in service. It was not until May that the first Sopwith 1½ Strutters with synchronised machine guns were at last delivered to 70 Squadron in France. In fact, the 'Fokker Scourge' was effectively combatted on the British Front by the Farnborough-trained Geoffrey de Havilland's Airco D.H.2 and the Royal Aircraft Factory's F.E.8 and F.E.2b fighters: all three having been developed under O'Gorman's administration. However, the aircraft that probably did most to end the Fokker's supremacy in the early months of 1916 was France's Nieuport 'Bébé' even though it was still only armed with a Hotchkiss machine gun mounted on the upper wing. From the very first this beautiful little aircraft comprehensively outflew the Fokker and did much to redress the balance of the air war temporarily in the Allies' favour.

★

It cannot be denied that a good deal of Pemberton Billing's fiery indictments were justified. The way in which aircraft were commissioned, designed and built for the British war effort was indeed inefficient, the delays often grotesque. In 1915 thirty-four different companies produced 1,680 aircraft.[15] This might sound like a lot but wastage was extremely high. Actual combat aside, training and ordinary accidents (which in those early days of aviation were very frequent) accounted for at least half the

---

* In the following year, 1917, nearly 800 pilots would be killed in the UK in training accidents alone.

casualties. What happened to the F.E.2b is revealing enough of
how the industry lacked a sense of real urgency. This aircraft was
a development of Geoffrey de Havilland's early design. Its first
version, the F.E.2a, had been planned as early as August 1913 as
a fighter: itself an indication that O'Gorman's Farnborough was
capable of forward thinking since at that time hardly a military
aircraft anywhere was being built for any role other than observation. It will be remembered that this was a 'pusher' type with
the gunner/observer sitting at the front of the nacelle with an
outstanding field of forward fire. In due course, with modified
wings and a more powerful Beardmore engine, it became the
F.E.2b. The future memoirist Louis Strange flew the first of four
examples to France in May 1915, just before the start of the
'Fokker Scourge'. Having already survived at least one pre-war
flying accident, Strange was destined to continue a charmed and
distinguished career as a pilot throughout the First World War.
He was to survive active service in World War Two as well, finally
leaving the RAF as a Wing Commander in 1945.

The F.E.2b Strange ferried to France was soon acclaimed as
an able fighter and was badly needed at the front. Yet it took a
scandalously long time for the type to be built and delivered in
any quantity. For all that production was contracted out to
several aircraft companies, a mere thirty-two machines had been
delivered to the RFC by the end of that year – by which time the
Fokkers had been doing their worst for some six months.
Evidently Pemberton Billing and Charles Grey had been wrong
in their repeated assertions that the private companies were so
much more efficient than Farnborough.

On the other hand PB was right that General Henderson's
Department of Military Aeronautics was doing a poor job of
overseeing the industry and ensuring that the RFC's aircraft
were built and delivered on time. Because aviation generally had
remained low on the Army's list of priorities for so long, the
supply of new aircraft – and particularly of engines – was slow
and disorganised. In the first year of the war the RFC was almost

completely reliant on French engines to power its aircraft, and even in 1916 roughly a quarter of the air force was still French-powered. The companies shuffled their feet and muttered about strikes at engineering works up and down the country, especially in Glasgow where Beardmore engines were produced. The national deficiency in machine-tools had delayed essential supplies and what could they have done? Such inefficiencies merely added to the scandal in 1915 known as the 'Shell Crisis'. This had caused a Cabinet split over the continued shortage of shells for the artillery in France, a shortage partly caused by industrial action. Yet the Munitions of War Act and the Defence of the Realm Act ('DORA') had given the army and police draconian powers to remove male strikers and send them straight off to the trenches. True, many factory workers were women, especially in munitions, but that was part of the problem because the government had had to promise male workers that once the war was over they would get their old jobs back again – which in turn made it clear to the women that they had no job security. Yet even with these bitter undercurrents, it still seemed inconceivable that in a time of national emergency things were so badly organised that the RFC should have to wait seven months to get a derisory thirty-two F.E.2bs that were, after all, of very basic wood-and-canvas construction.

Production of the otherwise excellent Bristol Fighter (the 'Brisfit') was also to be seriously delayed because Rolls-Royce failed to turn out its Falcon III engine in sufficient quantity and Bristol was obliged to substitute a less powerful Hispano-Suiza engine, built under licence, that considerably reduced the aircraft's performance. Many of the engines were also seriously defective mechanically. And the Sopwith company's failure to ensure its designs were built on time turned out to be at least partly down to poor standards in its Kingston drawing office as well as to sloppy supervision of its subcontractors. Such things led to a state of affairs (sadly familiar even a century later) when bought-in parts were found not to fit. The Royal Aircraft Factory,

by contrast, did at least make painstakingly accurate drawings
and keep a keen supervisory eye on its suppliers. It made sure
that wings from one factory would exactly fit a fuselage built at
another, and they almost invariably did.

*

The more the industry expanded, the more its work was farmed
out to concerns both large and small throughout Britain, just as
it would be in the Second World War. The actual construction of
all these aircraft was often severely affected by shortages of materials, as well as by the sheer logistics of organising adequate
supplies to factories up and down the land. The job of building
the wooden frames of the fuselage and wings went most naturally to the motor industry's coachbuilders, to furniture makers
and even to piano factories. The wood used was principally Sitka
spruce and Douglas fir, although since these were imported
from the USA and Canada supplies were affected as German
U-boats took an increasing toll of shipping. Not only that, but as
production grew and great swathes of forest were felled in
Oregon and Washington states, the increased haste led to imperfectly kilned or seasoned wood being used, with subsequent
warping. Other woods were resorted to, including white pine.
The different woods with their varying characteristics and
strengths could produce marked differences in durability and
handling between aircraft of the same type, and it was often difficult for aircraft manufacturers to ensure uniformity.

Some of the textile industry's capacity was diverted to making
fabric to cover the frames. This was chiefly cotton- or linen-
based as well as canvas, and shortages occurred because of the
regular Army's rival demands – to say nothing of the Navy's. (By
1918 30,009 *miles* of flannelette had been produced as pull-
throughs for cleaning rifles: enough to girdle the Earth with
another 6,000 miles to spare.) There also seemed no limit to the
amount of canvas needed for the millions of tents and awnings
and haversacks, as well as enough webbing to reach to the moon

– quite apart from the acres of canvas required for the RFC's Bessonneau hangars.

There were even pressing health issues to take into account. Once the frames of the aircraft's fuselage and flying surfaces were covered with fabric they were varnished with dope. This waterproofed and preserved them while at the same time the tautening effect added to the strength of the whole. A factory's doping area needed to be kept warm at around 20°C because the fabric was very susceptible to damp and mildew. Six coats of dope were applied, each being allowed to dry thoroughly before the next. The dope itself was a syrupy, colourless liquid consisting of cellulose dissolved in acetone, benzene and tetrachloroethane, and had a pungent smell vaguely reminiscent of chloroform. It remained extremely flammable even when long dried on an air-craft in service, where it added materially to the fire hazard so feared by aircrew. In the warm atmosphere dope vapour had a dizzying effect on the workers involved. These were usually women and they frequently needed to stumble outside into fresh air to recover.

Far worse, the vapour slowly poisoned them. Once the war began and production increased, so did the number of aero industry workers reporting ill with nausea, back pain, headaches and jaundice. Several died, and fear and disquiet began to spread among the work force. Late in 1914, as the result of another death at a Hendon factory, Britain's leading pathologist Bernard Spilsbury was called in. He was already known nation-ally for giving the forensic evidence that had sent Dr Crippen to the gallows two years earlier. He now set up a classic experiment with rats, exposing some of them to dope and others to just one of dope's several constituents. After eight days he killed and examined the animals and found that the worst damage, espe-cially to the liver and kidneys, occurred in the rats that had been exposed to tetrachloroethane. Back at the Hendon factory Spilsbury discovered that every one of the workers showed some symptoms of poisoning. He noted that dope fumes were heavier than air and tended to sink, so the air extractor fans mounted high up in the wall were useless. He recommended building separate, properly ventilated sheds exclusively for the doping process, as well as instituting twice-weekly medical examinations for dope workers.

The real difficulty was that although it only constituted 12 per cent of the dope, tetrachloroethane seemed to be the one vital ingredient. Dope made without it resulted in a much less tight, flexible and durable coating. While chemists searched for a substitute, Bernard Spilsbury's recommendations had a beneficial effect, if only for bringing the problem to wider recognition. No doubt factories took what precautions they could, but the urgency of the war's requirements must have taken priority since the reports of illness and occasional death persisted. The phrase 'toxic jaundice' became common and was also used in connection with the exposure to TNT dust of 'munitionettes', the women workers in munitions factories who, because it turned their skin yellow, were also nicknamed 'canaries'. 'Even though women workers wore rubber gloves, mob caps, respirators and leggings and coated their faces with flour and starch to protect them, their skin still turned yellow and there were fifty-two deaths from "toxic jaundice" in 1916 alone.'[16] In its 1st July issue of that year, *The Lancet* noted questions being asked in the House following the deaths of two women dope workers. The Under-Secretary of State for the Home Department, a Mr Brace, replied that 'The Admiralty and the War Office are developing as fast as they can a non-poisonous dope. They are doing their best.' A week later he assured the House that a non-poisonous dope would be available 'within a very short time.' On 12th August he was pleased to announce that non-toxic dope was now available and in wide use. Also, that notification of cases of toxic jaundice due to tetrachloroethane poisoning was now compulsory. As a footnote to this it would be interesting to know whether the Admiralty and the War Office had pooled their researches to discover a non-toxic dope or if, as so often, they worked separately in an atmosphere of mutual disdain.

Pemberton Billing was certainly right that a situation where the Army and the Navy competed with one another for Treasury funds and aircraft was ridiculously counter-productive. A good example was the Sopwith Triplane. In June 1916 the company sent its new prototype fighter to France for evaluation. This was a revolutionary aircraft with its three pairs of wings, good pilot's vision and manoeuvrability that rivalled that of their highly successful Pup. The design of the 'Tripe' was so influential it was quickly copied by no fewer than fourteen German and Austro-Hungarian manufacturers, and Richthofen's red triple-decker Albatros would probably never have existed had it not been for Sopwith's designers. However, it was the Navy that had a contract with Sopwiths and ordered it for RNAS squadrons, later cannily exchanging their old French SPADs with the Army for the RFC's own order of 'Tripes'. Thus it was that every one of the best new fighters wound up with the RNAS and the type never did see service with the RFC.

All things considered, then, it is a pity that Pemberton Billing and Charles Grey should have mounted so many *ad hominem* attacks on the wretched Mervyn O'Gorman when they would have done better to concentrate on the continuing failure of the military and the government to organise a properly unified air service. In fact, in April 1916 the far-sighted PB published an outline of his own for what he called an Imperial Air Service (a memorandum of which he sent to the Prime Minister, Herbert Asquith) that in many respects bore a considerable resemblance to the plan that was adopted for the Royal Air Force when it was finally created by amalgamating the RFC and RNAS two years later.

These days Noel Pemberton Billing's reputation has to some extent been made hostage to the more lurid episodes in his wartime career as an MP. He once had to be carried bodily out of the House of Commons on the Speaker's orders, and he had a bout of fisticuffs with a fellow MP, Lieutenant-Colonel Archer-Shee, that *Punch* gleefully described. 'Palace Yard was the scene of the combat, which ended in Archer downing Pemberton and Billing sitting on Shee. Then the police arrived and swept up the hyphens.'[17] Most notorious of all was PB's claim that an unnamed German prince had a 'black book' containing the names of 47,000 British homosexuals of both sexes (reaching, as always, to 'the very top of society' – not to mention government, since veiled gossip hinted that Asquith's wife Margot was a lesbian). PB's allegations in print resulted in a libel suit at the Old Bailey in which he defended himself and against all odds won. This earned him considerable popular acclaim. As the war dragged on in an apparently endless stalemate an increasingly fractious public was casting about for scapegoats, and it was easy for such papers as Horatio Bottomley's jingoistic rag *John Bull* to whip up paranoia about Germans blackmailing 'sodomites' into spying for them. (Barely forty years later a similar moral panic would surface in the Cold War, although this time it was Soviet Russia that was 'turning' homosexuals to spy for it.)

As a result of such escapades, PB is generally written off as a publicity-seeking crackpot. It is a vanishingly rare MP who shuns the limelight and PB undoubtedly courted it better than most, zealously and effectively. However, though often foolish, he was not stupid. In 1916 in the wake of the early Zeppelin bombings he published a book called *The Air War: How to Wage It* in which there was a section entitled 'The Protection of England. A Dream that MUST Come True'. This included a vision of how the country might be defended against aerial attack and invasion. He foresaw an operations room with one wall entirely covered by a map of Britain on glass divided into squares, with a smaller replica on a large table. The country was divided into sectors, all of which were linked to the room by telegraph and telephone. A reported sighting of enemy aircraft from any of them instantly lit up that sector on the wall and table maps. In addition to spotters on the ground was a network of 500 listening posts: wooden towers with large cones attached to microphones for detecting the sound of aero engines (a technique that was already in use by both Britain and Germany). In a way this was an almost uncanny foreshadowing of the Chain Home defence system eventually built in the 1930s with PB's acoustic 'ears' replaced by the new technology of radar. His visualised 'ops room' was also remarkably similar to that of the future Bentley Priory, the headquarters of RAF Fighter Command from where Britain's Second World War air defences would be directed.

Whatever else, PB did act as both lightning rod and stimulus for growing public dissatisfaction with the war's conduct as well as impatience with politicians' inability to break the apparent stalemate that was costing the country, and the rest of Europe, a fortune in blood and treasure (as he frequently put it). Indeed, by 1916 the war was costing Britain £5 million a day – something like £215 million at today's values. He was unquestionably right to keep on pointing out the absurdity and inefficiency of having the Army and Navy run competing air services, and for this reason it is perhaps not far-fetched to argue that he played a small but vociferous part in ensuring the RAF was finally created when it was, on 1st April 1918, rather than after the war was over. It is true that both the French and German armies, faced with much the same problem, also managed to create independent air forces before the war's end. Doubtless they had Pemberton Billings of their own: civilian public figures desperately trying to instil a little reason into the military and political maladministration of an insane war.

At any rate the inflammatory rhetoric in Westminster and the press had its effect. Together with the military impasse in France and the failure of the British authorities at home to make provision to counter the German air raids, it helped unseat Asquith as Prime Minister and install Lloyd George in December 1916. The new coalition government at once put the Ministry of Munitions in charge of the aircraft industry and made the new

Air Board responsible for allocating resources. From 1917 onwards British aircraft improved markedly in both quality and quantity – and this despite 281,600 working days being lost that year to strikes. The number of different types of aircraft was cut from fifty-three to thirty, a process of rationalisation that continued until the war's end. (It was much needed. In four years of war the Sopwith Aviation Co. alone produced some thirty different types.) By the time of the Armistice the British aircraft industry had 347,112 employees and in that final year of war it produced over 30,000 aircraft. In a little over four years and after a very poor beginning it had become the world's biggest aircraft industry.[18,19]

*

The sheer proliferation of early aircraft shapes and types that Britain flew in the first air war is examined in the following chapter. This variety can be construed as partly the result of administrative disorganisation. But even more, it was a product of the still experimental nature of flying itself, when 'suck it and see' designs and piloting techniques were often improvised with more optimism than understanding of aerodynamics. Merely getting airborne could be hazardous enough; staying there was by no means guaranteed. Powered flight using wings rather than gasbags to stay aloft took place in a realm that was new to *Homo sapiens*, who was obliged to deduce its laws from scratch the hard way.

## CHAPTER 2

# WHY BIPLANES?

It happened during the spring of 1914, at one of the famous Hendon Saturday afternoons. A very strong, gusty wind was blowing… The first machine to be brought out was an 80 h.p. Morane monoplane piloted by Philippe Marty, a Frenchman, who asked me whether I would like to accompany him as his passenger. With the enthusiasm of youth, I agreed to do so.

Marty taxied out to the far side of the aerodrome in order to take off into the wind; but the machine left the ground all too quickly, with the result that a strong gust lifted us up about forty feet in the air and then left us in a stalled attitude, with practically no forward speed. The machine staggered for an ominous moment and then stalled.

I have never forgotten the horrible sensations of the next few seconds, and I don't suppose I ever shall. The left wing seemed to drop out of sight, and I saw the right wing sweep round the sky above us like a sort of windmill vane. Then the roar of the engine stopped.

I thanked heaven that Marty had switched off in time, for a second later the Morane's nose hit the ground with a bang and a crash, just as she had settled into the position of a vertical nose-dive. As she cartwheeled over on to her back I ducked well down inside the fuselage, and there we were – upside down, unable to move an inch and fairly soaked with petrol from the burst tank.

Meanwhile the aerodrome staff had hastened to the scene of disaster. When the machine's tail was lifted up we both fell out of the fuselage, whereupon all our rescuers began to laugh. This only sent Marty off into spasms of mirth-provoking Anglo-French fury. All of which may have conveyed the impression that we were rather a heartless set of fellows, but although a pilot who was hurt in a crash came in for his due share of sympathy, it was the custom at Hendon to give him a dose of ridicule if he was fortunate enough to escape injury.[20]

This vignette of a typical flying accident a few months before the First World War is revealing on several counts, apart from acting as a reminder that even today, a century later, a stall on take-off still causes multiple fatalities each year around the world, especially in light aircraft like this. At the time it was a familiar occurrence and the writer, Louis Strange, was very lucky. Many such crashes caught fire and their trapped survivors, often still very much alive and all too audible, were burned to death in front of the horrified spectators and ground crews. Aviation spirit, together with the aircraft's wooden construction covered in doped fabric, could produce a raging bonfire within seconds. Despite the rapid developments in aircraft design that the war was to expedite, flying remained a high-risk pastime for many years, as the aeronautical engineer and future popular novelist Nevil Shute was to discover when working for the de Havilland company in the 1920s.

> The jocular phrase that one was going out to flirt with death was not entirely jocular in 1923. Humour was grim at times on Stag Lane Aerodrome. There was a crash wagon with fire extinguishers on it ready at all times when flying was in progress, as is usual, and this crash wagon was provided with a steel rod about eighteen feet long with a large, sharpened hook at one end. This was for the purpose of hooking the body of the pilot out of the burning wreckage when the flames were too fierce to permit any gentler method of rescue. It was the custom at Stag Lane when a pupil was to do a first solo to get out this hook, to show him that his friends had it ready…[21]

As it turned out, Louis Strange's luck went on holding to a phe-nomenal extent (as will shortly become even more apparent). He was the pilot mentioned in the previous chapter who had flown the first F.E.2b out to France and he was to have a most distinguished war, emerging practically unscathed from his years as a combat pilot and flying instructor, neither of which profes-sion was noted for longevity. His pilot that day at Hendon, Philippe Marty, was not so lucky. He was to die only a few weeks later from stalling his machine once again, this time at 200 feet.

The story shows vividly how very susceptible early aircraft could be to chance gusts of wind. This was because they were of the lightest possible construction, which in turn was the result of the aero engines of the day being generally weak. This further restricted what could be achieved by designers' limited under-standing of aerodynamics. Among the earliest pioneers the Wright brothers in America were the most consistently scien-tific and systematic in their approach to flight, and this undoubtedly formed the bedrock of their success. Not only did they build a primitive wind tunnel to test their wing shapes, they also designed the first true aero propeller. Various propellers had already been tried on dirigibles, but they were mostly based on ships' screws and even on paddles. It was the Wright broth-ers who broke decisively with the nautical model and reasoned that a propeller blade was in effect a little narrow wing that needed to be given a twist to ensure it created more lift than drag along its entire length as it revolved. Since the engine was mounted horizontally this lift simply became thrust. The pro-pellers they crafted out of wood for their 'Flyer' were a mere 4 or 5 per cent less efficient than are the best computer-designed propellers well over a century later. It was a stroke of engineer-ing genius for two men calculating with paper and pencil in a bicycle workshop.

Besides adequate thrust, powered flight depended on the aircraft being controllable. The Wrights and the German pioneer of man-carrying kites, Otto Lilienthal, are between them credited with having worked out the basic principles of aerodynamics and control. However, as the Wright brothers themselves acknowledged, credit for that actually belonged to an extraordinary Englishman, George Cayley, who was born in 1773. He was the first person known to have worked out that the four main forces acting on any aircraft as pairs of opposites are gravity and lift, thrust and drag. He also designed the first cambered wing for generating lift; this became the standard aircraft wing shape such as the Wrights tested in their wind tunnel and which has persisted to the present day. Cayley first constructed and flew a model glider as early as 1804, and in 1853 an employee of his bravely made the first manned glider flight in one of Cayley's designs at Brompton Dale in Yorkshire, nearly half a century before Lilienthal's experiments with what were essentially the first hang-gliders. Modern replicas of Cayley's glider have since been flown successfully in Britain and America to prove that, primitive or not, it really had worked.

As the Wrights and their contemporaries in Europe had learned from their kite-building, there are three basic axes in flight: roll, yaw and pitch. Roll is when an aircraft tilts or banks to one side or the other; yaw is when the tail swings from side to side like oversteer in a car; and pitch is its nose-up or nose-down attitude: climbing or diving. To steer their 'Flyer' by using yaw, the Wrights employed the same vertical rudder that they and others had used for their gliders, although they mounted this at the front, canard-style, rather than at the back. To achieve both pitch and roll they devised a system of wing warping, or bending the entire wing. This device was still used extensively on early aircraft like the Morane-Saulnier GB type in which Marty and Strange stalled and crashed at Hendon in 1914, although by then the method was obsolescent: a process that the Wrights themselves had unintentionally hastened.

For, in the wake of their epoch-making success of late 1903, the brothers made an error of judgement that was to cost

America the lead in aviation and cede it to Europe. This was to take out a patent on their aircraft's control system and then to become litigious. It was not only their own wing-warping they patented but *any* form of flight control that involved interfering with the airflow over the outer portions of a wing. Their lawyer was quick to bring legal actions against aspiring rivals in the United States and even against visiting aviators from Europe who experimented with any form of wing-bending to control their own aircraft. This was vociferously condemned as selfishly hindering progress, especially in Europe, where no pioneer was about to quit his own researches out of respect for an American patent. This attempt to monopolise the science of controlling an aircraft backfired even in the United States itself where another great figure of early aviation, Glenn Curtiss, was harried by the Wrights' lawyer. The mantle of leadership effectively passed across the Atlantic to men like France's Voisin brothers (who had opened their first aircraft factory as early as 1904), the Farman brothers, Armand Deperdussin and Louis Blériot. Other European pioneers included the young Dutchman Anthony Fokker and in Britain the American Samuel Cody, the Irishman J. W. Dunne, A. V. Roe, Geoffrey de Havilland and Claude Grahame-White. In the United States it was a measure of Glenn Curtiss's brilliance and determination that despite the Wrights' opposition he still managed to produce original and sound early aircraft as well as founding one of the great American aircraft companies. Generally speaking, however, after its pioneering start in aviation the United States rested on its laurels to such an extent that when it finally went to war on the Entente (Allied) side in 1917 American pilots were obliged to fight in French and British combat aircraft, with the honourable exception of a few Curtiss HS-2L flying boats that performed long-range escort duties for cargo ships running the gauntlet of German submarines.

British aviation owes a very large debt to Samuel Cody who, as mentioned in the previous chapter, was the first to achieve

powered flight in Britain. Calling himself Colonel Cody, he was a
barely literate Texan showman with a twelve-inch moustache. At
the turn of the twentieth century he was touring British music
halls giving 'Wild West' exhibitions of trick shooting and riding.
But what really fascinated him was flying, and he devised a series
of man-lifting box kites for military observation. These duly
caught the eye of both the British Army and the Royal Navy and
by 1906 Cody found himself at the Army's Balloon Section at
Farnborough. His problem was money, since at the time the military were still only interested in balloons and could see no future
in the powered aircraft he wanted to build. In the teeth of opposition, by one means or another (and mainly by sheer force of
ebullient charm) he managed to put together something he
called the 'British Army Aeroplane No. 1', and on 16th October
1908 he flew it. Like most of the pioneers he had taught himself
to fly and had no formal education in aircraft design. Carpers
accused him of having cribbed his machine from his fellow
American, Glenn Curtiss, but by now there were aeronautical
inventors in most European countries, travelling around to dis-
plays, swapping information, accusing one other of plagiarism
and promoting their own designs while learning from each other.
Nevertheless, at Farnborough Cody was often ridiculed as 'the
Texan showman' and 'the cowpuncher' for being no scientist and
generally self-taught.

In 1913 the *Daily Mail* offered a prize of £5,000 for the first
person to fly a 'waterplane' around Britain, including a flight
across the Irish Sea to Dublin. Cody, by then aged fifty-three,
built a new aircraft of his own to meet this challenge. It was his
sixth design: a biplane so large it was mocked at Farnborough as
'Cody's Cathedral'. The young Geoffrey de Havilland, who as
well as being a pilot had formally studied aircraft design, infuri-
ated Cody by sauntering over to his immense machine, plucking
its flying wires like harp strings and telling the old showman that
he really needed to double them for added strength. Cody
assured this whippersnapper that it was as strong as a house. On

7th August, the day Cody was due to fly his 'Cathedral' down to Calshot to have its floats fitted for the competition, he decided to give two friends the flights he had long promised them. On the second of these he took up W. H. B. Evans, the captain of the Hampshire cricket team.

> Two of Cody's three sons, Leon and Frank, were among those watching as Cody circled the clubhouse of Bramshot golf course and turned back towards Laffan's Plain. They saw the plane stagger and the wings fold upwards. Cody, easily identified by his white coat and cap, followed by his passenger, were catapulted from their seats at a height of between 300 and 500 feet. Their bodies, followed by the wreckage of the plane, fell into a clump of oak trees 50 yards apart. Cody's publicly expressed wish that, when it came, death would be 'sharp and sudden, from my own aeroplane, like poor Rolls', had been granted.[22]

'Poor Rolls' was the Hon. Charles Stuart Rolls, who had gone into partnership with Henry Royce in December 1904. On 12th July 1910 Rolls was piloting a Wright 'Flyer' at Bournemouth when its tail broke off and he was killed, the first person in England to die while flying a powered aircraft. As for Cody, the *Daily Mail* gave him an epitaph on 11th August in the form of a bitter poem by a certain J. Poulson.

> Crank of the crankiest, ridiculed, sneered at,
> Son of a boisterous, picturesque race.
> Butt for the ignorant, shoulder-shrugged, jeered at,
> Flint-hard of purpose, smiling of face.
>
> Slogging along on the little-trod paths of life;
> Cowboy, and trick-shot, and airman in turn.
> Recklessly straining the quick-snapping laths of life,
> Eager its utmost resistance to learn.

Honour him now, all ye dwarfs who belittled him,
Now, 'tis writ large what in visions he read.
Lay a white wreath where your ridicule killed him;
Honour him, now he's successful – and dead.

As a sacrificial victim of early aviation Sam Cody was hardly alone. He had his counterparts all over Europe and elsewhere: men with a mechanical bent who for ten years had been putting together flying machines of their own design in sheds and garages, each convinced that his would prove revolutionary, only for the dream to end in a tangle of wire and fabric in the middle of rough pastureland. 'The only bones left unbroken in the cadaver,' as one army medic bleakly observed, 'were probably those of the inner ear.'

The single flight that first made it clear aviation was a practical mode of transport and not just a spectacular way of getting killed was Louis Blériot's across the English Channel on 25th July 1909. His model XI was the world's first powered and truly airworthy monoplane and it was to inspire several other similar designs, including those by Morane and Fokker. Blériot's soon became the world's most-produced aircraft, being bought by flying schools and several European countries for evaluation of its military potential. Indeed, it was Anthony Fokker's derivation of it, the Fokker E.1 *Eindecker* (monoplane), that was to establish temporary German air superiority in the skies above France and Belgium in 1915. Yet by then early monoplane design was revealing its limitations. With the exception of the E.1's forward-firing machine gun the aircraft itself was rather old hat and could be outperformed by several biplanes at the time.

★

This prompts a question. Why was it – to judge from contemporary photographs and films and all the popular imagery of the first air war – that the vast majority of aircraft in those days were biplanes and even triplanes? Only part of the answer is that four wings produce more lift than two. Four wings can also be made much stronger, the struts and wires between the pairs producing the effect of box girder construction. A box girder resists torsion, or twisting; and twisting was the inherent problem of the wood-framed wings of the day. Because Blériot, Fokker and many others at first used Wright-style wing warping to control their monoplanes' pitch and roll, the wings *had* to be able to twist. But as speeds increased, together with a need for more manoeuvrability, so much torsion could be set up that the wing could be torn entirely off. Aircraft shedding their wings as Cody's 'Cathedral' had were a distressingly familiar sight at air shows and also accounted for a good many deaths in Fokker's and other monoplanes of the period. Blériot's famous model XI was similarly plagued by structural failure and earned itself the nickname of 'The Killer'. It was obvious that as a method of control, wing warping was doomed. Quite apart from anything else, it was mechanically complex. As Fokker himself later admitted of his own aircraft, 'To warp the wings for elevator action required twelve wires, running on rollers and centring on the control stick. This was bad mechanics, however good a theory it might be.'[23] The wings of a biplane, on the other hand, could be made remarkably stiff when built as a box girder, and pitch and roll could then be achieved by the far simpler method of ailerons: hinged flaps on the trailing edges at the ends of the wings. In this way pairs of stiff wings equipped with simple ailerons revolutionised control and effectively became the basic design for most of the aircraft that flew in the First World War.

However, designers soon found that doubling the number of wings did not double the lift. The reason for this is inherent in the way a wing works. Its cambered shape produces a drop in pressure in the airflow as it passes over its curved upper surface, creating a vacuum effect that 'sucks' the wing upwards. At the same time the flatter underside of the wing, at an angle to the airflow (the 'angle of attack'), produces an increase in pressure that 'pushes' the wing upwards. Both these forces together produce lift. In a biplane, though, with one wing above the other, there is interference between the positive pressure beneath the upper wing and the negative pressure above the lower, cancelling some of the potential lift. It was for this reason that, as the war went on, aircraft designers tried either increasing the distance between the top and bottom wings or else 'staggering' them so they were not directly above each other. Usually the top pair was placed slightly ahead of the bottom pair.

It was soon discovered that, with careful placing of a biplane's centre of gravity and by not designing it for stability at all costs, it could be made much more agile if often trickier to fly. This might be achieved by 'short-coupling': reducing the length of the fuselage so the aircraft became stumpier. There were subtleties of fine-tuning, too. The diagonal wires between the pairs of wings could be tightened or slackened by means of turnbuckles. By careful alignment of the tail with the centre section (the roofed 'box' of struts that surrounds the cockpit), the aircraft could be deliberately trimmed to fly in a particular way. 'Tuning' a biplane to suit its pilot became a valued skill on the part of his rigger mechanics.

Sundry variations in design were tried during the war, including that of adding a third pair of wings. The first triplanes to be seen were the big Voisin bombers of 1915 and 1916, when a third wing was very obviously a load-bearing measure. When Britain's Sopwith company came up with the first little triplane fighter in 1916 it seemed revolutionary. It was found that three pairs of somewhat shorter wings could confer amazing agility in the air and the design of the 'Tripe' was quickly copied. As mentioned earlier, a plethora of different triplanes came from Austro-German manufacturers, most notably Fokker's Dr.I which today is most associated with Baron von Richthofen. Yet the triplane craze was short-lived. While increasing the number of wings can indeed increase lift, it also adds weight and drag. The Dr.I was noticeably slower than many of its contemporaries and although initially it climbed well it soon became sluggish at altitude.

The French company Nieuport, which built some of the war's most successful fighters, went in another direction, that of the sesquiplane. This literally means 'a wing and a half', and the Nieuport design was a biplane in which the lower two wings were much narrower and shorter than the upper. They were pretty machines and generally very agile. The flying aces Eddie Rickenbacker, 'Billy' Bishop, Albert Ball and Charles Nungesser all flew Nieuports for preference at one time or another. They liked their manoeuvrability and responsiveness to the controls. But even they needed to be careful not to over-stress the aircraft because the narrow lower wings suffered from the same old problem that monoplanes had: they couldn't be built rigid enough to withstand too much torsion, and the twisting forces sometimes caused the wing to fail, which usually led to the break-up in mid-air of the entire machine.

The generic problem with biplanes of all kinds was always going to be that of drag, which in turn would limit speed and demand ever more power to overcome it. Biplanes needed struts and wires between the wings, and it hardly helped that they also had fixed undercarriages, a further potent source of drag. There was simply a mass of stuff obstructing the airflow and contributing nothing in the way of lift. In the earlier part of the war aircraft were practically always of all-wood construction, although as engines became more powerful and weight a little less critical metal began to be used for certain parts of the airframe. It was all a matter of weight and the availability of materials. Aerodynamicists realised that in the end the only way to make an aircraft fly faster was to reduce drag and go back to monoplane design; but the problem remained of how to make a cantilever wing stiff enough to withstand the twisting and flexing forces of high-speed manoeuvres. Wood and contemporary glues lacked strength. Making main spars of steel would be too heavy. What was needed were light alloys, but the sort of metallurgical research needed to develop and test them was very time-consuming and besides, even if the ideal metal – both strong and light – were found, the uncertainties of wartime supply made it unlikely that any sort of mass production could be reliably undertaken. At the same time aviation-quality seasoned wood of all kinds became progressively scarcer as the war went on and frames of steel tubing and even monocoque (stressed metal skin) construction were introduced here and there before the war's end, most notably by German companies like Junkers. It is a measure of the difficulties that only in the early 1930s did all-metal structures slowly become the norm for larger aircraft, while military biplanes persisted here and there even into the Second World War (the Gloster Gladiators that defended Malta in 1940, for example). These late biplanes now had metal frames even if their flying surfaces were still partially covered with fabric. Debatably the most impressive, as well as the fastest, biplane fighter of all time was the Italian Fiat CR.42 'Falco' that flew in numbers in several theatres in the Second World War. It was actually a sesquiplane, its lower wings being much shorter than the upper. Yet although outstandingly manoeuvrable and quick, it was ultimately no match for that war's potent all-metal monoplane fighters. Even so, wood continued to be used to advantage in certain airframes, most notably in the Hawker Hurricane and the de Havilland Mosquito.

★

Manoeuvrability was always going to be a critical factor in aircraft and its development was much accelerated by the requirements of war flying. For some time, though, what pilots could do in the air was limited not merely by their machines' structural weakness but by an incomplete understanding of aerodynamics. In addition, the conservative way in which pilots were trained deterred them from performing certain evolutions. By 1914 rolling, diving and even looping an aircraft were all crowd-drawing novelties at any air show, thrilling spectators with both the spectacle and the likelihood of disaster. However, at that time the RFC actively discouraged such 'stunting' by its own pilots as being no better than vulgar showing-off. This revealed how very far the British Army still was from recognising the need for pilots skilful enough to fight rather than just to act as chauffeurs for their observers. For at least the first two years of the war stalling and spinning remained aviation's great bugbears, to be avoided at all cost. In particular, spinning was a phenomenon that scared pilots everywhere simply because nobody really understood its cause, still less how to stop it and regain control.

It was recognised that the main way to trigger a spin was by losing flying speed. The stall at Hendon that Louis Strange survived showed classic symptoms, and had it occurred at a higher altitude – say 500 feet – the Morane would undoubtedly have spun into the ground. Strange's observation that the aircraft gave a 'stagger' is an exact description of the buffeting that occurs at stalling point. In his case the Morane's left wing stalled first, losing all lift and gaining drag, while the right wing maintained lift and so swung up and around. Luckily for Strange and Marty they were still low and impact with the ground prevented this from developing into a full autorotation that the pilot appears helpless to stop. Several showmen of the day claimed to be able to spin at will, but there is no reliable evidence for this. What they were probably doing was known then as a 'tourbillon' spin: essentially a tight downward spiral as opposed to autorotation. In other words they were maintaining airspeed and were under control, effectively rolling the aircraft but vertically downwards instead of horizontally. All they had to worry about was being able to pull out high enough above the ground without their wings folding up under the strain. A genuine spin was a very different matter and for a while it was nearly always fatal.

At six in the morning of 25th August 1912 a young naval lieutenant, Wilfred Parke, and his RFC observer took off from the Army's Larkhill aerodrome on Salisbury Plain in an Avro biplane for a three-hour qualifying flight. They returned to the airfield at nine o'clock at an altitude of around 700 feet and Parke banked the machine to lose height in order to land. Thinking his angle of descent too steep, he pulled back on the control wheel and the machine immediately stalled and whipped into a left-handed spin. The technical editor of *Flight* described it for the magazine's next issue:

> [T]he machine was completely out of control, diving head-long at such a steep angle that all the spectators described it as vertical and stood, horror-stricken, waiting for the end. According to Parke the angle was very steep, but certainly not vertical; he noticed no particular strain on his legs, with which he still kept the rudder about half over to the left (about as much as is ordinarily used in a turn), nor on his chest, across which a wide belt strapped him to his seat. His right hand he had already removed from the control wheel in order to steady himself by grasping an upright body strut... This he did, not for support against the steepness of the descent but because he felt himself being thrown outwards by the spiral motion of the machine, which he describes as 'violent'. It was his recognition of the predominating influence of the spiral motion, as distinct from the dive, that caused him to ease off the rudder and finally push it hard over to the right (i.e. to turn the machine outwards from the circle), as a last resort when about 50 feet from the ground.
>
> Instantly, but without any jerkiness, the machine straightened and flattened out – came at once under control and, without sinking appreciably, flew off in a perfect attitude, made a circuit of the sheds, and alighted in the usual way without the least mishap.[24]

This incident became famous in aviation circles as 'Parke's Dive', and remains the first known detailed description of an aviator surviving an unintentional spin. It so happened that the Royal Aircraft Factory at Farnborough had recently been asked to investigate the phenomenon of spinning and by good fortune the young Geoffrey de Havilland was present at Larkhill that day as their representative. He promptly debriefed Lieutenant Parke at length in the mess. It seems unlikely that Parke would have had much of an appetite for breakfast and his observer – who had worn no seatbelt and had been pinned helplessly to the side of the aircraft by centrifugal force – still less. But de Havilland, self-taught pilot that he was, must have clearly noted the lesson of Parke's Dive because at some date in 1914 he deliberately spun an aircraft knowing how to regain control.

Dunstan Hadley, a Fleet Air Arm pilot who flew Fairey Barracuda torpedo-bombers in WW2, made a particular study of the history of spinning and consulted records in the USA, France, Italy and Germany as well as in the UK. He concluded that Geoffrey de Havilland was 'the first British pilot to have spun intentionally, knowing he could recover; and until any earlier claim is discovered and verified, it stands as both the British and world record for the earliest known deliberate spin'.[25] As for Lieutenant Parke, he had just under four more months to live, being killed while flying a Handley Page Type F monoplane when it suffered engine failure on a flight from Hendon to Oxford in December 1912. He was twenty-three.

Thereafter, one would have thought the method for getting out of a spin would have spread like wildfire throughout the flying fraternity – reduced to a life-saving mantra such as *Full opposite rudder, stick centred, throttle back* or, a little later, *Throttle back, stick forward, pause, opposite rudder.* Yet the mere fact that spins were still almost superstitiously feared four or five years later shows it did not. Even a pilot as accomplished as Cecil Lewis was clear on that point:

In 1916, to spin was a highly dangerous manoeuvre. A few experts did it. Rumour had it that once in a spin you could never get out again. Some machines would spin easier to the left than to the right; but a spin in either direction was liable to end fatally. The expression 'in a flat spin', invented in

those days, denoted that whoever was in it had reached the
absolute limit of anger, nerves, fright, or whatever it might
be. So spinning was the one thing the young pilot fought shy
of…[26]

Even so, 1916 was also the year Major Lanoe Hawker, VC, put his
DH.2 through a series of spins above his squadron's airfield to
demonstrate to his assembled pilots that this aircraft's reputation for fatal spinning was unwarranted, and that it was perfectly
possible to spin it deliberately and regain control.

Part of the reason for this fear must also have been that for
many pilots the remedy for a spin was counter-intuitive. One
instinctive reaction was to freeze and steer *into* the spin, as
though to mollify the machine by going along with it before
finding a way of coaxing it out of its disorder. Yet any horseman
would know that was fatal. It required a masterful hauling of the
beast's head round, using strength. Full *opposite* rudder. Also, if
you were heading for the ground out of control, the last thing
you felt like doing was pushing the stick forward. Yet the chances
were the stall occurred in the first place because you had the
stick back and had lost flying speed. It was soon learned that
each aircraft, as well as every type, could have slightly different
stall and spin characteristics. Even so, it would not be until 1925
that the RAF made it mandatory for a company's test pilots to
complete spinning tests on any new aircraft before it was
accepted for trials by the RAF's own test pilots.

As combat became more aerobatic during the war, the more
adventurous pilots did learn to spin at will, knowing they could
recover, and it became a trick used to simulate being shot down
in order to fool an opponent. Yet by no means every pilot either
mastered it or wished to try. Spinning in general went on having
a bad reputation, while particular aircraft became notorious for
it. A centre of gravity too far aft was always a danger sign. An
additional problem was that the slightest alteration to the airframe – putting on an external mount for a camera or adding a

fairing behind the pilot's head – could sometimes drastically change an aircraft's spin characteristics and a new set of trials would be needed. As Dunstan Hadley observed, 'Even by the 1930s the dynamics of the spin were imperfectly understood and trial and error was very much the order of the day.' It should be added that much the same applied to the stall, which continues to be a problem to this day, as witness several recent accidents to commercial airliners involving the loss of all on board. Any complacency in flying of any kind sooner or later proves fatal, as does putting too much faith in training pilots entirely in simulators in order to save money. There is no substitute for live cockpit experience, preferably including a couple of hundred hours in light aircraft or gliders.

Quite apart from pilot training, though, it should be remembered that every light aircraft has a personality of its own: not just the different types but each individual machine. It can differ in ways no rigger or fitter or mechanic can account for, acquiring a reputation for docility or sluggishness, the engine not giving full revs in a steep turn or overheating, even occasionally making a mysterious faint whinnying sound like a pained horse. Some aircraft feel eager to fly as soon as the engine starts, others much less so. It can't be explained. (Many drivers feel the same way about cars.) This was especially true in the First World War when so much production was farmed out to various factories, each of which had slightly differing work practices according to what they had been making before the Munitions of War Act obliged them to build aircraft. The machines they turned out may have looked identical – may have *been* identical in the sense of meeting specifications – but they seldom flew identically.

★

In many ways it was the engine as much as a growing understanding of the basics of flight that determined the progress of early aviation. Weight was absolutely critical, and power-to-weight became a ratio that haunted every aircraft designer. It can be argued that an equal hero of the Wright brothers' first controlled and powered flights was their mechanic, Charlie Taylor, who was asked to provide an engine for what was essentially one of the Wrights' manned gliders. In the absence of any existing engine light enough to power an aircraft weighing only 604 lb, Taylor built a 12 h.p., four-cylinder inline engine whose block was cast aluminium. He did it from scratch in six weeks and the resulting engine weighed a mere 180 lb. For its time it was a masterpiece of off-the-cuff engineering.

On the other hand, it was weak. French aviation pioneers like the Voisin brothers were not satisfied with the Wrights' top airspeed of 30 mph in 1904. This was, after all, the year Henry Ford set a new land speed record of 91 mph. They turned to the rotary engine. This was originally a French invention, although by the turn of the twentieth century it had been developed elsewhere, notably in the United States for use in cars. Now the three Voisin brothers set up a rotary aero-engine business called Gnome, which along with Le Rhône and Clerget was to become a major engine supplier to the Allies during the war. Many companies also made Gnome rotaries under licence, especially in Germany. Trade was trade, even in wartime.

Rotary engines look like radial engines in that both have their cylinders arranged as a 'clock face', but they function quite differently. A radial engine, like a car engine, is stationary and turns a crankshaft in the normal fashion, whereas the rotary's crankshaft is fixed and the entire block of cylinders turns around it. If it is to be used in an aircraft, a propeller is simply bolted to the front of the rotating engine. By modern standards this may seem a bizarre arrangement but in the early days of aviation it offered important advantages over a conventional stationary engine, the main one being that it had an impressive power-to-weight ratio since it was very light. As the cylinders whirled around they cooled themselves in the air and there was therefore no need for a bulky system of radiators and water jackets. Secondly, a rotary engine ran very smoothly because the whole thing acted as a flywheel. And thirdly, it was extremely compact, amounting to little more than the clock-face of cylinders with its circular sump in the middle, like a fat hub surrounded by spokes. This compactness was a useful feature, and in a fighter like the Sopwith Camel it meant that the first seven feet of airframe could accommodate the entire 'works': engine, fuel tank, guns and pilot. This design led directly to that fighter's hair-trigger handling which was to gain it so many combat victories.

But back in the summer of 1914 it is practically certain that not a single British military aircraft that flew in the first batch to France had a British engine. Initially, our development of both aero engines and aircraft was seriously hampered by a chronic lack of machine tools, ball bearings and magnetos, as well as steel and alloys of sufficient quality. Britain, the erstwhile cradle of the Industrial Revolution, now had only a single ball bearing factory capable of bulk output and supplies had to be imported urgently from Sweden and the United States. As for magnetos, home-grown production proved equally inadequate and until mid-1916 the RFC relied largely on a pre-war stockpile of German-made magnetos to enable its aircraft to fight Germany.[27] By 1918 the desperate modernization of British industry had gathered considerable pace and things had much improved. Even research into new alloys had become advanced.

For the first two years of the war, however, the RFC was almost entirely reliant on French-designed rotary engines. In fact, in August 1914 there were only two British-designed aero engines being built, the 60 h.p. Wolseley that powered the earliest B.E.1 and Sunbeam's 120 h.p. Crusader. Both were V-8s and as such were bulky and heavy for their output. Rotaries were the obvious choice: it was a capable and ingenious design. Tens of thousands were built by all sides throughout the war, and yet they virtually disappeared the moment the Armistice was signed. By then their drawbacks had exceeded their usefulness.

While the rotating engine did indeed provide smoothness, it also produced a powerful gyroscopic effect that could make an aircraft easy to turn in one direction but less so in the other. This feature became notorious in Sopwith Camels, which were typically powered by the 130 h.p. Clerget engine. That aircraft also had a marked tendency to swing on take-off and landing, one of several tricky features that led to countless crashes in training. Because rotaries lacked carburettors they were tricky to control with a throttle. They tended to run 'full on', and the normal way to reduce power was by using a cut-out switch that prevented every other cylinder from firing and required repeated 'blipping' of the engine. This – together with a fuel-air mixture control that demanded constant monitoring – made flying all rotary-engined aircraft a handful, and the Camel most of all. Rotaries also worked on a 'lost oil' principle that used great quantities of castor oil, much of which was sprayed back half-burnt over the pilot.

None of this was ideal, although it had to be lived with at the time. The real reason why the engines fell out of fashion so quickly after the war was because aircraft designers wanted more and more power. Rotaries were comparatively slow-revving and the propeller could only turn as fast as the engine, unlike stationary engines where the power could be greatly increased and the propeller geared for maximum efficiency. (The underlying problem is that petrol engines reach their maximum efficiency at relatively high speeds, whereas propellers are more efficient at lower speeds.) During the First World War rotaries were developed as far as they could be, even acquiring a second bank of cylinders 'staggered' with respect to the first. The high point was probably reached with the Bentley BR.2, a magnificent 25-litre rotary engine whose single bank of nine cylinders produced 250 h.p. But rotaries had reached their limit for reasons of simple physics. The faster the cylinders whirled, the more the drag on them increased (since drag in air increases with the square of the velocity). But the power needed to overcome drag is the cube of speed, and very soon a point was reached when much of a rotary engine's power was spent in making itself turn.

★

Given the various armies' more or less dismissive attitudes to aviation at the outbreak of war, it is ironic how quickly they came to rely on aircraft as engines and airframes improved. It is now possible to view the whole development of aviation during the First World War as a direct consequence of the static trench and artillery warfare on the ground, with rapidly escalating demands for aircraft to fill different and more demanding tactical roles. By early 1915 more accurate anti-aircraft defences were forcing pilots up to 8,000 feet or so, over twice as high as they had been used to flying a mere six months earlier. But at 8,000 feet accurate observation by eye of what was happening within the intricate network of trenches was very difficult, particularly as so much was increasingly disguised from aerial spying by the burgeoning art of camouflage. An observer peering over the side of his cockpit, attempting to stop his goggles being torn off his face in the seventy-mile-an-hour gale while trying to draw maps and take pencil notes on flapping paper with frozen fingers – this was clearly no way to conduct a vital military survey. Thus cameras became more and more important while gaining in intricacy, size and weight, which in turn necessitated better aircraft performance at altitude.

Aeroplanes became increasingly vital for artillery observation, too, which meant it was essential to have quick and accurate communication with the gunners on the ground. No longer could an airborne spotter rely on signalling their hits and misses by shooting off a series of colour-coded flares from his Very pistol. He needed to carry a wireless transmitter, which in turn meant still more weight and improved engine and airframe design to cope with it. In time, aircraft with bombing capabilities were expected to fly to more distant targets with a heavier bomb load, which also meant having to fly higher to avoid anti-aircraft fire. Once aircraft were armed with effective machine guns, observation machines and bombers also needed them for their own defence, as well as increased speed and the ability to climb fast in order to avoid trouble. By the war's end combat aircraft were regularly reaching 22,000 feet, an unimaginable height only four years earlier.

In this escalating fashion the developing war on the ground fed directly into the way aircraft were built, and it all happened at a breakneck pace. The rival air forces watched each other closely for any new technology, eagerly tore apart their opponents' latest downed aircraft for its secrets, tried always to keep one step ahead. Serious aeronautical institutions like that at Farnborough did their best to work out the intricacies of flight theory; but in the companies that actually built the aircraft, practice was often more the product of hunches and bright ideas than of theory, and not all the hunches worked. Thus, aviation from 1903 to at least the end of the First World War can be seen as a constant series of experiments as little by little the basics of twentieth-century aerodynamics came together in a solid body of knowledge. The science of flight certainly did not stop there; but a good deal of the raw spadework was achieved in that first air war, albeit at prodigious cost in money and lives.

Many aspects of aircraft design were dictated by factors that had nothing to do with aerodynamics. The sundry French – and particularly British – 'pusher' machines were made necessary simply because at the time they had no synchronisation gear allowing a machine gun to fire forward through the propeller arc, therefore the propeller was most easily placed behind. They were not beautiful, those pusher biplanes with a blunt nacelle sticking out in front like a canoe while behind that an open trellis-work of bare metal tubing enclosed a yawning space wide enough to accommodate a whirling eight- or nine-foot diameter propeller. This trellis joined together some fourteen feet behind to support a fabric-covered tail. Pusher aircraft like the D.H.2 were often good for what they were, and usefully manoeuvrable, and at any time other than war they probably offered a pilot the most pleasant flying experience of the day, with all the noise behind him, no prop-wash blowing into his face, and wonderful visibility. But pushers also had inherent disadvantages. One was that any hard object sucked rearwards out of the open cockpit in front – as a pair of goggles or even a pencil might be – could damage or even shatter the propeller. But the chief disadvantage of the pusher type was that the open framework of the 'fuselage' caused a good deal of drag that would always put a limit on performance.

Another measure forced upon aircraft designers of the period (not to mention the pilots) was that no ordinary machine had wheel brakes. This was, of course, to save weight; but it did mean that landing in a restricted space could be tricky indeed. Instead, there was a tail-skid (sometimes steerable) that dragged along the ground and slowed the aircraft after landing: always crude but not always effective, especially if the ground was frozen. To limit the run-out trainees were taught to make 'three-point' landings: touching down on the main wheels and tail-skid simultaneously. If the machine's attitude at rest on the ground was at a particularly steep angle, this took practice. The propeller's size sometimes dictated how a tractor aircraft sat on the ground. A nine-foot propeller at the front of a typically stocky Sopwith design meant the aircraft sat at an angle that left the pilot staring up into the sky. This not only made the view ahead when taxiing almost non-existent without weaving from side to side, but until a pilot got used to it doing a 'three-pointer' could go badly wrong.

The same applied to the Royal Aircraft Factory's generally awful R.E.8, or 'Harry Tate' two-seater observation machine. This had been designed to sit with a very nose-high attitude on the ground, not to provide propeller clearance but so that the upward angle of the wings would produce more drag on landing and hence a braking effect when touching down in small fields. It took a lot of getting used to, and no-one was keen to botch a landing in a Harry Tate, an aircraft that already had an evil reputation for catching fire in a crash. (The fuel tank was sited immediately behind the engine, so when – as usual – it split on being forced forward, petrol promptly gushed over the red-hot exhaust manifolds.) Nothing could have made plainer the gulf between the boffins at Farnborough who designed this detail and the wretched men who had to fly the aircraft:

> I well remember one very windy day when I had been forced to land on an R.E.8 aerodrome owing to having received a bullet through my petrol tank. Flying conditions were abominable, and I watched four R.E.8s land, all within half an hour. Two pulled up safely, one crashed on landing, and the fourth turned over on the ground. In both latter cases the machines immediately burst into flames, killing pilots and observers. A tribute is due to the squadrons using these machines, and while we scout pilots laughed at them to their faces, behind their backs we heartily respected and admired them.[28]

On the other hand one Harry Tate became famous as a 'ghost' aircraft that never did catch fire. It was doing artillery observation one day in December 1917, flown by two Australians from No. 3 Squadron, Lieutenant J. L. Sandy and his observer, Sergeant H. F. Hughes. Hughes managed to shoot down an Albatros D.Va scout that attacked it and a larger battle ensued when two more R.E.8s from 3 Squadron turned up as well as some more German machines. In the end the Germans broke off the attack and one of the R.E.8s, noting that Sandy and Hughes looked fine, gave a wave and let them get on with their 'art. obs.'

> Somewhat strangely, no further wireless messages were transmitted from Sandy's R.E.8 and apprehension increased as the evening approached and the aircraft had not returned. To all intents and purposes the aircraft and its crew seemed to have vanished from the face of the Earth. The perplexing

mystery was not solved until 24 hours later, when a telegram was received from a hospital at St. Pol, stating that the bodies of Sandy and Hughes had been found in a crashed R.E.8 in a nearby field. It was ascertained that both men had been killed instantly during the aerial combat, when an armour-piercing bullet had passed through the observer's left lung and thence into the pilot's head. They had not been injured in the crash-landing, and the R.E.8 itself was only slightly damaged. Apparently, after the crew had been killed, the aircraft had flown itself in wide left-hand circles until the petrol supply ran out. This theory was supported by the fact that a north-easterly wind was blowing and the aircraft had drifted south-west before crash-landing about 50 miles from the scene of the combat. This extraordinary occurrence provided a striking example of the inherent stability in the flying characteristics of the R.E.8 – the aircraft had flown and landed itself without human assistance.[29]

*

The R.E.8's inherent stability regardless, few would dispute that overall it was a bad aircraft. How else describe a machine notorious for burning its crews alive? Statistics seem to bear this out since it sustained the second highest losses of all British aircraft on the Western Front, 661: a figure exceeded only by that for the Sopwith Camel at 870.[30] Debate becomes heated over the issue of which of all these dozens of First World War aircraft were good. Bar-room and internet forum discussions still take place between armchair aviators bickering over which was the 'greatest' aircraft of a hundred years ago. Given that few of these people are qualified to fly aircraft of that vintage, and even fewer have ever flown a Fokker D.VII or an S.E.5a or a SPAD S.XIII, the discussion is about as meaningful as those similarly impassioned debates about the greatest-ever Formula One car that regularly occur in pubs between stout and opinionated men who would never fit into one, still less be given the chance to drive it. In one sense there *was* no truly 'great' aircraft in the whole of the first air war, and for a very good reason. At the time, the development of aircraft was everywhere so rapid that almost none escaped becoming obsolete after six months' active service. Thanks to production delays many a type was already outmoded even as the first squadrons took delivery of it, having been leapfrogged in the interim by a new enemy machine: a syndrome that would reappear in both the Second World War and the Cold War. A combination of materials (or engine) shortage, battlefield emergency and administrative incompetence obliged several aircraft such as the B.E.2c to plod on above battlefields long after they should have been grounded.

The criterion for true 'greatness' surely has to reside in something more than a short-lived combat advantage, no matter how impressive that was at the time. A genuinely great aircraft must offer a more enduring quality such as longevity and all-round reliability (like the Douglas DC-3), utterly transcendent performance (like the Lockheed SR-71 'Blackbird'), overwhelming aesthetic beauty, like Concorde, or the capacity for constant uprating of its basic design like the B-52 bomber which, by the time the last one is scheduled to leave USAF service in 2040, will have racked up an astounding ninety years' active service. None of the First World War's aircraft comes close to measuring up to any of these yardsticks. That being said, a Sopwith Pup might still afford a skilled pilot immense pleasure even today, but the same could be said of a pre-1920 racing car without either machine qualifying for the timeless accolade of greatness.

This is obviously not to deny that hundreds of WWI pilots often found a new type wonderful and exhilarating to fly, usually because it was so much better than the machine they were used to and which had increasingly been feeling like a deathtrap when confronting the enemy. On the British side Sopwith's Pup, Triplane and Camel, as well as the Royal Aircraft Factory's S.E.5a, were a revelation to those who first flew them in combat; and at

the time, as also today, each aircraft had its dedicated support-
ers. W. E. Johns's punning title for an early collection of his
stories, *The Camels Are Coming*, shows that fighter still had a
certain legendary quality to it fourteen years after the war's end,
even though its active service life lasted a scant eighteen months
after its introduction in the summer of 1917.

The stumpy little Camel was neither beautiful nor easy to fly.
In fact it was notoriously tricky, 'a fierce little beast', as one
airman described it, although those who mastered it found it a
highly effective fighting machine. All the same, by late 1917
many German pilots reckoned their new Pfalz D.III was easily
the Camel's equal and in less than a year the Fokker D.VII was
plainly the better fighter. One aviation historian, the late Peter
Grosz (son of the German Expressionist painter Georg Grosz
and an acknowledged expert on German aircraft), described
the Camel baldly as 'probably the most over-rated and accident-
prone fighter in the Allied inventory', going on to add that
'surprisingly, only the D.H.5 was superior to the Pfalz in speed,
climb rate and manoeuvrability'.[31] 'Accident-prone' the Camel
certainly was, which must partly explain why it so easily heads the
list of British types lost. Many an experienced British pilot
dreaded having to convert to it:

> They were by far the most difficult of service machines to
> handle. Many pilots killed themselves by crashing in a right-
> hand spin when they were learning to fly them. A Camel hated
> an inexperienced hand, and flopped into a frantic spin at the
> least opportunity. They were unlike ordinary aeroplanes,
> being quite unstable, immoderately tail-heavy, so light on the
> controls that the slightest jerk or inaccuracy would hurl them
> all over the sky, difficult to land, deadly to crash: a list of vices
> to emasculate the stoutest courage, and the first flight on a
> Camel was always a terrible ordeal. They were bringing out a
> two-seater training Camel for dual work, in the hope of reduc-
> ing that thirty percent of crashes on first solo flights.[32]

Nevertheless, once in the air the Camel had an agility all its own, partly down to the lightness of its construction and the weight of engine, guns, tanks and pilot all being concentrated in the nose. The gyroscopic effect of the engine was very marked, as might be expected with a mass of 350 lb whirling around at 1,250 rpm. Seen from the pilot's little wicker seat the propeller rotated clockwise. This meant that if he climbed or turned to the right the nose would drop sharply, and if he dived or turned to the left the nose would rise. It also meant that lightning-fast right-handed turns were easily performed. Left-handed turns were another matter, however, and pilots found they could often turn 90 degrees left quicker by making a right turn of 270 degrees. This is not an ideal characteristic in any aircraft, but the most skilled pilots eventually found ways of instinctively going with rather than against the engine's gyroscopic pull. The Camel is credited with being the top-scoring fighter of any side in the war, with 1,294 victories.[33] On the other hand it killed 350 trainee pilots, or more than one non-combat death for every four enemy air-craft downed (but not necessarily with a fatality): a high price to pay.[34] Like the contemporary French SPAD S.XIII, it stalled readily and spun viciously. Because of its tail-heaviness it could never for a moment be flown 'hands-off' and was therefore a very tiring aircraft to fly. Its combat success rate unquestionably makes the Camel one of the best fighters – and by that sole yardstick *the* best – of WWI. Yet that still does not make it a great aircraft because it so obviously could be improved, as was demonstrated by Sopwith's next aircraft, the Snipe, which came late in the war and was willy-nilly adopted as the RAF's first postwar standard fighter because there was nothing else available at the price. The Snipe was derived from the Camel and was equally manoeuvrable (hence its name), but it was much easier to control while afford-ing the pilot far better all-round visibility. It was also slightly faster, being fitted with Bentley's powerful BR.2 rotary engine.

Some biplanes were undoubtedly a good deal more elegant than others, and aircraft with the longer stationary (especially in-line) engines often looked more streamlined and better-proportioned. In this the German machines predominated because their designers were less wedded to rotary engines than were the French, the British, the Italians or the Russians. But the Royal Aircraft Factory's S.E.5a with its stationary Hispano-Suiza or Wolseley Viper V-8 engine had the look of a serious modern fighter and was much respected by German pilots. Once initial problems with the supply and reliability of the engines had been overcome, the S.E.5a was looked on as the equal of the new Fokker D.VII, which ended the war with a fearsome reputation for all-round competence. After the Armistice the Allies, in punitive mood, impounded Germany's entire fleet of Fokker D.VIIs as being too dangerous to be allowed to fall into others' hands. This was really pure superstitiousness because by then the Fokker was already dated. Its top speed was only about 118 mph whereas Britain's new Martinsyde F.4 'Buzzard' was capable of a top speed at low level of 146 mph and was technically the fastest aircraft of the war. Unfortunately, it came too late to make the game-changing impression it otherwise might have done.

Long before then the war had determined the trajectory of aviation and of flying itself. A quirk of history ensured that what had started out as an entirely civilian enterprise had been comprehensively hijacked by the military. This is why considerations of a pilot's pleasure – or even of his safety – did not figure on the list of specifications to which aircraft designers worked. This was also made clear in the matter of how to arm aeroplanes, where guns and bombs soon became the most significant part of many an aircraft's payload, outweighing the aircrew both literally and metaphorically. The next chapter deals with this subject which, in the case of machine guns, was to afford a turning point in aerial warfare.

## CHAPTER 3

# ARMED TO THE TEETH

——— ·– ———

WHEN THE WAR ended in November 1918 the Germans were perfecting a flamethrower that could be deployed against troops from the air, and their increasingly threadbare and outnumbered air force was also taking delivery of the formidable twin-barrelled Gast machine gun capable of firing 1,800 rounds a minute. The French were adapting their four-engined 'Henri Paul' triplane bomber to take a massive 75 mm cannon (the calibre of a small artillery field piece) for trench strafing and general ground attack. And with the advent of the Handley Page V/1500 bomber the British had already begun dropping the 1,650 lb SN bomb they had developed, a munition whose weight and size would have made it inconceivable a mere four years earlier. Domination of the enemy's airspace by sheer force of arms was now universally recognised as modern warfare's *sine qua non*.

Back in August 1914 none of the high commands could possibly have imagined such hectic technological progress. In fact, at that time the question of whether to consider an aircraft itself as any sort of potential weapon revealed a good deal about the different armies' reactions to the new technology and their varying ability to see its possibilities. Certain individuals had long since made up their minds, however. In 1912 a far-sighted Italian officer, Giulio Douhet, wrote a manual entitled *Rules for the Use of Aeroplanes in War* that advocated bombing from a high altitude. This was based on his own military experiences in Libya the previous year, when in November 1911 Italy had become the first nation in history to use a heavier-than-air winged machine in war. Lieutenant Giulio Gavotti in his Blériot had hand-dropped four bombs of four pounds apiece on Ottoman troops in Libya, leaning out of his cockpit and letting them go one by one. In the same campaign Captain Carlo Piazza became the first man in a reconnaissance aircraft to take aerial photographs during an actual war. The Futurist and poet F. T. Marinetti was in Libya at the time and fancifully described a new being: the air hero. 'Higher, more handsome than the sun Captain Piazza soared, his bold, sharp-edged face chiselled by the wind, his little moustache crazy with will.'[35] However, dropping explosives on the heads of those below was one thing; the idea of using aircraft to fight duels in the sky quite another. In 1911 the French pilot Ferdinand Ferber gave an interview for an aviation journal in which it became clear that it had never occurred to the journalist that one aircraft might actually fight another in the air. Why not? asked Ferber. If such a combat could take place between a falcon and a raven, why might it not between two armed airmen?

The fact is that practically as soon as the Wrights' 'Flyer' left the ground in 1903 there was speculation about the new technology's military potential, something that has no doubt always been true of any new technology. Many who had foreseen the possibilities were not military men at all. In his writings and public speeches the libertine Italian poet and Futurist Gabriele d'Annunzio had been a noisy enthusiast for the glories of mechanised warfare since at least the turn of the century. He first went up in an aircraft in the summer of 1909 from an airfield in Rome where Wilbur Wright was teaching Italians how to fly. This aerial baptism turned d'Annunzio into an ardent devotee of flying and its military possibilities, and he was certainly not alone in this reaction. It was all of a piece with the fashion of the day for power and speed as already epitomised by the car and the train and celebrated earlier that same year by Marinetti's *Futurist Manifesto*. H. G. Wells's *The War in the Air* (1908) has already been alluded to for its novelistic vision of a London razed to the ground by aerial attack. Ironically, Wells was writing his book even as the new Hague Convention was being promulgated. Article 25 stated: 'The attack or bombardment, by whatever means, of towns, villages, dwellings or buildings which are unde-fended is prohibited.' This particular Article was itself destined to become one of the war's earliest casualties.

Wells was by no means alone in his anxieties. Many of his con-temporaries were also rendered thoughtful by the military possibilities those spruce-and-fabric early aircraft offered. As soon as Blériot had made his epic flight across the Channel in July 1909 the British journalist Harold F. Wyatt wrote an article, 'Wings of War',[36] in which he wondered how many of the crowds assembled on the cliffs of Dover to welcome the Frenchman realised they were 'assisting at the first stage of the funeral of the sea power of England'. In this new air age, Englishmen would be 'doomed helplessly to gaze into the skies while fleets which they are powerless to reach pass over their heads,' a prediction des-tined to become true within six years when the first German bombs fell unopposed on London. This was to become a common theme in British journalism of the day, joining a strand of thinking in continental Europe whose misgivings about the malign potential of airships and aircraft was in marked contrast to attitudes in the United States where, thousands of miles away and unmenaced by warlike neighbours, Americans generally saw aviation more naively as a liberating technology that would spread Progress for mankind.

Few armies have ever been remarkable for their eagerness to embrace novelty, the British Army least of all. (One Chief of the Imperial General Staff wrote triumphantly in his retirement: 'There have been many changes in the British Army during my term of office, and I have opposed them all.'[37]) The formation of the Royal Flying Corps in 1912 was the Army's reluctant acknowledgement that aircraft might conceivably be useful as 'eyes in the sky'. They could act as a more mobile adjunct to observation balloons to watch for enemy troop movements and take photographs of things like supply trains and ammunition dumps. With a bit of ingenuity they might even be able to tell artillery batteries where their shells were falling. But these envisaged roles were essentially passive and defensive. At the level of high commands there was little serious thought given to a more aggressive role for aircraft, such as fighting or bombing.

Such attitudes must have been intensely frustrating to those younger officers – German as well as British – who perceived the military possibilities beyond mere reconnaissance that the new aviation offered. They were abreast of developments that were already turning futuristic dreams into a primitive sort of reality. It is unlikely that any of them would have read Giulio Douhet, who remained largely unknown outside Italy for another twenty years; but they would have known about the Italian Army's use of aircraft against the Ottoman Turks they had successfully evicted from Libya. They would also have known that French aircraft had similarly dropped bombs in their campaign against rebels in Morocco between 1912 and 1914, as had the Spanish Army in its campaign in the Moroccan Protectorate in 1913 (using four Austrian Lohner aircraft). In 1914 Italy was not yet at war in Europe and it would have been to France that young aviation-minded officers looked as leading the field in treating the aeroplane as a potential weapon, not least because the French had the most advanced aircraft. It should be added that at this stage Britain's Royal Naval Air Service seems to have contained more progressively minded men among its high command than the RFC, a characteristic that in certain ways would persist.

Germany's position in 1914 was also equivocal in that its army had long since committed itself to the development of airships, a field in which it held unchallenged world supremacy. Seen from the army's point of view its Zeppelins and Parsevals could easily outperform any contemporary aircraft in terms of endurance, to say nothing of being able to carry a considerable bomb load. To many in the German high command there seemed little point in jumping on the bandwagon of an inferior technology simply because it was newer. Besides, nobody was expecting the war to last beyond Christmas. The German Air Force thus began the war at a disadvantage, aware that such airmen and machines as it was able to field were not only still prone to all sorts of teething troubles but were undervalued to the point of contemptuous dismissal by much of the Army's high command.

Well before either Germany or Britain, however, France had understood how useful aircraft could be in artillery spotting, bombing and aerial warfare in general, and had already envisaged arming them. As early as 1910 the brilliant aviation pioneer Gabriel Voisin had bolted an enormous 37 mm naval gun to an improvised mounting in the nacelle of one of his pusher-engined biplanes. It looked, and was, ridiculously unwieldy – a motorised kite with a cannon – and it caused some derision. However, enough influential military men took it seriously for Voisin to persevere with his experiments. In 1913 he gave a demonstration of a Hotchkiss 37 mm gun more flexibly mounted in one of his aircraft, shooting at a bedsheet laid out in a field from an altitude of 1,500 feet. Roughly 70 per cent of the shots were hits, a degree of accuracy that was not lost on the military observers that day, who must have gone home imagining the awful damage a number of similarly armed aircraft might inflict on massed cavalry or infantry. Anyone at the time would have been impressed that Voisin's aircraft could not only fly with the weight of a substantial cannon and its explosive ammunition but that it could be flown steadily enough to score hits on a small ground target 500 yards away.

★

By August 1914 the battle lines were drawn between the Central Powers (Germany, Austria-Hungary and, later, Bulgaria and the Ottoman Empire) and the Triple Entente (of France, Britain, and France's ally Russia). Although according to treaty Italy was pledged to side with Germany, it remained non-combatant until eventually joining the Entente, principally against Austria-Hungary. Each one of these combatant nations had an air force of sorts, ranging from the best-prepared (France) to the most rudimentary (Turkey).

At first light on 13th August the ragbag assortment of fifty-six flying machines making up the four squadrons of Britain's entire army air power flew in stages to Amiens. Most were already obsolete. Gallantly unprepared, they afforded an authentically British spectacle. 'We patched up anything that could stagger off the ground,' as Arthur Edwards remembered from his apprenticeship at Farnborough as a 'Trade Lad' learning how to use a lathe. 'We sent off a total of about seventy aircraft, some of them hardly capable of flying. Twin-seaters were fitted with rifle-clips and a rifle, and single-seaters supplied with a revolver or a Very pistol.'[38] Soon both sides were making observation flights over each other's territory in two-man machines, the opposing pilots and observers waving cheerily at each other with the comradeship of men conscious of being members of an international winged elite. Indeed, a good few of them could well have known each other from private training and flying clubs scant weeks earlier. This 'brotherhood of the air' was, needless to say, not popular among their respective army generals and it was quickly made clear that since observing such things as troop deployments was of vital military significance, every effort should be made to prevent the enemy from carrying out their reconnaissance in the first place, and certainly from flying back with the information. Despite this, and despite the as yet unimagined horrors of the next fifty months, there is ample evidence that a lingering spirit of comradeship amongst airmen on all sides did survive the conflict. Certainly it was widely considered a matter of honour throughout the war to drop message bags and streamers – often at great personal hazard – over opposing airfields to give news of those who had been shot down. Both sides also held funerals with full military honours for their respected adversaries.

Within weeks aircrew had begun taking pot shots at each other with their service-issue pistols and rifles, plus various weird weapons devised and pressed into service at the whim of the individual, such as (in one case) a black-powder blunderbuss loaded with nails. One German officer later recorded earnest top-level discussions about the etiquette of carrying a cavalry sword in the cockpit. He also remembered nailing a gramophone horn to the stock of his carbine so that, in the event of an aerial duel, he might better give an illusion of being armed with a terrifyingly large-calibre weapon.[39] Other combatants were even more inventive. In early 1915 Lieutenant Alexander Kozakov of the Imperial Russian Army Air Service took off in his Morane-Saulnier Type G with a boat anchor attached to a length of rope. Tied to the anchor was a slab of gun cotton. His theory was that he could throw out the anchor while flying above an enemy aircraft, snare it, trigger the gun cotton and blow it to bits. He actually tried this in March with an Albatros he met near the River Vistula but the rope tangled in his own slipstream. Abandoning the idea, Kozakov gave up and rammed the German instead, who duly crashed. By sheer luck the future Russian ace managed to land his own crippled aircraft, but in terms of damage inflicted on an enemy it was something of a Pyrrhic victory.[40]

At that stage in the war, though, improvisation was the order of the day and at least one British airman saw quite clearly what was required. Louis Strange, who had survived the Hendon crash described in the previous chapter, arrived in France as a young lieutenant. He at once fitted a Lewis machine gun in the observer's cockpit of his Farman 'Shorthorn'. This occasioned much scoffing from the rest of his squadron, especially since the extra weight of the weapon and its ammunition limited his aircraft's ceiling to 3,500 feet, but Strange was soon proved to have the right idea. After astonishing adventures he was to survive the war and eventually he met his German counterpart and sometime opponent, Bruno Loerzer (whom he mistakenly called 'von Leuzer' in his memoir). Loerzer recalled an absurd aerial duel he had had with a British machine back in the early months of warfare in 1914:

When the combatants had exhausted all their rifle and revolver ammunition they blazed away with their Very pistols, with which they made very poor shooting. After a while both pilots realized that the only chance of scoring a hit was to get close up, but when they laid their machines alongside, the humour of the situation struck von Leutzer forcibly, so that he roared with laughter at the sight of two observers solemnly loading up and taking deliberate aim, a green light answering a red one. Evidently the observers were also too tickled to shoot straight, for neither got anywhere near his mark.[41]

In fact, the first aircraft ever to shoot down another was probably the French Voisin that downed a German Aviatik on 5th October 1914. Thereafter there must have been fewer opportunities for opposing crews to be reduced to helpless laughter. With the murderous autumn battles of Mons and the Marne, followed by the winter conflict of Champagne, the war on the ground turned deadly serious and the war in the air had to match it. The pressure for technological improvement was urgent. It was developing into an artillery war, and anti-aircraft guns were driving aircraft ever higher.

At this early stage there was as yet little 'specialisation' in any of the air forces. There were no dedicated bombers as such, nor fighters – or 'scouts', as the British soon knew them – in service, even though the Royal Aircraft Factory's F.E.2a of 1913 was intended as a fighting aircraft and the French had planned a bomber in the same year. Scarcely a single machine had yet been designed from scratch for a specific role other than general observation. (Once the war had begun the Imperial Russian Air Force's gigantic and precocious four-engined 'Ilya Muromets', which the aviation genius Igor Sikorsky had designed and built in 1913, was redesignated as a bomber although originally it had been intended – and many times flown – as a luxury passenger aircraft seating sixteen. It even had a lavatory. Just how extraordinarily advanced this record-breaking aircraft was compared with any other in 1914 can be judged by the fact that it continued in service until 1922.) If anything, most aircraft designers were still aiming for the characteristics best suited to reconnaissance: stability, easy handling, and duration in the air. Things like altitude, top speed and manoeuvrability were not yet reckoned of much importance. Pilots and observers were prepared to be sent aloft for any task they might be ordered to perform, from taking photographs to dropping bombs and *fléchettes* on enemy troops.

*Fléchettes* or 'aeroplane arrows', which the French had already used in their pre-war Moroccan campaign, were simple steel darts a few inches long equipped with stabilising fins. All three principal combatants dropped their own designs. There is an early account that a Dr J. Volkmann gave to the Stuttgart Medical Society of two British aircraft at a height of around 4,000 feet dropping *fléchettes* on three German companies of bivouacked Uhlan cavalry. Volkmann reported that out of fifty or so *fléchettes* dropped, fifteen soldiers and several horses were hit, two men being killed outright while others were badly wounded, one pinned to the ground by a dart through his foot. Though lacking the lethality of explosive weapons they were definitely demoralising and half a century later would be used in American munitions in Vietnam to dreadful effect. At the time many RFC and RNAS airmen thought *fléchettes* 'unBritish' and disliked dropping them on account of the dreadful wounds they could inflict. But squeamishness was another of the war's early casualties.

It had been clear from the first that it was nearly impossible for one aircraft to down another by means of pistols. No observer standing up in a lurching cockpit in a sixty mile-an-hour gale trying to hit another with a service revolver could hope to score, barring a one-in-a-million fluke. As Louis Strange had quickly realised, machine guns were absolutely essential for serious aerial combat. (He would have been amazed by the story dating from the Second World War claiming that the pilot and co-pilot of an American L-4 light aircraft, Lieutenants Duane Francis and Bill Martin, opened fire on a German Fieseler Storch observation machine with their .45 service automatics, forcing it to land and its crew to surrender.)[42]

The problem with machine guns was chiefly one of weight: not merely that of the weapon itself but of the ammunition. Both the RFC and the RNAS opted for the American-designed Lewis gun as their standard weapon but left the question of how it should be mounted to individual taste. This was both logical and absurd: logical because the design and position of the mounting depended critically on the type of aircraft, and absurd because the lack of standardisation gave each man the responsibility for cobbling something together that might work. The Lewis gun weighed 28 lb, which was manageable. By far the easiest aircraft to arm were the 'pusher' types with the engine at the back like the British F.E.2d and the French Maurice Farman 'Shorthorn'. As already noted, this design afforded the observer-gunner in front an unobstructed field of fire upwards, downwards and on both sides, although it was highly vulnerable to attack from the rear.

This set-up contrasted strongly with 'tractor' biplanes (like practically all the German types) with the engine and propeller in front. This arrangement soon proved hopeless if the observer remained in the forward cockpit, as convention at first seemed to demand in British two-seaters. Sandwiched between the upper and lower wings the gunner had no field of fire at all, hemmed in as he was by the birdcage structure with its delicate struts and the vulnerable propeller immediately in front of him. Close behind him was his pilot and, further to the rear, the aircraft's fin and tailplanes. In fact, if one had set out expressly to design an aircraft for a machine gun that could never be safely fired, something like the British B.E.2c or the Avro 504 with their observer-gunner in the front seat would have been it. Yet this was no more than a reflection of the fact that the Royal Aircraft Factory had designed the B.E.2c before the war for the express purpose of observation and photography rather than for fighting.

Here it is worth noting that in the German air force the observer was usually in the back seat. He was generically known as 'Franz' and was almost always an officer, while the pilot ('Emil') was his subordinate, no matter that with experience both men would form comradely bonds of mutual trust. By contrast it seemed logical to both the French and the British that the pilot should be in command of the aircraft, regardless of rank. German culture evidently saw things differently, perhaps by analogy with an officer in the back seat of a staff car giving directions to the driver/chauffeur, who was also expected to double as a mechanic in case of breakdown.

With remarkable swiftness the RFC's new commander in France, Hugh Trenchard, appreciated that the attack must be taken to the enemy and that, used correctly, aircraft were nothing if not offensive weapons. For this they needed to be properly armed. The Lewis gun initially deployed by the RFC and the RNAS was air-cooled. Its .303 ammunition, which was identical to the standard round used in the infantry's rifles as well as in its Vickers machine guns, came in flat drums that revolved on top of the weapon. When it didn't jam the Lewis achieved a rate of fire of about 550 rounds per minute. The French had already settled on their 8 mm Hotchkiss, a reliable design that was also air-cooled and at first belt-fed until it too was converted to a drum feed with a rate of fire of about 450 rounds per minute. The Germans' drum-fed 7.9 mm Parabellum MG 14 could fire up to 700 rounds a minute. In terms of airborne offensive weapons the three main air forces were thus fairly evenly matched at the outset. That is, until the next great step, which was devising a way to fire a machine gun through the aircraft's propeller arc without reducing the propeller itself to matchwood: the Holy Grail of early air warfare.

The value of a pilot being able to deploy his own machine gun rather than relying on his observer's was self-evident. The obstacle in a front-engined aircraft was obviously that of the propeller, and worse could result from damaging it than merely losing motive power. According to German accounts the early ace Max Immelmann died when, through a mechanical fault, his gun shot a single blade off his propeller. Before he could throttle back the severely unbalanced engine tore itself off its bearers and the Fokker monoplane broke up in the air. (This is eminently possible, although Allied accounts suggest this was a face-saver and Immelmann was actually shot down, which in Germany would have been a severe blow to morale since by then he was a public hero.) Sundry efforts had been made to devise gun mountings that ensured the stream of bullets missed this vital part. As already mentioned, one had the machine gun mounted outside the cockpit beside the pilot but pointing out-wards at an angle, which obviously required flying an oblique line at an opponent. Calculating the angle of deflection accord-ing to range and speed also made for very difficult shooting, although the future British ace Lanoe Hawker VC became famously adept at this with a single-shot rifle. The more usual solution in a biplane was to mount the gun above the pilot on the centre section of the upper wing, firing just over the arc of the propeller. The advantage of this arrangement was that the gun aimed where the aircraft was pointed. The drawback was that if the gun jammed (as machine guns of the period fre-quently did) or needed reloading, it was beyond easy reach. In the early days the pilot would have to stand up in the cockpit in a seventy-mile-an-hour gale to hammer at the cocking handle or wrestle with a spare drum of ammunition, all the while trying to control the aircraft. In combat this was all but suicidal.

Once again Louis Strange supplies a vivid example. On 10th May 1915 he was at 8,500 feet in his single-seat Martinsyde biplane trying to shoot down an Aviatik of Bruno Loerzer's squadron with the Lewis gun mounted on his upper wing. Strange was annoyed by the German 'Franz' taking rather too accurate pot shots at him with his pistol. Provoked, he shot off

an entire drum of ammunition at the Aviatik but without discernible effect. When he tried to replace the empty drum it
jammed and refused to come loose. What happened next is best
told in Strange's own words, bearing in mind that like every
other airman of the day he had no parachute:

> After one or two fruitless efforts I raised myself out of my seat
> in order to get a better grip, and I suppose my safety belt
> must have slipped down at the critical moment. Anyhow, my
> knees loosened their grip on the stick just as the Martinsyde,
> which was already climbing at its maximum angle, stalled and
> flicked over into a spin.
>
> As I was more than half out of the cockpit at the time, the
> spin threw me clean out of the machine, but I still kept both
> my hands on the drum of the Lewis gun. Only a few seconds
> previously I had been cursing because I could not get that
> drum off, but now I prayed fervently that it would stay on for
> ever. I knew it might come off at any moment, however, and
> as its edge was cutting my fingers badly I had to get a firmer
> hold of something more reliable. The first thing I thought
> of was the top of the centre section strut, which at that time
> was behind and below the Lewis gun, but as the machine was
> now flying upside down I had sufficient wits left to realize
> that it was behind and above me, though where exactly I
> could not tell.
>
> Dare I let go the drum with one hand and make a grab for
> it? There was nothing else for it but to take the risk. Having
> achieved this firmer handhold I found my chin rammed
> against the top plane [wing] beside the gun while my legs
> were waving about in empty air. The Martinsyde was upside
> down in a flat spin, and from my precarious position the only
> thing I could see was the propeller (which seemed unpleas-
> antly close to my face), the town of Menin, and the adjacent
> countryside revolving apparently above me and getting larger
> with every turn.

I kept on kicking upwards behind me until at last I got first one foot and then the other hooked inside the cockpit. Somehow I got the stick between my legs again and jammed on full aileron and elevator. The machine came over the right way up and I fell off the top plane into my seat with a bump. I grabbed at the stick with both hands but to my surprise found myself unable to move it. I suddenly realized that I was sitting much lower than usual inside the cockpit; in fact, I was so low down I could not see over the edge at all. The bump of my fall had sent me right through my seat, with the result that I was sitting on the floor of the machine as well as on the control cables, which I was jamming.

Something had to be done quickly as the engine was roaring away merrily and taking me down in a dive which looked likely to end in the wood to the north of Menin. So I throttled back and braced my shoulders against the top of the fuselage and my feet against the rudder bar, pulled out the broken bits of seat and freed the controls. I was then able to put the machine's nose up and open the throttle again. I rose and cleared the trees on the Menin road with very little to spare. I felt happy to be alive and thought it simply marvellous that I was still able to control the machine.

I went to bed early that night and slept for a good solid twelve hours, but Lord! how stiff I was the next day! It took a long time before I was able to move about with any comfort.[43]

It was not long before the over-wing 'Foster' mounting was devised that enabled the pilot to pull a Lewis gun back and down to him on a downward-curving rail. It didn't make the jams any less frequent but it did make it a good deal less hazardous to clear stoppages and change magazines. It also enabled a pilot to shoot at an aircraft from beneath it. Both the German and French air forces devised similar mounts. Even so, this solution was still not as good as having the gun fixed accessibly in front of the pilot and firing through the propeller, and everybody knew it. In fact, this problem had been widely considered well before 1914. The pioneer aviator August Euler (who held the first German pilot's licence) tried in 1910 to patent the idea of fixing a machine gun to a 'pusher' aircraft's nose so the gun would be aimed by pointing the entire aeroplane at a target. It seems doubtful that a patent would have been awarded simply for an idea, especially one that must have been obvious to many, and in fact Euler's 'invention' was really no more than a copy of the French Voisin designs already mentioned. At the time the German Army, having concentrated so much of its inventive prowess on airships, had little interest in arming aircraft. Furthermore, its aircraft designers favoured tractor rather than pusher types, being especially keen on their 'Taube'-type mono-planes. These were unusually stable, and as we know in those early days of aviation stability was prized over agility. Thus the Germans were faced with an urgent technical challenge: where on a monoplane with the engine in the nose could one accessi-bly fix a weapon *without* it firing through the propeller arc? It was no good putting machine guns out on the wings because once they had jammed or needed reloading the aircraft would be defenceless.

In 1911 the Swiss engineer Franz Schneider was working in France for the Nieuport aircraft company where he devised an ingenious scheme for mounting a gun that fired through the hollow propeller shaft of an inverted inline aero engine. Turning the engine upside down had the additional advantage that the six bulky cylinders were now underneath and no longer obstructed the pilot's view. The following year Schneider was offered and accepted a job at the German aircraft company LVG, based at Johannisthal airfield, Berlin. He suspended work on his idea of firing through the engine's prop-shaft as being better adapted for a cannon than for a machine gun. (The prin-ciple was adopted later in the war for the cannon in the French SPAD XII fighter and in the Second World War for arming such high performance designs as the Messerschmitt Bf 109, the French Dewoitine D.520 and the Russian Yak-9U.) In 1913 Schneider published a patent for a different approach in which a cam activated by the crankshaft would block the trigger of an automatic weapon so that it couldn't fire if a propeller blade was directly in front of the muzzle. He installed this in one of LVG's two-seater E.III monoplanes but unfortunately the aircraft was almost immediately lost in a crash.

The epithet 'unfortunately' is appropriate because the whole subject of synchroniser (or interrupter) gear has since turned into an aviation historian's battleground. The engineering problem was complex enough: how to make a machine gun's set rate of fire coincide with the gaps offered by however many propeller blades were spinning in front of it (generally either two or four) and regardless of the engine speed. The matter has become contentious because there are several other claims to have been the first practical design, by far the best known being Anthony Fokker's own account in his ghosted autobiography, *Flying Dutchman* (1931), a book that is probably not much more self-serving than are most of its kind. In a chapter modestly headed 'I Invent The Synchronised Machine Gun' he alleges that 'the invention and development had all been completed in forty-eight hours of day and night work, after I had hit upon the essential idea'. Just how disingenuous this description is can be judged by recalling that, like Franz Schneider, Fokker was himself based at Johannisthal and in 1915 as a young aircraft designer and engineer of growing reputation he would have been privy to the projects of the various companies based around the same Berlin airfield. There is no way he could not have known about Schneider's work.

Meanwhile in France the pioneer Morane brothers had formed the Morane-Saulnier aero company with the engineer Raymond Saulnier, who invented and built a synchronised gear mechanism for which he took out a patent just before the war. The late British aviation historian Harry Woodman is unequivocal on the matter:

'There is no doubt in this author's mind that Saulnier invented and built the first practical gun synchronisation gear in April 1914.'[44] Roland Garros, the pioneer French aviator who in 1913 had flown the first-ever crossing of the Mediterranean (Fréjus to Bizerta), joined the army as a pilot at the outbreak of war. On 1st April 1915 he took off in his Morane-Saulnier Type L 'Parasol' (high-winged) monoplane fitted with a machine gun using Saulnier's system to fire through the propeller. Because variations in individual loads meant that some cartridges fired fractionally quicker or slower than others it was still not possible to guarantee that the occasional bullet might not hit the propeller. So Saulnier fitted protective steel deflector plates to the inside of the propeller blades. That day Garros made history by shooting down a German aircraft, the first-ever aerial combat victory by an aircraft using a machine gun firing through its propeller. He thus has claims to be the first true fighter pilot and his single-seat Parasol the world's first real fighter aircraft. During the course of the same month he went on to shoot down two more German aircraft, causing consternation in the *Fliegertruppen*. This French aircraft clearly represented a technological leap forward that they urgently needed to understand and master. Luckily for them they didn't have long to wait to learn the secret of Garros's success. On 18th April he was obliged to force-land behind the German lines and failed to set fire to his machine before he was captured. A team led by Anthony Fokker soon pulled the Parasol apart and all was revealed.

Within three months Fokker had designed a monoplane fighter of his own, the E.1 *Eindecker* which he fitted with a forward-firing machine gun using his own synchronising system that was efficient enough not to require deflector plates on the propeller blades. This can now be seen as arguably the single most revolutionary aircraft of the entire war, a true game-changer in that in its primitive way it set the pattern of the typical attack aircraft that in one form or another was to last for the next hundred years: a highly manoeuvrable monoplane with a reliable system of fixed guns firing forward. That summer of 1915 began the six months of German air supremacy that Noel Pemberton Billing described as the 'Fokker Scourge'. It was not that Fokker's aircraft was itself so superior or, indeed, original in design (it was very closely modelled on Morane-Saulnier's pre-war Type H). It had good manoeuvrability but a tendency to shed its wings in dives. What gave it terrifying superiority was its forward-firing Spandau machine gun. A development of Hiram Maxim's original design, this was the 7.92 mm IMG 08 whose ammunition came in cloth belts each containing 250 rounds. For a good half-year the French and especially the British air forces could do little to counter it.

Fokker's *Eindecker* was a good example of how a new technology can enforce a radical change in military thinking. Once the single-seat fighter was established as an effective type it took on specific functions for itself that were to endure for at least the next half-century, well beyond the Second World War, to be modified only when advances in aerodynamics, jet engines and avionics made it possible to revert to the 1914 idea of a non-specific, multi-role aircraft equally useful according to mission as a fighter or bomber, in ground attack or reconnaissance.

The 'Fokker Scourge' effectively lasted from July 1915 until early 1916. Like other monoplanes of its day the E.1 at first proved a tricky aircraft to fly, but once the German pilots had mastered its foibles it took a toll of RFC aircraft that made it vital for Britain to acquire its own synchronising gear as quickly as possible. The German tactics with the new Fokker were to hunt in pairs or even in threes, to climb to 10,000 feet and then swoop down on Allied aircraft, firing continuously before passing them at speed and climbing back up again. Britain's Vickers 'Gunbus', a two-man pusher aircraft, won German respect for its sturdiness as well as for the machine-gunner in its nose with an excellent field of fire; but it was not really a match for this sort of tactic. Neither were other two-seater 'scouts' of its generation, the 'Fee' (the F.E.2 series) and the R.E.7. The Fokker held too much of

an advantage in speed and climb. The RFC had to resort to formation flying with Fees and Gunbuses escorting the fatally
defenceless B.E.2c observation machines over enemy lines, but
this did little more than make it easier for the Germans to spot
them and pick them off.

From early 1916 the RFC at last began to reorganise its squadrons according to dedicated roles so that each flew the same type
of aircraft. Hitherto, any squadron might field a motley assortment of types and vintages to which sorties were assigned
somewhat at whim. But the coming of Fokker's single-seat fighter
made this amateurish approach impossible to sustain. In February
1916 24 Squadron, under Major Lanoe Hawker VC, flew to
France as the first RFC single-seat fighter squadron. They were
equipped with the de Havilland D.H.2. This was still a 'pusher'
type of aircraft in which the pilot had both to fly and aim his gun:
a type of design that synchronisation gear had made old-
fashioned at a stroke even though the D.H.2 was probably the
best of all the pushers in terms of performance and toughness.
Like many another true fighter it at first proved difficult to fly for
pilots used to the almost bovine stability of the old Avros and the
government's aircraft from the Farnborough establishment. It
had a tendency to spin, and following one occasion when a spinning D.H.2 caught fire it was dubbed 'the Spinning Incinerator'.
As we know, in those days spinning was hardly understood and
less confident pilots tended to be almost superstitious about it.
However, among those who mastered it the D.H.2 gradually lost
its fearsome nickname. It also helped that it was fully aerobatic,
which naturally appealed to the better pilots who, once in France,
began systematically to deal with the Fokker Scourge. By late May
Sir Henry Rawlinson, General Officer Commanding the Fourth
Army, could report that 'the de Havilland machine has unquestionably proved itself superior to the Fokker in speed, manoeuvre,
climbing and general fighting efficiency'.

Nevertheless, pushers were not as efficient as were front-
engined aircraft and the British had yet to make the breakthrough

of coming up with a suitable way of allowing a machine gun to fire safely through the propeller arc and installing it in a fighting aircraft. From the first, German pilots flying the Fokker *Eindecker* had been forbidden to venture over the British lines for fear the secret of their synchroniser might be revealed. At last, on 8th April 1916 one was downed on the British side of the lines and Anthony Fokker's mechanism could be taken apart and examined in detail. But although a British equivalent had lagged behind both the Germans and the French, the engineers had not been idle and six weeks later the first RFC machines equipped with synchronising gear, the new Sopwith 1½-Strutters of 70 Squadron, arrived in France. The gear was made by Vickers and the aircraft mounted a single Vickers machine gun on the cowling in front of the pilot. In the long run this particular gear proved less significant than the type of gun. Because of the way its action worked the ubiquitous Lewis gun was impossible to synchronise, and from now on the Vickers took its place as a forward-firing machine gun.

Meanwhile the Royal Navy, individual as ever, favoured a synchroniser called the Scarff-Dibovski. 'Scarff' referred to Warrant Officer F. W. Scarff of the RNAS who had already invented the 'Scarff ring' mount for the gun of the observer/gunner in the rear cockpit of two-seaters. As the name suggests this was circular, and by means of bungee suspension to cancel the weight of the gun it enabled the gunner to swivel the weapon quickly through 360 degrees. As with most other advantageous developments it was swiftly copied by other air forces and the Scarff ring and its derivatives went on being used in aircraft long after the First World War.

Like the Vickers, the Scarff-Dibovski synchroniser was not a great success and the British tried other types including one made by the Sopwith company, the Sopwith-Kauper gear. But like the Fokker system, all these variants were purely mechanical. The synchronising gear the British finally adopted, and which was to remain in service until the Second World War, was the so-called Constantinesco [*sic*] or 'CC' gear. It was the invention of a Romanian scientist with a fertile mind, George Constantinescu, who had settled in London in 1912. It employed his theory of sonics, which used hydrosonic impulses transmitted through oil-filled tubes to synchronise the gun with the propeller. The theory behind the system remained an official secret until after the war even though it used the same basic principle as that of hydraulic brakes in a car (which the American Fred Duesenberg had pioneered for his racers in 1914).

Unfortunately the sheer speed of development and the hectic pressures of wartime manufacture did not allow for much in the way of re-equipping existing aircraft with better weapons and weapon systems as they became available. Thus Arthur Gould Lee, in a letter to his wife from France dated 29th June 1917, could still write:

Scott left us because he'd shot away half his propeller. The Sopwith-Kauper interrupter gear with which the [Sopwith] Pup is fitted is complicated mechanically and sometimes goes wrong, and then the bullets go through the prop. It's this gear which slows down the rate of fire of the Vickers. In the air when you press the trigger, instead of getting the fast rattle of a ground gun you have a frustrating pop! pop! pop! pop! The Huns have a much more efficient gear, for the Spandau fires very fast. In fact, when you hear the twin Spandaus of the Albatros opening up on your tail they sound like some vast canvas being ripped by a giant. And your answer is pop! pop! pop![45]

Even the Constantinesco gear was not infallible, being highly dependent on correct maintenance, as were all the synchronisation systems. The ease with which guns jammed, invariably at a critical moment (otherwise why would a pilot be firing?), was a permanent source of complaint in all the air forces in the First World War. One of the commonest reasons was a swollen or split cartridge. Cockpits were usually equipped with a small pouch containing a hammer with which the wretched pilot could bash away at the gun's cocking handle until the cartridge was cleared. This usually happened when under attack, the pilot cursing and hammering at his gun even while trying to dodge about and avoid collision. It was noticeable that many of the pilots who became 'aces', or others who realised that being an accurate shot was every bit as important as being able to fly well, would spend time before sorties hand-loading their own machine gun belts and checking each round rather than going off to the mess and leaving the job to some ack-emma (air mechanic, in the Army's phonetic alphabet). They would then taxi their machine over to the testing butts (the 'gun pit') on the edge of the air-field and zero the guns afresh, according to the range they preferred for attacking. Any gun they found unsatisfactory they would take to the Armaments Officer's hut and swap for some-thing better. On such attention to detail their lives depended. As the ace Mick Mannock succinctly advised anyone posted to 74 Squadron: 'Sight your own guns. The armourer doesn't have to do the fighting.' He was unequivocal about the importance of constant shooting practice, of going up in a spare half hour to try to hit a petrol tin in a nearby field at various distances and speeds. 'Good flying never killed a Hun yet,' he would say. 'And when you shoot, don't aim for the plane – aim for the pilot.'[46]

In fact many of the most successful pilots like Mannock and McCudden spent a good deal of time tinkering with their air-craft's engines and guns, trying out various modifications of their own invention for improving performance. Each gun – like each aircraft and each engine – had a log or record sheet of its own on which the armourer noted its history: whether and when it had jammed, the total number of rounds it had fired, plus any mechanical defects such as barrel wear. Mannock is reported to have increased his Vickers' rate of fire by the judicious addition of a washer somewhere in its mechanism. But none of these critical tweakings and tunings was proof against a substandard load in a single cartridge, or a primer cap whose mercury fulminate failed to ignite the charge.

Often behind such things lay the labour problems in Britain's munitions factories. There, the predominantly women workers would be working long shifts doing repetitive and heavy tasks with potentially dangerous explosives. As time went on they became increasingly unionised and despite emergency legislation mounted ever more frequent go-slows and walkouts. Endemic alcoholism and drug-taking hardly helped the situation, and under the intense pressure to maintain and increase production quality checks could be variable or skimped altogether. Since working conditions – and especially lighting – were often poor and there was increasing panic over German air raids and the toxicity of the chemicals the munitions workers were using, it is hardly surprising that some of the millions of cartridges they churned out varied in quality.

Aside from that, though, a common reason for guns stopping in the air was extreme cold, particularly at high altitude. The various kinds of grease and oil, so vital to the proper functioning of these high-speed mechanisms, thickened and sometimes froze solid. The RFC's Chief Armament Officer, Major J. L. T. Pearce, devised an electric heater to keep a gun warm and Mannock enthusiastically adopted it. Low temperature oils and lubricants were also introduced but they didn't work at the subzero temperatures of patrols at very high altitude (from 1917 up to 20,000 feet). Then, a pilot's only recourse was to fire half a dozen single shots every so often to keep the breech warm in case of a sudden attack. It was wasteful of ammunition but better than being caught defenceless.

★

The First World War saw the rapid development of existing types of bullet such as armour-piercing (AP), tracer, incendiary and explosive, most of which occasioned moral outrage and accusations of 'frightfulness' at one time or another. It should be pointed out that all of them had been produced before the war by this or that country. Only one type of bullet had already been outlawed by the Hague Convention in 1899. This was the notorious creation of the British Military Arsenal at Dum-Dum, Calcutta, a few years earlier. The dum-dum was not an explosive but an expanding bullet. The problem with sharp-nosed jacketed bullets designed for maximum range is that they tend to go straight through a target and carry on beyond. It was obviously better to devise a round that gave up all its energy on impact to cause maximum damage. The British military achieved this by cutting a slit in the nose of the bullet so it would mushroom on hitting anything. It was this type that was outlawed, as well as other soft-nosed bullets designed to expand, such as hollow points. As the First World War progressed, so new propellants were adopted and the velocities of bullets greatly increased. Particularly if they tumbled after a ricochet they could cause gross injuries that field doctors wrongly but excusably assumed could only have been caused by 'exploding' bullets.

True exploding bullets were not really practicable simply because they were too small to contain a significant explosive charge. But tracers ('sparklers') were devised that left a smoke trail and glowed in the dark to tell the gunner where his shots were going. However, not only did they quickly become erratic as their charge burned, often misleading the gunner as to whether the rest of his shots were on target, but their corrosion and residues fouled gun barrels and jammed mechanisms. Pilots usually had their own private preferences for the best combinations of bullet types in their machine gun belts, selecting from a mixture of ordinary rounds, tracer, armour-piercing and incendiary.

Incendiary rounds were originally devised for use against hostile airships (Zeppelins, for instance) or observation balloons. A frequent and unloved mission – usually rated by airmen on all sides as semi-suicidal – was to shoot down enemy balloons that were directing artillery fire. These were always heavily protected by nests of machine guns and anti-aircraft guns as well as by aircraft waiting high overhead. It was wrongly believed that incendiary ammunition would easily set fire to the hydrogen in the balloon and several different British types of bullet were invented, among them the Pomeroy, the RTS, the Brock and – best-known of all – the Buckingham. They all contained phosphorus in one form or another, were sensitive to heat and could be quite hazardous to the user in a highly flammable aircraft. The Buckingham incendiary round achieved notoriety because it was soft-nosed and at the beginning was officially made available for use only against Zeppelins flying over Britain. Nevertheless it became widely employed in France against balloons, although with trepidation as it was said that any pilot who was downed over the German lines with Buckingham ammunition would be shot out of hand. Station commanders sometimes gave a pilot an official letter in English and German stating that his Buckingham rounds were for use exclusively in sorties against gas-filled balloons.

As usual in war, complaints by one side of 'inhuman' weapons used by the other were purely hypocritical. As early as 1914 the French pioneered the use of tear gas in artillery shells. This seemed to constitute a carte blanche for the use of chemical agents by all sides and it was only a matter of months before both the Germans and the British adopted the mass release of chlorine, and later mustard gas, phosgene and worse on the battlefield. That all these contravened the 1899 Hague Declaration as well as the 1907 Hague Convention on Land Warfare knocked none of the combatants off their self-claimed moral high ground. Compared to the horror of young men trapped in trenches being burned alive with flamethrowers (a German invention), the Buckingham bullet now looks almost humane.

★

How these basic component parts – the assorted weaponry and the aircraft themselves – were brought together and deployed for an ever-widening variety of hazardous military purposes is the subject of the next chapter.

# CHAPTER 4

# COMBAT AND OTHER MISSIONS

---

'By this time we were near the trenches and as we approached – still of course with the sun behind our backs – I saw an enemy scout machine diving into our trenches and firing at the troops. It was easy to take him in our stride for home, and diving steeply I met him nose-on as he turned to make another dive. I nearly hit this machine, for we were approaching each other at something like 300 miles per hour. After firing I saw a burst of steam come from his radiator and he took a steep dive towards the River Scarpe. At the time I thought I had set him on fire and he was going to try to come down in the water to extinguish the flames (this fight took place at under 1,000 feet), but I was attributing thoughts to a dead man, for he bit the earth in No Man's Land, sending up a great cloud of dust, since he fell with the velocity of a shell. This was one of the few occasions when I was sufficiently near to the ground to feel sick at the sight of a vertical plunge to earth of what was, but a few seconds previously, a breathing fellow-man mounted on wings of silk, but now unrecognizable amidst the twisted mass; death dealt to him while he was dealing death.

And so we flew home, landed and made our report. Four, possibly five of the enemy had been brought down before breakfast. We ourselves were untouched save for a few small holes in our wings from the anti-aircraft fire and, by virtue of

living on the surface, by turning away our faces and refusing
to acknowledge death, by casting off that thin veneer of civi-
lization with the excuse that we were, after all, hired assassins
in the cause of patriotism, we were able to sit down and enjoy
a good breakfast. How marvellously can the human mind
adapt itself, how easily persuade itself that its course is right,
from a nation to the individual; so that all experience, all
knowledge, even religious beliefs can be laid on one side
until the lust to kill is satisfied, leaving a charred and black-
ened earth and the sweet sickly smell of blood.'[47]

This is part of an undated account by an RNAS flight commander of a dawn patrol that took place over Flanders,
somewhere between Arras and Douai, probably in late 1917 or
early 1918. It is merely one of hundreds of such descriptions of
First World War combat left by aircrew of all nations. The sentiments, too, were clichés even at the time. It was a very blunt
sensibility that failed to appreciate the thinness of civilisation's
veneer and did not at some point think itself no better than a
hired assassin.

As we know, this was emphatically not how the air war began.
For the first few months the respective armies were mostly
content for their aircraft to 'see over the hill', to use their own
jargon. But it was not long before it became obvious that with
the infantry largely bogged down this would primarily be an
artillery war, and the need became urgent for artillerymen to
have an eye in the sky to tell them what to aim at and whether
they were hitting it. At the same time it was obviously necessary
to attack the enemy's observation balloons, just as in time it
became imperative to carry out patrols, take photographs, spot
for the artillery gunners, prevent hostile aircraft from doing the
same, shoot up troops in their trenches, drop bombs, and finally
do much of this work by night as well as by day. In short, to adopt
the modern military cant, it was a good example of generalised
'mission creep'. Airmen and aircraft laboured to keep up with

the armies' expanding demands, while the armies themselves struggled to deal with what they saw as aviation's shortcomings. Behind this lay a real difficulty that aggravated both parties' problems: that of communication. The situation would have been utterly transformed had there been a reliable way of talking to each other during operations. This one great lack must indirectly have cost hundreds of thousands of infantry lives, as well as those of many hundreds of airmen.

The trouble was that radio, or wireless as it was then known, was almost as much in its infancy as were aircraft. The great Italian pioneer Guglielmo Marconi had sent the first Morse transmission across the English Channel in 1899, almost exactly ten years before Blériot became the first man to fly it. The first dots and dashes faintly crossed the Atlantic only in late 1902 – a year to the month before the Wright brothers first left the ground in their 'Flyer' – but such transmissions were unreliable and weather-dependent in that a kite needed to be launched first in order to pull a couple of hundred feet of aerial wire into the sky. Not only was Marconi's spark transmitter crude, he knew little about wavelengths and nothing about how radically the range of a transmission could be affected by whether it was sent by night or day. But knowledge grew and by 1912 wireless was installed on most oceangoing liners; and in the sinking of the *Titanic* that year the technology proved serviceable enough to summon RMS *Carpathia* belatedly to the scene.

However, it was one thing to install a wireless room aboard a ship and quite another to reduce the equipment in size and weight so it would fit into an early aircraft. It was a real achievement in August 1910 when John McCurdy in the United States transmitted the first Morse message from an aircraft to the ground, a feat that was repeated a month later in Britain by the pilot-actor Robert Loraine, flying a 50 h.p. Bristol Box-kite above Salisbury Plain during the Army's autumn manoeuvres. By the end of 1911 the British Army had designed a wireless transmitter suitable for its aircraft and in June 1914 the RFC Lieutenants B.

T. James and D. S. Lewis flew from Netheravon to Bournemouth
with transmitters and receivers in their two B.E.2s. They flew ten
miles apart and kept in touch with each other by Morse the
whole way. This seemed auspicious.

Yet as the Army soon discovered, there was a big difference
between experimentally installing wireless equipment in a
couple of aircraft and gearing that up to widespread use,
together with aircrew well enough trained in Morse code to be
able to send and receive messages while flying. Airborne wireless
telephony – the transmission of speech – was not achieved until
1915; and although by the end of that year a British transceiver
capable of both telephony and Morse, the TWA Mk.1, was produced in small numbers, it was never more than experimental.
For the duration the war, and for the overwhelming majority of
aircraft on all sides, airborne wireless was by Morse. As has been
amply indicated, weight in those early days of aviation was critical and wireless equipment was bulky. It also required an external
power source: an accumulator fed by a generator bolted beneath
a wing or on a strut and driven by a little wooden propeller.
Apart from its extra weight the equipment caused significant
drag. Although it only provided 6 volts with an output of 30-40
watts, the system was also potentially dangerous. The Morse key
was wired directly into an induction coil that stepped up the
voltage to produce a spark across a gap when the key was pressed
(the origin of the later generic name for radio operators,
'Sparks'). This was less than safe in a flammable aircraft with
petrol vapour seeping into the cockpit, and the problem was
only solved, presumably many fireballs later, by encasing the
spark gap in a sealed box. An additional weight was the spool of
copper aerial wire the observer needed to lower before he could
transmit. This had its own drawbacks, and not only when the
aircraft needed to take evasive action.

> Half a dozen of us were sitting having tea in the orchard
> behind the sheds when a machine was heard. Soon it came

in to land, passing overhead. We looked up at it casually. It
was Hoppy, out with another pilot (for my machine was dud)
returning from patrol. Suddenly the camp table on which the
tea was set flew up into the air, described a pretty parabola
above the grass, and landed ten yards farther down the slope
– a debris of broken china and spilt jam. We all jumped up,
very annoyed.

'That silly little bastard, coming down without winding in
his aerial!' – for the meteoric flight of the tea table was
caused by the lead weight attached to the end of the aerial
catching it as it swept past at sixty miles an hour. The peace
of the orchard was gone, tea entirely ruined. 'Besides which,'
added the Major, 'the damn thing only missed my head by
six inches.'[48]

The technological and supply difficulties meant that air-to-
ground wireless communications only gradually took hold in
the various air forces. For some time yet ordinary observations
of potential targets had to be marked on a squared map which
was then dropped in a message bag for the gunners to make a
decision. A harder and even more valuable role for airmen was
in 'art. obs.' or spotting for the artillery: observing where their
shells were landing and giving instructions on how to correct
their aim. This marked the armies' shift in attitude from viewing
aircraft as an extension of the cavalry to being an extension of
artillery. Although by May 1915 many RFC airfields in France
had a wireless hut and a call sign, only a few individual aircraft
carried Morse transmitters and those were in constant demand
by the gunners. Despite this, even by the war's end airborne
wireless was still neither widespread nor reliable, many pilots
preferring to do without it altogether in exchange for having
less weight and drag. The alternative was signalling between
observer and battery using Very flares or flash lamps in a prearranged code. Such methods were obviously crude and fallible
but often there was no alternative.

An added difficulty in mid-1915 was the so-called 'Shell Crisis'. The military on all sides had miscalculated, largely through thinking the war would be brief, and supplies of big shells ran short. In Britain this was also down to industry's chronic inability to produce steel of high enough quality to make reliable shell casings. This had to be imported hastily from the United States and the inevitable delays and U-boat depredations of merchant shipping caused a scandal that threatened the government. For a while British gunners in France were rationed to four rounds per gun a day:[49] not enough even to give the spotters overhead a couple of ranging shots, while a brief barrage could exhaust that gun's ration. Once supplies of munitions increased, though, artillery observation became a major daily task for the RFC and the RNAS. A few aircrews seemed to like it, but for most it was simultaneously boring and horribly dangerous. It involved stoogeing around in the sky in an antiquated and largely defenceless machine (usually a B.E.2c) over the same spot for anything up to half an hour or even longer, by which time every 'archie' battery within range was well zeroed in and putting up its own barrage. Despite this the pilot had to circle round and round in a hail of shrapnel while his observer watched for the smoke-puffs of shells landing below and laboriously tapped out the codes for 'Over', 'Short', 'Left', 'Right' and – in the event of a bull's eye – 'OK'.

It is small wonder that the RFC's continuing reliance on the pre-war B.E.2c should have earned that aircraft the heartfelt contempt of so many airmen. Today it has its admirers; but none of them ever had to fly sorties in it against far more advanced machines armed with twin synchronised machine guns. It was a disgrace that it went on being flown for so long and in such numbers, and the men knew it. As late as June 1917 Arthur Gould Lee heard a mess performance of a parody of Psalm 23 known as *The Pilot's Psalm*:

The B.E.2c is my bus; therefore shall I want.

He maketh me to come down in green pastures.

He leadeth me where I wish not to go.

He maketh me to be sick; he leadeth me astray on all
cross-country flights.

Yea, though I fly o'er No-Man's-Land where mine
enemies would compass me about, I fear much evil,
for *thou* art with me; thy joystick and thy prop
discomfort me.

Thou prepareth a crash for me in the presence of mine
enemies; thy R.A.F.* anointeth my hair with oil, thy
tank leaketh badly.

Surely to goodness thou shalt not follow me all the days
of my life, else I shall dwell in the House of Colney
Hatch** for ever.[50]

A further danger was the real possibility of being hit by the shells
fired by the very battery the aircraft was directing. 'At two thousand feet we were in the path of the gun trajectories, and as the
shells passed above or below us the wind eddies made by their
motion flung the machine up and down as if in a gale. Each
bump meant that a passing shell had missed the machine by
four or five feet.'[51] There are even accounts of observers or
pilots actually glimpsing a big artillery shell as it howled past.
Some aircrew were less lucky. Cecil Lewis wrote of his friend and
observer Pip, who carried on art. obs. duties with another pilot
while Lewis was away on leave:

One morning, on the dawn patrol, they, flying low in the arc
of our own gunfire, intercepted a passing shell. The machine
and both the boys were blown to bits.[52]

---

* i.e. the engine designed by the Royal Aircraft Factory, Farnborough.
** Colney Hatch mental hospital at Friern Barnet, universally known as
the 'loony bin'.

But the real objection of most aircrew to spotting was the sense of being helpless prey for any enemy aircraft that happened by. The chief problem was that it was impossible to take any sort of evasive action with 120 feet or more of weighted copper wire trailing beneath the aircraft. Very often the observer would not have enough time to wind it all in before the attack and he had to leap to his gun instead. The chances were excellent of one's own machine becoming entangled in the aerial, wrecking the propeller or fouling the controls and leaving the aircraft help-less. This went on being a difficulty throughout the war (Stuart Wortley refers to a pilot's complaint about it as late as September 1918) and it was not until the war was well over that the technol-ogy had developed enough for RAF aircraft finally to acquire fixed aerials contained within the fuselage. It is equally clear that with the exception of some experimental installations, pri-marily in Home Defence, there was no regular use of wireless by British commanders on the ground to control a pilot in the air during the war.

This lack of easy communication was particularly noticeable in contact patrols. These were designed to keep the generals in the rear constantly informed about where their infantry were, espe-cially during a rapid advance. Apart from the tactical reasons, this was vital to avoid the gunners shelling their own troops. Down on the ground Royal Engineers signallers laid skeins of field telephone cables like spiders' webs across a dawn meadow, most immediately lost in the mud. Being static, they were largely useless in quick advances or retreats, and entirely so if a platoon became cut off or surrounded. The RFC was therefore instructed to maintain contact with the troops from the air and report back their position to the brigades' or divisions' headquarters. They also had to report on the enemy's position, how well it was defended, and whether or not he had reserves to bring up.

As from late spring 1916, the RFC's contact patrol aircraft had broad black bands painted on the underside of their wings and flew blue streamers from their struts in the hopes that trigger-happy British troops would not machine-gun them from their trenches, as had frequently happened. The pilots were also issued klaxon horns, and if they needed to draw the troops' attention they would fly low and slow over them repeatedly sounding the letter A in Morse code (short–long) on their klaxons like the harsh cries of some giant prehistoric bird. Hearing this, the infantry were expected to lay out a panel of white cloth on the ground with black letters in a prearranged code displayed on it. ('NN', for example, meant 'Short of ammunition'). This was communication, First World War-style. Needless to say, it was exceedingly unreliable, especially if the troops were under fire. No sane man wanted to leave the shelter of a trench or cover in order to lay out large pieces of cloth, and particularly not if there were enemy aircraft around since it simply drew attention to his position.

From the airmen's point of view, too, flying contact patrols was immensely frustrating because they could often see trouble on the way for the men on the ground and had to resort to dropping hastily scrawled messages in bags with streamers attached, provided they still had some left (in dire need the observer's cigarette case might have to be sacrificed). In reverse, a signaller was expected to communicate from the ground in Morse by means of a black-and-white venetian blind affair with strings that uncovered one or other colour, a method that was laborious to the point of impossible, especially under fire, and extremely hard for airmen passing overhead at seventy miles per hour to follow.

After the armies' initial scepticism about aviation's usefulness, by 1916 their reliance on it and their expectations of what aircraft could do were often downright unrealistic. A notorious instance of this became apparent in the first days of the costly Somme offensive in July. It was fundamental to the British Army's plan that observation aircraft should not only reveal the size and position of the German forces behind their front lines, but also direct the artillery barrage so it could blast aside the barbed wire that lay in massive entanglements in front of the advancing British troops. At the same time aircraft were also required to attack troops in the trenches as well as to bomb railways and supply lines behind the German front. Some of this was gallantly achieved. Yet no matter how good the RFC's and RNAS's cameras were, they could not show what was happening underground in the German dugouts and elsewhere: how, safely hidden from aerial scrutiny, the well-disciplined German forces went on with their target practice and machine-gun drills in underground shooting ranges. Nor were photography or observation even possible if ground mist or clouds of gas obscured the view, as was often the case. In several places the artillery completely failed to clear the barbed wire or annihilate the Germans inside their fortifications as directed, and much of the reason for this was an absence of reliable communication between the aircraft and the artillery batteries as well as a lack of visibility. The wretched infantry advanced believing the barbed wire was gone, only to be brought up short by it and shot to ribbons.

The Germans had exactly the same problems during the protracted battle of Verdun. The usual forms of ground communication (runners, field telephones, even messenger dogs) having failed, aircraft were sent up. But even from 1,000 feet there was nothing to be seen. 'The muddy uniforms of our troops were hardly distinguishable from their background of shell holes,' as one pilot remarked later.[53] In fact, in those days long before GPS aircrew would have found it impossible to give a map reference for almost anything they saw, the destruction below them being so complete. Since whole French villages had literally vanished, the pre-war maps were useless and the German infantry frequently became lost, there being absolutely no landmark left on which to take a bearing.

★

Other forms of patrols that RFC pilots carried out included line offensive patrols (LOPs) and distant offensive patrols (DOPs).

The line offensive patrol required cruising up and down the enemy lines in a fighter to protect the vulnerable 'art. obs.' aircraft from attack as they circled around. This inevitably drew ground fire, and out of self-defence LOPs could degenerate into pure and simple trench-strafing.

As Arthur Gould Lee was to remark, 'every fighter pilot heartily abominated trench-strafing, not only because of poor results for much jeopardy, but because blind chance played too big a part.'[54] In fact, it was as near as an RFC airman came to understanding what the PBI or 'poor bloody infantry' felt like. Suddenly, his individual skill as a pilot counted for nothing and his fate was completely arbitrary, settled by randomly flying pieces of lead or steel. The trench-strafer's job was perpetually over the edge of suicidal since it involved flying low along an enemy trench and shooting up men who were well protected in the narrow, zig-zagging slit and who were meanwhile shooting back at close range with all the rifles, machine guns and anything else they possessed. No pilot ever felt other than mother-naked, perched as he was on a wicker seat with only a flying suit and some doped fabric between his cringing skin and the hail of supersonic metal hurled up at him personally from a mere eighty feet below. All in all, it was an efficient way of getting killed without having achieved anything commensurately useful. As Arthur Lee Gould put it:

> Low-flying attacks were, with few exceptions, a wasteful employment of highly trained pilots and expensive aeroplanes. A 30 percent rate of casualties meant a new squadron every fourth day and one rendered useless for normal air fighting duties. This situation developed in 46 Squadron when after a week's losses, all but a handful of our pilots were straight out from England.[55]

One obvious way of improving the airman's chances was to provide him with some protective armour. The engine and cockpits of a few B.E.2cs were given 445 lb of steel plate, but the effect on the performance of an already sluggish and outdated machine can be imagined. It was really only once aero-engines had become powerful enough towards the end of the war that armour plating became practicable. Once Camels entered service in 1917 they were extensively used for ground attacks and a prototype armoured Sopwith Trench Fighter (T.F.1) version was built. However, the project was shelved in favour of the Sopwith T.F.2 Salamander, conceived from the first for a trench fighting role. It carried 650 lb of armour to protect the pilot and the fuel tanks, and after field trials in France production was begun in the summer of 1918 despite the ridicule voiced by diehards like Biggles (*see* Chapter 9, p.246–7). However, as so often with new British aircraft, production was too slow and only a handful of Salamanders were delivered before the Armistice. The sole successful armoured aircraft of the war was the German Junkers J.I, a remarkable piece of design since the engine, tanks and pilot were protected by a one-piece 'bathtub' of steel that also doubled as the fuselage itself, monocoque-style. It was introduced in the late summer of 1917 and was well liked by its German crews since it offered them immunity from just about anything short of armour-piercing cannon shells. RFC pilots, meanwhile, had to content themselves with sitting on cast-iron stove lids, just as in World War II bomb-aimers lying prone in the nose of their aircraft used car hub caps, and in Vietnam low-flying helicopter pilots sat on their flak jackets rather than wearing them.

★

Distant offensive patrols were a distilled expression of Trenchard's aggressive policy of carrying the fight to the enemy.[*] Several flights of aircraft would carry out a sweep well behind the German lines, and many pilots could see little point in that,

* Today, DOPs would be CAPs, as the RAF calls combat air patrols.

either. Had the sortie had a particular objective such as a photo recce or a bombing raid, nobody would have raised a murmur. But to fly off deep into enemy territory either looking for trouble or just hoping to represent a demoralising presence seemed mere risk-taking for no useful purpose. DOPs were particularly unpopular because something as trivial as engine trouble could lead to an airman having to glide down and crash-land deep inside German territory, with almost inevitable capture and internment for the duration. On many of these patrols not a single enemy machine was seen, so it was not as though being downed was always the result of combat. It might merely mean a careless mechanic had failed to tighten a nut sufficiently and the last oil had drained out of the engine twenty miles on the wrong side of the line. In such circumstances a harsh stretch in a prison camp for an unknowable number of years seemed a cruelly unearned punishment, as well as a waste of a trained airman and his aircraft.

DOPs in the last two years of the war could easily lead to combat if they ran into a Jasta (German fighter squadron) patrol. A real set-piece battle could take place if they had the misfortune to encounter a flying circus like that of Richthofen himself, with massed fighters waiting 'upstairs' for just such victims. Certainly in the early stages of an encounter like this the lack of communication between aircraft made it almost impossible for the leader to employ a particular tactic once the fight had started. Formation flying without wireless required extreme alertness on the part of the wingman to what his leader was doing. It was all a matter of a pilot rocking his wings, firing off a prearranged colour of Very light with his flare pistol or simply waving his arms in the slipstream and pointing. The way a battle would commence was almost entirely determined by which side had the height advantage and could decide when and how to attack. Once the higher aircraft dived, the lower formations quickly split up to avoid becoming sitting targets, and without the cohesive force of a leader being able to communicate his tactics it quickly became a free-for-all. It seldom degenerated into a mass dogfight like the whirling knots of midges so beloved by film-makers and soon to be expected by cinema audiences. A pilot would pick out a potential victim and concentrate on him, make an attacking run and then pull out to see its effect.

However, it did sometimes happen that the number of combatants was big enough for the fight to become a mêlée, with a great risk of collision. It was a terrifying business for any pilot who was comparatively inexperienced. Everything took place at bewildering speed, with brightly coloured machines flashing past at every angle at closing speeds of 200 mph or more, and in the concentration of the moment all notion of where he was in relation to the earth beneath or to his companions was completely lost. There was the staccato sound of machine guns above the roar of his own engine, the intimate smell of other men's exhaust fumes and castor oil as well as the cordite smoke from his own guns. And then abruptly something quite extraordinary. He would complete a turn and find himself utterly alone. The guns were silent, the sky empty of aircraft, whether enemy or friendly. He would look wildly around but see nothing other than dissipating tendrils of black smoke standing in a corner of the sky to mark someone's fall. Scanning the ground he might finally spot a couple of machines low down, heading somewhere but already too far away for him to tell whose they were. Disorientated, he might follow them in the manner of a small dog tagging on at the end of a parade just so as not to be left behind. Years later, W. E. Johns wrote about a neophyte's bewilderment in combat:

> The first dog fight I was ever in, it seemed to me that one minute we – that is, my formation – were sailing along all merry and bright, and the next minute the air was full of machines, darting all over the place. I didn't see where they came from or where they went. I didn't see where my formation went, either. By the time I had grasped the fact that the

fight had started and I was looking to see who was perforating my plane, the show was all over. Two machines lay smoking on the ground and everybody else had disappeared. While I was considering what the dickens I should do I suddenly discovered that I was flying back in formation again! The fellows had come back to pick me up and formed up around me. I didn't even see where they came from.[56]

As the war went on and aircraft grew more capable, many DOPs effectively changed into bombing sorties against enemy infrastructure and finally into retaliation raids against cities. Again, these missions seemed to have a purpose – or at least they had targets – and airmen were more easily resigned to them.

As mentioned in the previous chapter, another suicidal pursuit was that of balloon strafing. Observation balloons were obvious targets, and the men who went up in their creaking baskets for hours on end with high-powered binoculars and a field telephone offered examples of some of the least-rated heroism of the entire war. Quite apart from the cold and the motion sickness often brought on by windy conditions, it must have been most unreassuring to dangle beneath an enormous tethered bag of hydrogen, the most prominent thing in the sky for miles around and famously a challenge to any passing enemy airman who fancied immortality. True, observers on both sides had a parachute that was carried in a canister outside the basket, which was more than the pilots had. True also that this worked more often than it failed, even though it sometimes happened that an observer might make it safely back to earth just in time for the blazing remains of his balloon to fall on top of him. Balloons could be hauled down if an attack were spotted in time, although the speed of their descent depended on the alertness of the ground crew and the power of the winch. Balloons' real defences lay in their usually being surrounded by ack-ack guns and machine gunners who between them could send up a lethal barrage towards any aircraft that fancied its chances. German balloons were also reputed to be defended by powerful flame-throwers, but how those were to be deployed against a rapidly moving aircraft was not clear.

Great personal acclaim accrued to those who downed a balloon, and in a pilot's tally it counted as a victory equal to shooting down an enemy aircraft. It was generally agreed that 'balloon-busting' was a mug's game, a pastime reserved for those who were radically tired of life. The greatest balloon-buster of all was the Belgian Willy Coppens. Flying his favourite French aircraft, an Hanriot HD.1, Coppens accounted for thirty-four balloons in a scant five months between May and October 1918. On more than one occasion he actually landed on top of a balloon to hide from ground fire, a brilliant dodge as well as evidence of superb airmanship. He undoubtedly had what people thought of as a charmed life because although his war career was ended by an incendiary bullet that led to the amputation of one leg, Coppens lived to be ninety-four, dying in 1986.

He had several miraculous escapes when balloon-busting, not least in surviving booby-traps. These were decoy balloons, worn-out sacrificial envelopes complete with a dummy observer leaning pensively on the rim of the basket that also contained a huge charge of high explosive fired electrically from the ground when the attacking aircraft was close enough. Each time Coppens somehow contrived to emerge unscathed in his sturdy Hanriot, rocking wildly in the blast and fumes.

Apart from the bristling defences, the main problem with shooting down balloons was the need to get in close despite the fact that they offered a very large target. Given hydrogen's noto-rious habit of exploding, it was ironic that it should so often have proved remarkably hard to set on fire. Ordinary tracer rounds seldom did the job, which was why Allied balloon-busters would load up with incendiary bullets – as already mentioned, the only permissible use of Buckingham ammuni-tion. Even this did not always work and the pilot was obliged to fall back on Le Prieur rockets. He usually carried eight of these, four on each side of his aircraft attached in racks to the outer struts between his wings. Fired electrically, the rockets had barbed heads for tearing a hole in the balloon's fabric before the main incendiary charge exploded inside. They worked, but they were seriously inaccurate and needed to be fired at close range to guarantee a hit.

Another kind of flying that hand-picked pilots were some-times asked to do was dangerous for rather different reasons. This was dropping or picking up agents in enemy territory, a mission usually but not always carried out at night. It required exceptional knowledge of the local country, which tended to mean a pilot who had been in the area for some time, plus the airmanship to find a particular field, land safely in it, turn around and take off again. Obviously it demanded good nerves as well as skill, for even though an RFC pilot might be uni-formed, dropping an agent was sometimes considered the same as being a spy since it facilitated espionage, and he stood a good chance of being shot if caught. In addition to the spy – often a nondescript Frenchman wearing peasant clothes – he would probably carry a basket of homing pigeons strapped to one wing: the spy's best chance of getting a message back. These were useful birds and RNAS seaplanes frequently carried pigeons in case the aircraft was forced down on the water. On such ancient methods was the new machine age obliged to rely, and it was astonishing when they worked, the pigeons stoically flying through appalling weather and sometimes through much worse:

> Today one of them performed an act of gallantry worthy of Napoleon's famous drummer-boy. The bird in question struggled into the pigeon loft, and having delivered its mes-sage fell dead upon the floor. It had been shot in the chest and one of its legs had been blown away, undoubtedly while crossing the trenches, for the enemy are always on the

look-out for westward-flying pigeons. The men buried it with pomp and circumstance…[57]

Certainly picking up an agent at a prearranged time and place was, as one pilot put it, 'a very ticklish business'. Obviously there was no knowing whether the spy had been caught and compromised, in which case there might be quite a reception committee waiting for whoever kept the rendezvous. There was also a good chance the field had been 'trapped', with wires stretched invisibly across it to snag the wheels of any aircraft attempting to land. There are accounts of agents being fetched out of fields from under the noses of search parties, with the aircraft doing a rolling turn-around at the end of its landing run and the sprinting agent not even having time to climb aboard but simply flinging himself onto one wing and hanging on for dear life as the aircraft took straight off again. If lucky he might cling on with frozen hands for as long as it took to get back across the lines – provided he wasn't hit by gunfire as they crossed or didn't fall off if the pilot had to make a sudden swerve.

In fact, there are numerous accounts of men surviving flights outside a cockpit (and engineers/gunners in the massive German Zeppelin-Staaken R.VI bombers were expected as a matter of course to climb an external iron ladder in flight to reach their guns in the upper wing). It was not uncommon for observers to leave their cockpit in the air – naturally, without a parachute or safety harness – and clamber around outside in the tearing slipstream in order to try and fix something. There are celebrated instances of observers hugging a strut on the outer section of a wing in order to balance a crippled aircraft as it flew, and even an instance of one managing to land his burning aircraft with its dead pilot by standing on the wing next to the cockpit with a hand on the joystick in the machine's blazing interior. In 1916, following a bombing raid on a British airfield on the island of Tenedos off the Turkish coast near the

Dardanelles, a German pilot suddenly discovered that his throttle had jammed shut:

> With astonishing coolness and agility the observer climbed
> down onto the wing and found that the control rod to the
> throttle had worked loose and that the spring on the throttle
> had automatically shut it. He therefore held it open and was
> obliged to remain standing on the wing throughout the
> whole of the homeward flight, which lasted nearly an hour.[58]

Obviously, this sort of thing was only possible in a biplane. Probably one of the very last instances of such heroics occurred in the absurdly gallant but doomed attack in February 1942 by six Fleet Air Arm Fairey Swordfish aircraft of 825 Squadron on the German battle-cruisers trying to slip through the Channel to their home port in the so-called Channel Dash. The leading Swordfish attempting to torpedo the *Scharnhorst* was a wood-and-fabric biplane designed in 1933. It was pitted against defending Messerschmitts and Focke-Wulfs and inevitably it was hit. 'Tracer tore through the junction of tail plane and fuselage, setting the fabric afire. The rear gunner, Clinton, calmly climbed out of his cockpit, sat astride the fuselage and beat at the flames with his hands. He put the fire out and clambered back.'[59]

★

Bombing became ever more common on all sides during the First World War as aircraft were designed to carry increasingly significant loads. A technique for aiming had to be developed from scratch, and a great deal of practice was called for. With practice of the kind described by one pilot it was amazing that anyone survived, even though the bombs were inert:

> After a week's constant practice most of us became fairly pro-
> ficient in the art of bomb-dropping. Sometimes one or other
> of us would be deputed to stand out on the aerodrome and

'mark' for another observer who was doing his tests. This was
a rather trying job. We used to call it 'death-dodging.' You
would take your scoring-card with its bull's eye and concen-
tric circles marked upon it, and proceed to a spot as near to,
or as far from, the target as your temperament dictated.
Some fellows would stand in the geometric centre of the ring
and allege that they felt safer there; others would hang about
near the edge of the field, and with the fall of each bomb
would dash forward, measure roughly its distance from the
bull's eye, then retreat once more to the comparative safety
of the hedge.[60]

Very British, the whole thing ('a rather trying job') in its lethal
and primitive way. Was it really not possible to devise a method
of scoring for bombing practice that didn't threaten to turn a
valuable trained pilot into a potential target on the ground?

This particular airman had been trained as a night bomber.
In the last two years of the war air activity continued through
the night. As in the case of the German bombers over London,
night flying conferred obvious advantages until defending
pilots also learned the technique. In France this skill was developed principally because the various armies soon learned the
benefit of moving troops and supplies at night. Accordingly,
these movements were targeted by the opposing artillery, which
in turn demanded 'art. obs.' aircraft to carry out their normal
daytime tasks as best they could by night. They, and night
bombers like the old F.E.2s still doing service, also carried
parachute flares that for a short while could bathe the ground
below in the unearthly white light of burning magnesium.
Apart from that, anti-aircraft and artillery guns below were
unable to suppress the muzzle-flashes that reliably betrayed
their position, just as their 'blazes' showed up in daylight on
grass and in snow.

Flying at night required very different techniques, and some
pilots never adapted to it. It was exceedingly daunting, regardless

of how courageous you were. The Canadian future ace Billy Bishop described being assigned to fly a B.E.12 as a night fighter with 37 (Home Defence) Squadron, based in Essex. It was December 1916 and he was a newly-qualified pilot. In common with everyone else at the time he had no radio, no parachute, and precious little training:

> Night flying ... in small aircraft was a fearsome business ... We took off between two rows of flares and soared into the night sky, praying to goodness we would be able to find our aerodromes when the time came to return. Our knowledge of navigation was completely elementary. We had a lecture or two ... and a rudimentary knowledge of the stars in their courses, but ... whenever we flew by night, it was strictly by the seat of the pants. I would pick myself a few shadowy land-marks and try to orient myself by them. There was no ... voice contact with the ground ... and no control tower tell-ing [us] what to do and when to do it. Consequently, it was always an awesome business to get back to the starting point and ... to land.[61]

Some pilots, no matter how courageous, never did adapt to night flying, often for physiological reasons. Men with perfect daytime vision discovered that their eyes failed to adjust to low levels of light – 'night blindness' – which ruled them out. This was also age-related: yet another reason why airmen in this first air war were generally reckoned to be over the hill at twenty-six. Some men found they became hopelessly disorientated in the dark and lost all sense of direction and even balance. They, too, were scratched from night-flying rosters, assuming they had sur-vived training long enough for their names to be put down in the first place.

Surprisingly, pilots unaffected by such conditions often adjusted very well and even found it easier to navigate at night than they had imagined – provided the weather was reasonably clear and they didn't need to make an emergency landing. Certain things became particularly visible from the air (as Anthony Fokker had already noticed before the war when flying over towns by day: a costermonger's barrow heaped with oranges in a market square stood out like a beacon, for instance, which is why a particular shade of orange-yellow is still used today for visibility at airfields). At night, and even without a moon, the stars shed an unexpected amount of light. Rivers showed up well (the German navigators heading for London needed only to pick up the mouth of the Thames and follow its sheen like a flarepath). Roads were distinguishable even in the days when by no means all roads were asphalted, especially in the country. They appeared a slightly different colour to the surrounding fields. The high polish of railway lines was also prominent, as were the signals. Railways were prime navigation aids in aviation's early days when lost pilots only needed to pick up and follow a line because sooner or later it would reach a town (in Britain this mode of navigation soon became known as 'Bradshawing', after the well-known railway timetable). At night the steam engines pulling the trains sent up billows of sparks from their chimneys, while each time a stoker opened the furnace door to throw on more coal the glow lit up the smoke overhead and was visible for miles in the darkened landscape.

Systems were developed on both sides for marking landing grounds at night. The RFC used flares laid out in an inverted 'L' shape. The pilot could land anywhere within the space the arms enclosed, depending on the direction of the wind, while the shorter arm marked the safe limit of his run. Additionally, a series of beacons could be lit in response to a Morse message – which was fine in an aircraft carrying wireless and an observer, but not available to a solo 'scout' or fighter pilot. As Billy Bishop found, the first scout pilots sent up in desperation over the Thames Estuary as part of Britain's Home Defence against German night raiders were at all sorts of disadvantage besides the likelihood of becoming lost. Perhaps the most crucial difficulty was that their instrument panels were unlit. They were therefore without any way of knowing their air speed or attitude to the horizon. It suddenly became extremely easy to edge into a stall without knowing it, and only the wind on one cheek told them if they were side-slipping. Worse still, they could not read the fuel gauge or (if they had one) the rev. counter; and worst of all they had no idea of the oil pressure, which was critical for rotary engines. A further unexpected problem was the exhaust pipe. This glowed cherry red and sent back bright rags of blue flame. Depending on how it was sited it could seriously interfere with a pilot's night vision as well as being a useful giveaway for an attacker searching for a target.

Whereas night tactical missions such as bombing and observation were feasible, if difficult and dangerous, the interception of enemy aircraft at night proved virtually impossible. If aircraft could seem to disappear with the greatest of ease in daylight – there one moment, an empty sky the next – trying to find a lightless and probably black-painted aircraft at night was generally reckoned a mug's game, although naturally squadrons of mugs were sent up to try, if only to defend their commanding officers against censure for having made no effort. Searchlights could occasionally make it easier to shoot down a bomber that had become caught in a beam, but they could also destroy night vision and leave a scout pilot temporarily blind.

★

By 1918 aircraft had long since become maids-of-all-work. In June 1918 the Independent Air Force was formed under the command of 'Boom' Trenchard with the remit of bombing German targets deep inside the Rhineland. The raids, carried out by day and night, quickly led to several Jastas of German fighters being sent down to the Nancy area from which squadrons like W. E. Johns's No. 55 were flying their shows. In some ways this represented the climax of aerial combat in the war, in the sense that at last the aircraft on both sides were more evenly matched in terms of capability. By this time no pilot any longer thought in terms of gallantry or considered for a moment that he was a knight of the air. His was 'a simple, vicious struggle for existence. There were endless days of struggling out of bed before daylight, almost too tired to gulp down the cup of tea brought in by a persistent batman with his eternal "Early morning show, sir. Fine morning, sir." Pilots would make their way, half-dazed, half-dressed and unshaven to the sheds; flying in all weathers; flying at all hours; flying when they were ill but would not say so because the squadron had lost men on the previous day and was short-handed; flying with their souls sick at seeing their friends go down in flames...'[62] From being so recently an adventure, flying had become a nightmare:

> Only politicians saw the romance in it then, with their beautiful speeches about 'our boys' – 'to be an immortal, undying symbol – a wonderful spirit of self-sacrifice – the unquenchable fire which must bring us glorious victory' – and so on – you know the stuff. Glorious victory, my hat. With most of us the war was a personal matter. Another fellow shot at you and you shot back; you shot at another fellow and he shot back; and it jolly well served you right. That's all there was to it.[63]

It might be hard to believe that two-seat bombers could be any sort of match for flying circuses (although the Red Baron himself was no longer there as inspiration, having been killed in April 1918). Yet the D.H.4 that Johns's squadron flew was a highly capable aircraft. With its 300 h.p. Rolls-Royce V-12 engine, the Eagle VIII, this two-seater could reach a ceiling of 23,500 feet and a top speed at low altitude of 143 mph (compared with the average Camel's 115 mph, for instance; while Fokker's much-feared D.VII fighter could just manage 117 mph). A bomber's vulnerability at the time was that it had to 'lay its eggs' at quite low altitude to stand much chance of hitting a specific target, and this obviously gave a diving fighter an excellent opportunity. Quite apart from the weight of the bombs it carried, the D.H.4 could not manoeuvre with the agility of a Fokker Triplane even though it could out-run or out-climb it with ease. From these facts some gruelling air battles developed:

> Bell took a formation of six machines over and came back alone after fighting twenty-seven EA [enemy aircraft] for the best part of an hour. Dowswell brought his bus back over the lines but force-landed at Pont St. Vincent. Gompertz was his gunner. He got two EA, but what a mess he was in when the tender brought him home! This was due to the fact that Dowswell had an aileron shot off and could only fly dead straight. Gompertz's Sidcot (a one-piece flying suit) [see p.212] hung on him in ribbons; it had been literally shot off his back; and those who read this who saw him will confirm that this is no exaggeration. Only one bullet hit him – in the shoulder. He didn't seem in the least upset. He just sat in the door of his hut with the rags still hanging on him, and laughed.[64]

It was small wonder that aircrew became semi-mad with exhaustion. Looking back over his notes and log books, Arthur Gould Lee found that the thirteen men in his squadron had between them flown eighty-seven hours in one day (the best part of seven hours each), that he himself had flown nearly forty combat hours in one week and one of his colleagues notched up *fifty*.[65]

Ultimately, of course, what the survivors carried away from all this was a burden of death, often in the form of vignettes not necessarily drawn directly from combat in which they took part. Random scenes became engraved on the mind, such as an airfield where one machine had just landed with long strips of shot-up fabric flapping from its wings even as another was being prepared for starting. In the background was the familiar litany exchanged between pilot and mechanic: 'Switch off', 'Switch off'. 'Suck in', 'Suck in'. 'Contact!' and the roar of the engine and a thick cloud of castor oil smoke drifting back over the returned machine from whose rear cockpit men were now gently lifting the observer, leaving his intestines behind as they did. But it was the injured man who kept weakly repeating 'Sorry... sorry...' until within seconds he died. As his pilot climbed shakily down to the ground and vomited an air mechanic assigned to that aircraft was crying, softly punching the fuselage in impotence as he wept.

Or else men would be standing in silence on the tarmac at dusk waiting for a flight's return. A blackbird would be perversely singing its evening song from a tree behind the hangars, almost loud enough to mask the dull thudding of the guns in the distance. The men would react to every distant hum or speck in the darkening sky until it was clear that by now all the aircraft would be out of fuel. There was always the hope that the phone might ring in the CO's office saying that one or other had force-landed somewhere, and maybe news would come in a week's time that someone was injured and a prisoner in Germany. Otherwise the whole lot had gone west and there was nothing to be done about it but to send urgently for a batch of fresh-faced replacements from home. And all the while the blackbird sang.

We were duly joined by this young, golden-haired blue-eyed child who looked about 16. I never met anyone so keen and literally bubbling over with enthusiasm. His letters home to relatives and friends, which at times it was my duty to censor, were a fine example of British spirit. I remember one particular letter just after he got back from a scrap with bullet holes in the petrol tank, and his machine generally shot about. It was a letter to a school friend and he said: 'I've just landed back with holes in my petrol tank, but you simply don't know or feel the danger, it's just one big thrill, hurry up and come out, it's just wonderful.' He only lasted a couple of months, poor boy, and was shot down in flames on our side of the line. In my letter home to his people I particularly avoided any reference to the way he met his death, so it was more than distressing for them when some tactless infantry officer who reached the wreckage first took his cigarette case and pocket book, which were of course badly charred, and sent them direct to his father.[66]

CHAPTER 5

# THE MAKING OF A
# FLYING MAN

———  ·  ———

THE TRAINING OF British military airmen in the First World
War followed a patchy trajectory: at first indifferent, then
often sinking to appalling before improving somewhat in the
last eighteen months of the war to finish better. How well a
country trains its aircrew is a good measure of how seriously it
values its air force; in the emergency of wartime it also inevitably
reflects the pressure to match demand with supply. Britain
began the war with a chronic lack of flying instructors and
training airfields, and although numbers of both increased
considerably, overall quality usually lagged far behind. This was
revealed in the RFC's accident rate. It is estimated that 60 per
cent of all British aircraft accidents during the war occurred
during training.[67] According to the RFC's own estimate made
in the spring of 1917, out of 6,000 pilots then in training 1,200
(a fifth) would be killed in accidents before they could qualify.[68]
These are shocking figures, although it must always be borne
in mind that in those days flying was a recent phenomenon
and both airframes and engines were very much less reliable
than they would become even twenty years later. No matter
how good an instructor and his pupil, neither was proof against
an engine failure immediately after take-off or of a wing
collapsing in mid-air.

As we have seen, at the war's outbreak Britain was caught unprepared. Although a Central Flying School had been established at

the same time as the RFC in April 1912, the impression remains that it was all done less from a conviction of aviation's vital military importance than because the War Secretary, J. E. B. Seely, had perhaps read in *The Times* one morning over breakfast that the French Army already had some 200 aircraft in service and the Germans even more. In Britain, by contrast, the chairman of the Defence Subcommittee on Aviation could observe: 'At the present time we have, as far as I know, of actual flying men in the Army about eleven, and of actual flying men in the Navy about eight, and France has about two hundred and sixty-three; so we are what you might call behind.'[69] '*As far as I know…*' Any Briton of a certain age will recognise the dry, ironic tone of the officer class whose real concerns are elsewhere – probably at Ascot or in White's. There was also perhaps the languid implication that what those foreigner Johnnies got up to was scarcely a matter for Britons to worry about unduly.

That was in 1912, and although the number of pilots and observers the RFC went on to train in the next two years increased, the pace still reflected a less than panicked ambition to catch up with the Continent. By the outbreak of war the RFC and RNAS combined could field 197 officers, many of whom were observers or non-flying. With assorted personnel plus all available aircraft and spares they between them constituted precisely four squadrons. (Five years later in April 1919 the RAF would have 27,906 officers and over a quarter of a million other ranks.) In 1913, though, the British Army could no doubt console itself by thinking that when push came to shove it always had a pool of civilian pilots to call on: young men who had earned their certificates in flying clubs and schools like Claude Grahame-White's.

Grahame-White had learned to fly at Blériot's flying school in France, in 1910 becoming the sixth holder of a Royal Aero Club pilot's licence. At that time flying clubs were springing up everywhere in Europe, most of which offered flying lessons. With the energy and enthusiasm of the true convert, Grahame-White decided on a site at Hendon as suitable for London's Aerodrome – possibly the first-ever use of that word – and bought the land and set it up. (It is now the site of the RAF Museum.) His club and flying school were typical of many others started at much the same time, whether run by keen individuals or by recently founded aircraft companies such as Bristol, which opened two schools in 1910 – one on Salisbury Plain and the other at Brooklands. Eager young men scrimped and saved to enroll at flying schools at home and abroad. The future commander of the RFC in France, Hugh Trenchard, learned to fly at Thomas Sopwith's school at Brooklands. He was nearly forty years old. Within ten days he went solo, his two and a half weeks' tuition having cost him £75 (the equivalent of over £5,000 today). All in all he had spent just sixty-four minutes in the air. Over in France Louis Blériot already had several flying schools while in Germany by 1911 there were fourteen where students could qualify for their Deutsche Luftfahrer Verband (DLV) private pilot's licence, as well as two aircraft factories (Albatros and Aviatik) producing training machines at a rate that by the war's start had supplied some 300. Private aircraft manufacturers like DFW (Deutsche Flugzeug-Werke) with its associated flying school went on being contracted throughout the war by the military to supply trained pilots, especially when – as in 1916 – the urgent need for them outstripped the Army's ability to keep up with demand.

In 1914 such enterprising young Britons as already had a private pilot's licence were exactly the volunteers the RFC badly needed to supplement those officers it had already trained at its Central Flying School in Upavon. Anyone who had had the private means or gumption to get himself into the air was plainly officer material. However, the world of pre-war flying had acquired a very definite ethos of its own, and by no means every qualified pilot was suited to military discipline. Aviation everywhere had started as a private venture and was at heart an entirely civilian enterprise. Anthony Fokker vividly remembered how, as an earnest country boy from Holland, he had moved his fledgling business to Berlin in 1911 and was amazed by the international coterie that aviation had enticed there:

> Johannisthal was a thriving little cosmopolis. Aviation was a sport which had attracted daring spirits, ne'er-do-wells, and adventurers from all over the world. There were sober, industrious pilots and designers present, too, but they were in the minority. Many of the amateur pilots were rich men's sons who found this spot a fertile ground for the sowing of wild oats. Dazzled by the dare-devilry of these men, beautiful women from the theatre and night clubs hung around the flying field, more than a little complaisant, alluring – unstinting of favours to their current heroes.[70]

This was the same crowd that aviation was attracting everywhere. Fokker's description of it as a 'sport' was apt. By no means every pilot was either very experienced or skilled, and many were easily tempted into showing off to girlfriends and admirers, performing ever more hair-raising stunts in aircraft that had a habit of coming apart in the air. The turnover of what today would be known as 'silly young buggers' was brisk. Once Adolphe Pégoud, a Blériot company test pilot and instructor, had followed the Russian Pyotr Nesterov's example a few days earlier in September 1913 and made his name by looping a Type XI monoplane, 'looping the loop' became a huge novelty crowd-pleaser and for a year or so acquired a death-defying mystique all its own. Pégoud went on to become an early ace until shot down in 1915 by one of his own German ex-students, who reportedly wept when he learned what he had done. Meanwhile, over in America a brilliant barnstorming pilot named Lincoln J. Beachey made his own short-lived name and fortune by performing multiple loops, the final one of which killed him when his aircraft broke up over San Francisco Bay and he drowned. Such 'stunting' manoeuvres were soon to become a necessary part of aerial combat, but by then aircraft were better designed for such harsh treatment. In the pre-war years it was widely recognised that a solid proportion of airshow spectators came in the expectation of thrills, death and disaster, just as they went to motor races, and they seldom left disappointed.

It was obvious to the British Army that while dash and pluck were as essential to its pilots as they were to its cavalrymen, they were qualities needing to be reined in and subjected to stern military discipline. Observation aircraft were to be crewed by sober men taking careful notes from the air of enemy troop movements; the Army made it quite clear it was not in the market for reckless daredevils looping the loop above the battlefield. And yet, as we can guess and as the Army was to discover, there always was something about airmen and flying that was inimical to the sort of discipline it expected. Even at the Central Flying School there was something ad hoc and unsystematic in the instructors' methods, and before long the need to set up other training squadrons to cope with the RFC's rapid expansion resulted in tuition that could depend entirely on the whims and prejudices of the individual instructor, not to mention the condition of the aircraft assigned.

The RFC's standard elementary trainer was French, the Maurice Farman MF.11 'Shorthorn', universally known as the 'Rumpty' or 'Rumpety', possibly because of the clattery sound its 8-cylinder inline Renault engine made until it had warmed up. It was a two-seat pusher biplane with twin curved wooden skids projecting in front of the wheels like the runners of a toboggan. (Its predecessor, nicknamed the 'Longhorn', had vastly bigger skids.) These 'horns' were intended to prevent the aircraft from tipping on its nose in a bad landing. Students (often known as 'Huns' because of their habit of destroying the RFC's aircraft) who nervously confronted their first mount found

a queer sort of bus like an assemblage of birdcages. You climbed with great difficulty through a network of wires into

the nacelle and sat perched up there, adorned with a crash
helmet, very much exposed to the wondering gaze of men ...
The CO, a pompous and bossy penguin, Major Beak, maintained that Rumpties were good buses when you knew how
to fly them ... He was sufficiently senior to be able to avoid
flying, and work off his bad temper on junior people who did
fly. According to him Rumpties were fine, and it was only
damned junior stupidity that jeered at them ... The trainees
would have to unlearn later all that they learned then, but
young pilots must begin at the beginning, and the Rumpty
was certainly only just beginning to be an aeroplane. Flying
with their antiquated controls was a mixture of playing a har-
monium, working the village pump, and sculling a boat.[71]

'It was, in fact, only slightly in advance of the machine which the
Wright brothers had first flown some ten or twelve years before,'
was Arthur Gould Lee's scornful assessment of the Rumpty half a
century later when describing his first flying lesson in one. Given
that this took place in August 1916, it is astonishing that RFC
pilots were still being trained on such a primitive aeroplane. It is
similarly unbelievable that even by then the Initial Flying Training
programme at Netheravon had little idea of how best to introduce
apprehensive youngsters to the dangerous science of flying.

[The Major] opened up the engine, took off, climbed to 300
feet, tapped me on the shoulder again and yelled 'Take her
over!'
    I was petrified. I had no idea what to do. I gazed at the
control, a sort of cycle handlebar with looped ends, known as
the spectacles, set on a central column. Below was a rudder
bar for my feet. I timidly rested my hands on the loops and
let my toes gently touch the rudder. For a minute the plane
kept on a straight course then the right wing started to drop,
the looped bar followed, and she began to slip sideways. I was
fascinated, waiting for something to happen.

'Straighten her up, you bloody fool!' came a bellow in my ear. Desperately I pressed the bar down further to the right. The right wing dropped steeper, and went on dropping.

'What the f...ing hell are you trying to do, you bleeding idiot?' came the bellow.

In a panic, I pushed the handlebar away from me. The Rumpty dipped her nose indignantly, shuddered, banked suddenly over. Then the controls were snatched from my feeble hands and during a full, unbroken minute of bellow-ing in my ear I learned what a wonderful flow of expletives a Flying Corps instructor could possess. Then we turned for home and landing. I at once received a flood of vituperation such as I had never known before. I tried to explain that I'd not been given a single lesson, but he wouldn't listen and threatened to have me sent back to my regiment. Then he stalked off.[72]

It was this sort of thing that set the tone in far too many RFC training squadrons. Too much depended on the character of the individual instructors and, in turn, on the station CO's ability and willingness to ensure they were up to the job. What was lacking was not merely sympathetic tutors but a modern, standardised approach to tuition that prescribed a series of clear steps, each of which every trainee had to master before proceeding to the next. Those who had learned to fly at the Grahame-White school before the war looked back at that system with admiration. At Hendon any pupil who made a mistake in the air when up with his instructor was firmly grounded for more tuition until he thoroughly understood the theory of what he had done wrong. Only then would he be allowed back up. Meanwhile, another pupil would take his place in the air. This was salutary rather than punitive. When in the autumn of 1915 Louis Strange was posted to Gosport to take command of 23 Squadron's training he remembered how he himself had been taught at Hendon and promptly instituted a similar regime, starting by carefully vetting his instructors. Obviously there were other similarly enlightened men at training squadrons up and down the country; but it was still largely a matter of luck whether a pupil was taught in a way that significantly increased his chances of survival in everyday flying, let alone in combat. The RFC was still seriously inconsistent in the way it taught men to fly.

★

France, by contrast, had instituted a rigorous and uniform regime of tuition through which all its pilots went. At least, they did so after a confused start in 1914 that was almost as hesitant as that of the British, and for some of the same reasons. Their Army high command believed that for economic as well as strategic motives the war could not possibly last more than a few months – certainly not much beyond Christmas. Consequently General Bernard, Directeur de l'Aéronautique Militaire, announced there was little point in going on churning out aircraft and pilots at the current rate. He closed down most of the flying schools and sent trained mechanics off into the infantry. It was not long before the gravity of this misjudgement was apparent and the position hastily reversed.

One big difference between the Aéronautique Militaire and the RFC was the French insistence that their prospective pilots should arrive already knowing – or at least willing to learn – about engines. The British had a variety of opinionated but vague ideas about what sort of man 'the pilot type' was, and left it at that. Provided an airman acquired some sort of competence in the air, that was enough. Anything that went on under the cowling of his engine could be considered a mechanic's job. Of course there were exceptions to this among pilots, like Louis Strange who was quite happy to spend a day taking out all his engine's inlet and exhaust valves, cleaning them and grinding them in again. The Canadian ace Billy Bishop was similarly able to work on his engine when forced down within 150 yards of the

German lines, and obviously there were many others whose peacetime hobby had been cars and motor racing who were willing to get their hands oily and knew what they were doing. But for the first two or three years of the war British pilots were taught next to nothing about the engines on which their lives depended and they had to get by on what they chose to pick up from colleagues and the squadron ack-emmas. To the British Army, officers and gentlemen were not grease monkeys.

The French Army's flying tuition was considerably based on the course that Blériot had developed for his school at Buc, near Versailles. Blériot had taken one of his own monoplanes and clipped its wings so it was unable to take off. This *rouleur* was familiarly known as *le Pingouin*: a flightless bird used for the first lessons in which students learned how to taxi at increasing speeds. The Penguin was by no means easy to hold straight, and only when pupils could do unswerving runs along the ground at full speed with the tail up were they allowed to proceed to the next class: that of *décoller*. In this they learned to 'unstick' a full-winged aircraft, rise a few feet into the air while holding it straight, and then come back down. These flights were gradually lengthened until the pupil was ready for his *tour de piste*, his first solo that entailed flying around the airfield at about 600 feet. The noteworthy thing about the French system of training was that, unlike the British, instructors did not initially fly with their pupils. The first time a pupil took to the air he was on his own. If he survived that he went on to make cross-country flights and practise basic manoeuvres like flying spirals. But well before then the student would have been thoroughly instructed on the ground. He learned how aircraft were built; how they could be rigged so as to fly with a different attitude by altering the tension of their various wires; about rotary engines and the problems of torque; about dealing with wind and weather; about basic navigation and many other things. Finally there came a high-altitude flight and a cross-country test, at the end of which the successful pilot was awarded his brevet and could put up his wings on the uniform of his particular army regiment, which he continued to wear. After that he usually went off to an operational training squadron where he would be given advanced instruction in flying a particular type such as a bomber or a fighter.

In the last two years of the war promising pilots, after graduating from one of the major French Army flying schools like that at Avord, near Bourges, might be sent down south to Pau on the edge of the Pyrenees to the School of Aerobatics and Combat. There they would find up-to-date Nieuport fighters, all maintained in peak condition, in which they were encouraged to spend as much time in the air as possible. Once their skills and flying hours had reached a satisfactory point they graduated to the final stage: the aerobatics course – the Haute École du Ciel.

The German system was like the British only in that instructors flew with their pupils from the first. Otherwise it was much more punctilious about avoiding training accidents: the Germans had a much smaller reserve of potential pilots to draw on than did all the Entente forces combined. For much of the war the British system led to new pilots being sent over to France and often straight into combat, a situation that many squadron COs themselves described as 'murder'. In 1916 the Germans considered their student pilots needed at least six months' instruction before being sent to an active squadron, although by 1918 under the pressure of demand this period had been reduced to three months. What was more, unlike Allied practice, the newly qualified German pilot was not immediately awarded his 'wings' but had to carry out several missions (usually with an experienced observer) before getting his *Flugzeugführer Abzeichen*. From the spring of 1917 pilots whose record in an ordinary squadron merited selection for any of the crack new fighter squadrons (*Jagdstaffeln*) were sent to one of the new single-seat fighter schools (*Kampfeinsitzerschulen*) in Paderborn and Grossenhain, after which they went for advanced training at *Jagdstaffelschule* 1 in Valenciennes.

Britain had nothing like these specialised fighter schools. But it should be emphasised that, regardless of how much better organised and uniform the French and German systems of training were, standards inevitably varied during the war, partly according to the quality of available instructors but also because of battlefield campaigns that made sudden and urgent demands for fresh supplies of pilots in the minimum time. Also, accident rates were high everywhere if only because it was not yet fifteen years since man's first-ever powered flight. No amount of pilot training could reliably be proof against every eventuality in the air. It was small wonder that somebody's brainwave to correct a particular machine's tendency to stall might appear to work very well until it was discovered too late that it could now easily tip the aircraft into a fatal spin. 'It spun into the carpet with all the ferocity the type could display when it was out of humour,' as W. E. Johns would remark laconically when he himself was in training, as though of a horse that had shied unexpectedly. 'It took the mechanics most of the day to dig Tony out, so I heard.'[73]

★

Although a big generalisation, it is probably justifiable to say that until at least the autumn of 1917 the majority of the RFC's pilots were nothing like as well trained as were their French and German counterparts. The reason was no secret, still less a mystery, particularly after the losses of 'Bloody April' that year. 'Boom' Trenchard's strategy of using air power aggressively inevitably resulted in a high rate of casualties who had to be replaced as quickly as possible. The figures are revealing: by the end of the war the Entente had lost 2.2 aircraft for every one lost by the Central Powers.[74] The corollary to this was a faster turnover of aircrew with the increased need to rush men through basic training to fulfil Trenchard's other policy of 'no empty chairs' in an active squadron. This kept the messes full 'even though it meant offering up the inexperienced and the partly trained as human sacrifices,' as one author commented later.[75] It is conceivable that

Trenchard was using his own experience of going solo with only sixty-four minutes' airtime back in 1912 as a yardstick for how long it ought to take to train new pilots. Bad as even the Germans' casualties were in training as well as in combat, their attrition rate was still significantly lower than that of the British. Quite simply, they took more time and care in teaching a pilot how an aircraft flew and how he might best fly one. This revealed a distinct difference of aviation cultures, in that a strand of thinking in 'official' British circles held it was probably better for an airman *not* to understand how his aircraft worked. The rationale for this bizarre viewpoint was summed up in late 1918 by an RAMC captain attached to the RAF writing for the august medical magazine *The Lancet*. He admitted to a

> definite conviction that the less the fighting scout pilot knows about his machine from a mechanical point of view the better. From the very nature of his work he must be prepared to throw the machine about, and at times subject it to such strains that did he realise how near he was to the breaking-point, his nerve would go very quickly.[76]

In other words ignorance was bliss. It was better for a pilot to risk losing both his life and his aircraft through bad flying than it was for him to risk losing his nerve.

With official opinions as perverse as this circulating it is hardly a surprise to find that even as late as the last days of December 1917 Stuart Wortley's fictitious letter-writer (based later on his own wartime correspondence and diaries) was exasperated both by a lack of training and an absence of keenness in the new pilots he was sent. 'I regret to say that many of the new recruits not only don't know how to fly or how to manipulate a machine gun but they fail to display any eagerness to learn. My wretched flight commanders have had to give up most of their spare time trying to train them, and even then some of them have to be sent back home for further instruction.'[77]

As the war went on the RFC's more outspoken commanding officers of active squadrons in France often agonised at being ordered to send men up who had no right to be in the air at all, still less in combat. It seemed a needless slaughter of the innocents and added to the steadily growing pressure for Britain's air wing to break with the Army and rid itself of the constant need to do the military's bidding at whatever cost. In the view of many RFC officers neither the infantry nor its commanders understood how best to use air power although they broadly supported Trenchard's approach, possibly because as a pilot he, too, was one of them.

Apart from that, there were the children who slipped through the Army's lax net. In late 1915 Cecil Lewis, who had falsified his age and enrolled in the RFC at seventeen (the minimum was eighteen), was sent up by his instructor on his first solo after a mere ninety minutes' dual flying. Young as he was, he was still not as juvenile as the RNAS pilot whom W. E. Johns met in Landshut POW camp after he was shot down in September 1918. This boy had also been shot down and was celebrating his seventeenth birthday as a prisoner. He had run away from school to join up, and many years later Johns might well have used him as the model for the main character in his novel *The Rescue Flight*.

Soloing after only one and a half hours' dual experience in the air was not uncommon in the RFC. Lewis's first solo was successful, Johns's rather less so since he stalled on take-off and crashed. The terse entry in Johns's log book reads:

Time: 8.30 a.m.
Pilot: Self
Type and number of machine: MFSH [Maurice Farman Shorthorn] 2113*
Passenger: None
Time in air: Five seconds
Height: 30 feet[78]

* There is a discrepancy here. No. 2113 is listed as a B.E.2c

He was lucky to survive. His instructor, a Captain Ashton, was one of those who subscribed to the commonly held view that pilots, like riders after a nasty fall, should get straight back into the saddle in order not to 'lose confidence'. He sent Johns up again the next day for a ten-minute flight 'at the most'. In the event it lasted ninety minutes on account of Johns getting completely lost and only finding the airfield again at dusk when he was down to his last thimbleful of petrol.

In May 1917 Arthur Gould Lee, another fledgling pilot who had just arrived in France, could note: 'Most pilots average 15–20 hours' flying when they arrive here, with maybe 10–12 solo and five on the type they're expecting to fight on. With that amount of piloting they can't even fly, let alone fight.'[79] He himself found he had done more flying than any of the others with whom he was posted: 85 hours all told with 72½ solo, including 18 hours on Sopwith Pups – the aircraft he subsequently flew in France. He had trained with Bristol at Filton but had been injured in a flying accident 'due to incompetent instruction'. This turned out to be a heavily disguised blessing since, as he admitted, recuperation had allowed him to stay in England long enough to learn to fly properly. Cecil Lewis, on the other hand, had flown just thirteen hours' solo when he was posted to his squadron in France, 'hopelessly inequipped and inexperienced'. It was only very much later in the war that – in theory, at least – no RFC pilot was supposed to cross the lines until he had done sixty hours' flying.

Yet perhaps the most scandalous practice surrounding the RFC's training methods was the way in which the instructors were chosen. Again, Johns's experience is illustrative. After his harrowing experiences in Gallipoli, Salonika and Egypt – not to mention a severe bout of malaria – he began learning to fly shortly after arriving at No. 1 School of Aeronautics, Reading, on 26th October 1917. Once he had earned his 'wings' his very first posting was on 20th January 1918 as an instructor with No. 25 Flying Training School, Thetford. Thus a man with fewer than three months' flying experience from scratch had himself become a tutor. True, this was a sign of the RFC's desperation at a time when almost anyone with a rough idea of what an aircraft's controls did was press-ganged into flying combat missions in France, with a consequent dearth of experienced pilots to teach new volunteers and conscripts. At this point the life expectancy of new pilots was three weeks. A good many were dead within three days. Seasoned airmen with real experience who had survived a few months' active service were of inestimable value to any squadron. They were far too valuable to be wasted back in Blighty teaching Huns to fly Rumpties. They were either inveigled into doing another tour or, as was common after perhaps four months, they were too shattered for further combat and became as much a menace to themselves as to any German opponent. They were often reluctantly posted back home as instructors to a flying training school like Johns's. With their half-crazed fatalism, thousand-yard stares and often bitter rage at being banned from returning to the action in France they, too, were usually not best suited to training beginners.

★

One of the most revealing accounts of what it was like learning to fly in the RFC only a year before the Armistice comes from an American, John MacGavock Grider, who was sent with his comrades to the UK in late 1917 to be trained as a pilot for service with the RFC until such time as the United States could organise squadrons of its own. Grider's first memory of the journey out was of being satirically regaled in Halifax harbour by a boatload of New Zealanders who paddled around their troopship singing: 'Onward, conscript soldiers, marching as to war,/You would not be conscripts, had you gone before.' After arriving in Britain Grider was first billeted in Oxford before being posted to the machine-gun school at Grantham.

> *November 18th*: There were a lot of young English kids that had been there for some time swinging the lead. [The new

CO] sent for them all and lined them up. He told them there was a war on and that pilots were needed badly at the front and they were all going solo that afternoon. They nearly fainted. Some of them had had less than two hours of air work and none of them had had more than five.

We all went out to the airdrome to see the fun. I guess there were about thirty of them in all. The squadron was equipped with D.H.6s which are something like our Curtiss planes [the JN-4 'Jenny' trainer] except they are slower and won't spin no matter what you do to them. The first one to take off was a bit uneasy and an instructor had to taxi out for him. He ran all the way across the field, and it was a big one, then pulled the stick right back into his stomach. The Six went straight up nose first and stalled. Then it did a tail slide right back into the ground.

Another one got off fairly well and came around for his landing. He leveled off and made a beautiful landing – a hundred feet above the ground. He pancaked beautifully and shoved his wheels up through the lower wings. But the plane had a four-bladed prop on it and it broke off even all around. So the pupil was able to taxi on into the hangar as both wheels had come up the same distance. He was very much pleased with himself and cut off the engine and took off his goggles and stood up and started to jump down to the ground which he thought was about five feet below him. Then he looked down and saw the ground right under his seat. He certainly was shocked...[80]

The afternoon progressed in similar fashion with smashed undercarriages and aircraft turning turtle. 'They finally all got off, and not a one of them got killed,' Grider commented. 'I don't see why not, tho'. Only one of them got hurt and that was when one landed on top of the other. The one in the bottom plane got a broken arm.' The tally in written-off and broken aircraft was considerable. The cost of a D.H.6 trainer at the time was £1,363 (without instruments),[81] or roughly £65,000 at today's prices. Needless to say, not a single one of the pilots that day ought to have been allowed up without an instructor.

*November 20th*: These old short-horn Farmans are awful-looking buses. I am surprised they fly at all. We have the same sort of wild kids here for instructors that we had at Oxford, only more so, – wilder and younger. I was told that they kill off more instructors in the RFC than pupils, and from what I've seen I can well believe it. I have a Captain Harrison for an instructor. He seems to be a mere kid. He's about nineteen and is trying hard to grow a mustache. Classes are a joke.

*December 6th*: I have been flying for three days and Capt. Harrison says I can go solo to-morrow if it's calm. ... I have put in two hours and twenty minutes in the air and I would have soloed this evening if it had been calm enough.

*January 1st, 1918*: I have done my four hours' solo on Rumpties and am done with them forever, thank God. I have done two hours on Avros [i.e. the Avro 504J]. They are entirely different and I have to learn to fly all over again.

Grider's months in England are a litany of drunken parties, girls pursued ('horizontal refreshment'), aircraft flown and crashes witnessed. He noted 'wholesale funerals' and that one of his fellow-Americans had already been to twelve in five months.

*February 9th*: A horrible thing happened today. We were all out on the tarmac having our pictures taken for posterity when somebody yelled and pointed up. Two Avros collided right over the airdrome at about three thousand feet. God, it was a horrible sight. We didn't know who was in either one of them. I was glad I was sitting next to Cal. They came down in a slow spin with their wings locked together and both of them in flames. Fred Stillman was in one machine and got out alive but badly burned and Doug Ellis was in the other one and was burned to a cinder. As I sat there watching I kept trying to imagine what those poor devils were thinking about as they went spinning down into hell. It made me right sick at my stomach to watch. We all went up later and felt better after a little flying. We went into town for a party with Capt. Horn…

Later, Grider would say that most pilots were killed by structural defects or by having the aircraft catch fire in the air. This was probably true, and there is hardly a diary or journal from airmen at the time that doesn't record several cases of wings either coming off entirely in the air or just folding up like tired sun-shades. Grider himself had only four more months to live. He was shot down on 18th June 1918 some twenty miles behind the German lines, leaving an ex-wife and two young sons back in the United States.

Certain other accidents were less accidental than self-willed. Any airfield could witness examples of the plain old showing off that was a hallmark of a certain kind of aviator then as now. In its way this, too, was a sign of poorly learned basic lessons. W. E. Johns described sitting smoking a cigarette outside the hangars at Thetford one day when a machine that was strange to him landed and taxied up. The pilot climbed out, leaving the engine ticking over, and greeted him.

'What's that?' asked Johns, nodding towards the strange machine.

'An S.E.5,' the pilot replied scornfully.

'Pretty useful?' asked Johns.

'Useful?' replied the pilot. 'Useful! I should say she is. She'll loop off the ground.'

Johns's expression must have betrayed his incredulity, for the pilot muttered, 'Watch me!' and climbed back into his machine. The S.E.5 took off and soared in a circle, swinging over the top and coming down. It hit the ground at well over 100 mph. Johns did not move. He could not. When the ambulance took away the pilot's remains and the air mechanics started to pick up the pieces, Johns noticed he was still smoking the same cigarette as when the S.E.5 had first landed.[82]

No matter how commonplace flying was to become over the next decades it lost little of its original glamour, and the fatal urge to shine as a demonstrator of a new type of aircraft or simply as a skilled daredevil was to persist. In 1931 Douglas Bader was famously to lose both his lower legs in a crash while attempting to slow-roll a Bristol Bulldog too close to the ground. It was pure showing off and he was lucky to get away with his life. Hundreds of other pilots down to the present day have killed themselves as well as spectators in similarly misjudged crowd-pleasing aerobatics at airshows. No matter how much safer modern aircraft are, Newtonian gravity and the laws of aerodynamics remain inflexibly unchanged.

For whatever reasons, the casualty rate at RFC training stations in Britain was often worse even than on active squadrons in France. Johns later wrote in his magazine *Popular Flying* that in early 1918 when he was stationed in Norfolk no fewer than thirteen pilots and observers were burnt to death in crashes in as many days and the local village blacksmith, who had been a juryman at all the inquests, committed suicide, overcome by the horror of it all. Structural failure may have accounted for some of the carnage (in this case deliberate sabotage was suspected), but poor training was most likely to have been at the bottom of the rest. Yet by the time Johns first arrived at the School of Aeronautics in Reading, RFC training was in a transitional stage, having at last embraced a new system, and the course on which he embarked required him to study a good few subjects on the ground besides the hours of actual instruction in the air. He learned such things as how aircraft were rigged and how their instruments worked. He learned about engines, navigation, observation, signalling, aerial gunnery and much else besides. It was a revolution in the way the RFC trained its pilots – belated, undoubtedly, but a revolution nonetheless. And it was almost entirely down to one man, Major Robert Smith-Barry.

Smith-Barry had a reputation as a considerable eccentric as well as an experienced airman. One of his early school reports at Eton described him as 'an awful little boy. He has no aptitude whatever,'[83] although he must at least have had a talent for music since he spent two years practising the piano for eight hours a day with a view to a career as a concert pianist. However, he was bitten by the aviation bug and learned to fly in 1911. Three years later he was in the first batch of pilots sent to France with 5 Squadron in August 1914. He was severely injured in a crash following engine failure in his B.E.8, badly breaking both his legs, and after several operations was left with a life-long limp. While recovering in England he flew in anti-Zeppelin night patrols and acted as an instructor. He returned to active duty in France in May 1916 as a major in command of 60 Squadron. There he became steadily more obsessed and upset by the feeble flying abilities of the young pilots he was being sent and began bombarding Trenchard's RFC headquarters with letters. These were not shy of using emotive phrases like 'Fokker fodder' to emphasise how appallingly vulnerable these airmen were, but they were also full of practical recommendations about what should be done to improve things. A letter he wrote on 10th December 1916 is worth quoting in full since it was probably the first time that an officer of his experience and seniority had sum- marised the deficiencies of the RFC's training and brought them to the attention of the high command. His frankness must have struck his superiors quite forcibly.

Up until the end of last May when the writer left England no attention whatever was paid to the fundamental importance of instruction in the mere manual part of flying. This was left to those who were resting, those who were preparing to go overseas, and those who had shown themselves useless for anything else. The first two classes had other interests paramount; the third had no interests at all. The present-day pupil is being taught to fly by people who are altogether without enthusiasm and whose indifference is, as always, contagious.

It is submitted that a good way to remedy this would be a school of training for instructors, where they could (*a*) have their flying brought up to the very high standard necessary before they can teach with confidence and ease, and be combed out if they do not speedily reach this standard; and (*b*) be given definite lines upon which to instruct. The institution of such a school would tend to produce an *esprit de corps* among the instructors and could improve the atmosphere surrounding the whole business.

The writer has been surprised to notice how little interest in flying is taken by many young pilots who come out to the Front. Though very young, and quite fresh, they have to be ordered to go up from the very first; they never ask permission to go up even for a practice flight. Before the war young flyers were always begging to be allowed up. It is thought that this, though in part due to the difference between volunteers and conscripts, is largely due to the mental supineness of instructors in England.[84]

This letter cogently made the point that in order to improve flying standards it was necessary first to train the trainers. By implication it was a fierce criticism of the Central Flying School, which was where the RFC's instructors were taught, and it had an immediate effect. The officer in charge of the RFC's training, General John Salmond, had a high personal regard for Smith-Barry and promptly posted him back to England as CO of No. 1 Reserve Squadron at Gosport, giving him a free hand to institute a system of his own. It is not clear when he arrived there how much was left of the regime Louis Strange had introduced during his command a little over a year earlier. In any case it was at Gosport that Smith-Barry began the process that finally managed to institute radical change throughout the RFC by revising the entire way in which flying instructors taught and pupils learned.

As an enthusiastic and veteran combat pilot himself, Smith-Barry considered that provided a pupil was accompanied by a genuinely inspirational instructor, he ought to be encouraged in hands-on flying from the very first. The essential was to have a man in the back seat who was as calm as he was experienced, someone who didn't curse and shout obscenities at his hapless student but was reassuring and encouraging. It may seem odd to us today that such a regime had not been made general far earlier; but it is perhaps not so surprising since in 1914 no pilot anywhere had combat experience and thereafter nearly anyone who could fly was needed for active duty rather than to instruct. In private, Smith-Barry probably acknowledged that the French and German systems had been much better planned from the beginning, if subject to the vagaries of demand, but that maybe in the final analysis they relied a little too much on the academy approach: a degree of methodical plodding at the expense of inspirational teaching.

One of Major Smith-Barry's first moves was to order the antique Rumpties banished from all flying training schools as quickly as possible. To replace them he selected the Avro 504J as the RFC's basic trainer, a controversial choice in some quarters that considered this excellent aircraft 'too advanced' for beginners, whatever that meant. It had many advantages, among them a rotary engine that enabled pupils to become used to the characteristics of the type of engine they would most likely be flying in France, as well as handling that was a good introduction to genuinely advanced machines like the Sopwith Camel and the S.E.5. The Avro must have been a good choice because it was to remain in service for many years. In all, 5,446 were built and in due course it became the aircraft in which the future King George VI learned to fly.

The reason for choosing the Avro was that Smith-Barry was no longer thinking in terms of airmen sent to France being able to fly in an ordinary way. Traditional RFC practice had been for instructors to drum into their students the situations to avoid at all costs, like getting into spins. Smith-Barry could see no point in telling future combat pilots what to avoid, given that by that stage in the war combat could involve advanced aerobatic manoeuvres they needed to master in order to be safe. To have no more than mere 'ordinary' flying expertise was just asking for trouble.

His new system therefore involved pupils being deliberately faced with exactly those situations their predecessors had been told at all costs to avoid: spinning, for example, which in many pilots' minds still represented something fearsome that was easily slipped into and practically certain to end fatally, like going over Niagara Falls in a barrel. The job of Smith-Barry's instructors was to take their students to the brink at a safe altitude, push them over, and show them how to stop the hypnotically approaching earth from revolving around the aircraft's nose. To be fair to the older methods of teaching, in the days of the Rumpties anything much more athletic than gentle turns and shallow dives risked the machine breaking up. For at least the first two years of the war nobody in any air force bothered to teach combat flying as a skill in its own right, partly because it was still not really needed and partly because so few machines were safely capable of anything very dramatic in the way of agility. The spectacular aerobatic 'dogfighting' so beloved of film-makers in the late 1920s and 1930s (*Wings, Hell's Angels, Dawn Patrol*) was almost entirely confined to the war's last eighteen months. But by 1917 the construction of aircraft had greatly improved and the Avro 504J could safely handle enough basic aerobatic manoeuvres to make conversion to an advanced fighting machine like a Camel or an S.E.5 a logical progression instead of potentially fatal.

Thus piloting skills had to keep pace with technological development. By the end of a Gosport-style course a pilot would have unlearned any residual dread of stalls and spins and could initiate and correct them at will. What was more, the installation in the Avros of what became known as the Gosport speaking tube that connected the pilot's and instructor's helmets at last made it unnecessary for instructors to whack their pupils over the head and bellow in their ear above the noise of the engine.

Within a short while Smith-Barry's experiment was acknowledged a success and the RFC adopted his system as quickly as it could. The Army being what it was, especially in wartime, this was not as fast as he wished, as witness Stuart Wortley's letter of December 1917, a year after Smith-Barry's posting to Gosport, noting there was still a lack of enthusiasm in young pilots. The American John Grider's diary entries of exactly the same date make it clear the old Rumpties were even then still in service although he did progress to Avros. Additional testimony of change can be found in the fascinating letters home written by a Canadian from Toronto, Roderick Maclennan, who began his own training as a pilot in England in July 1917. His experience reveals both the Gosport influence and the time it was taking to implement fully. His first week was spent either in a classroom or in a hangar studying rigging and engines. 'We had four hours of practical work on [engines],' he noted on 1st July, 'running them and starting them by turning the propeller. This is usually done by a mechanic but an officer has to learn how it is done in case he has to make a forced landing and then has to restart his engine to get home.'[85] Later that week Maclennan had to sit an exam in '(1) Rotary engines, (2) Stationary engines, (3) Bombs, Instruments, Photography, Wireless, etc., (4) Rigging and Theory of Flight, (5) Aerial Observation, and (6) A practical test in reading Morse on the buzzer.' The range of the syllabus is impressive, even though it can hardly have been covered with much thoroughness in only six days. He first went up in an aircraft on 8th July and flew his first solo on the 22nd. Obviously the RFC had shifted into high gear where turning out pilots was concerned since in November that year Maclennan was able to remark: 'There are so many pilots now that after they have done about four months in France, nearly all are returned to England as instructors…'[86]

He himself was not to be so lucky. He arrived in France on 28th November. On 15th December he wrote home: 'I can hardly express what a wonderful thing flying is, and what a hold it gets on one. I am having the time of my life… Aside from flying we get lots of motoring, football and even riding. Certainly it pays to go to the war on wings.'[87] Three days later he flew his first patrol over the lines. Two days before Christmas Roderick Maclennan was burned to death. He was twenty-four.

In spite of delays, the implementation of the new training regime did gradually spread and its influence take hold, with results that became visible even in the air. V. M. Yeates's semi-fictional character Tom Cundall, newly posted to his squadron in France, watched an old hand 'put his bus down almost in the hangar mouth with a pukka sideslip Gosport landing that reduced his forward speed to ten miles an hour, or so it looked.'[88] The name of Gosport had already become shorthand for a recognisable style of competence and panache. In some respects even the French system of aerobatics taught at their Hautes Écoles du Ciel was evidently not as comprehensive or advanced as Major Smith-Barry's. Gosport taught the side-slip as a matter of course for losing height quickly and especially to get back on the ground in a hurry. In the event of fire, for instance, pilots might side-slip to fan the flames away from the cockpit. It was a manoeuvre new and dramatic enough to take a group of French pilots by complete surprise when they first saw it practised in France. They assumed the British pilot was completely out of control until by what they took to be sheer luck he regained it at the last moment.

Not that the Gosport School (as the system became known) was for the faint-hearted. Geoffrey de Havilland remembered it in his 1979 autobiography as being run on the 'survival-of-the-fittest' principle. 'After only a few hops, the pupil was taken up and treated to a rapid series of evolutions, from loops to rolls and spins. On return to earth, if the pupil staggered away groaning, he was considered unworthy of further instruction; if he was still sane and obviously in his right mind, the training programme continued.'[89] This was probably a slight exaggeration and makes it sound more brutal than encouraging; but Smith-Barry was bullish, and undoubtedly some way was needed early on in the course to weed out those pupils who for physiological or other reasons would be unable to cope with the demands of combat flying. In any case the fame of his system soon spread to become a model for flying schools world-wide. Perhaps its true excellence can be judged by the fact that even the French came to adopt it.

★

A final word should perhaps go to the indestructible Louis Strange, who in May 1918 was a lieutenant-colonel commanding the 23rd Training Wing of what was now the RAF, stationed at South Carlton, near Lincoln. In that month

> the 23rd Wing did 4600 hours' flying, which was 2000 more than any previous month. The number and standard of service pilots we turned out were greatly increased, while crashes were reduced from one to every thirty hours' flying to one in sixty hours, and write-offs of machines fell from one in eighty to one in 145 hours' flying. ... No particular credit was due to any one individual for this improvement. We were only putting into practice a lesson that some of us had learned at Gosport and the CFS ...
>
> But others will bear me out that the work in a training Wing in those days was no joke. The write-off of one machine for every 140 hours' flying meant the loss of something between thirty and forty machines a month, in addition to

some seventy or eighty minor crashes. In the May of 1918, for instance, we had sixteen fatal accidents... higher than usual owing to a collision between two machines, the wreckage of which fell by ill luck upon another on the ground, so that the personnel of three machines were involved in the one crash. But the work had to go on at a still more feverish pace in order to cope with the overseas requirements, for at that time the monthly output of pilots from the Home Establishment was well in the neighbourhood of 400.[90]

These improved standards still represented an average daily toll of four crashes of various kinds, with a death every other day. Yet spread out over a wing it was an impressive advance and a tribute to the courage of a one-time 'awful little boy' in speaking out to his seniors.

Even so, for much of the war the slipshod and unsystematic manner in which Britain trained its aircrew was patently a false economy, given the expense and shortage of pilots and aircraft. Although the chaotic urgencies of wartime explain much, it is sometimes hard not to invoke that always-questionable category of national character. The over-valuation of the amateurish, the perennial excuse of the country having been 'caught on the hop', the lack of proper planning from the first, the improvising, cutting corners and doing everything on a shoestring all seem grimly familiar to this author. So, too, does the ability to turn 'muddling through' into an indomitable British virtue, even when muddling through in training led to the reckless squandering of so many young lives.

Another aspect of the same cavalier attitude will become evident in a later chapter where it needs to be explained why it took well over two years of German air raids on London before the authorities were at last moved by public rioting and political uproar to institute a properly co-ordinated system of home defence.

CHAPTER 6

# HOW THEY LIVED

———

ENOUGH HAS BEEN said in previous chapters to suggest that from its inception the RFC was never going to be like any other corps in the British Army. The experience of flying, like the physical skill itself, was too different from anything else. Once in the air, a man metaphorically left the Army and reverted to being a lone individual largely free to go where he wanted and act on his own initiative. True, on a particular mission he might be ordered to fly in formation, but even so he was a free agent within the constraints of rapidly changing circumstances such as weather, engine failure or enemy attack.

Yet there was another important way in which the airman differed from the infantryman. In all but the most granitically unimaginative, a pilot's aerial viewpoint could at unexpected moments become almost philosophically detached, even lordly. Contemporary letters, diaries and memoirs are full of passages like this:

> I explore the vast emptiness in which I am a proud but insignificant speck, look up into the violet of the furthest heavens, into the infinite zenith, and blink at the glaring sun, then gaze around me to the faraway horizons, apparently on my level. There comes an awesome feeling of loneliness. I and my companions are utterly remote from our mundane existence on the earth which we cannot even see. The three of us are as one, seemingly stationary, with no sensation of speed, just placed here for always in the void. Everything is still. The

engine is soundless. The leader's fluttering pennants are pet-
rified movement. Even time is at a standstill. There is nothing
between us and eternity, in space, in time.

  Almost in wonder, I realize that I am one of the few thousand human beings in the history of mankind who have been
chosen to experience this celestial vision. Compared with
ordinary earthbound mortals I am an Olympian god,
enthroned high in the heavens, free, serene, uninvolved.
Compared with the wretched millions locked in earthly combat, I and my companions are a winged aristocracy among
warriors, looking down on the invisible trenches below in pity
and amazement.[91]

'Winged aristocracy' says it all. This is hardly the ideal soldier as
promulgated in the various handbooks and manuals of the British,
German or French armies, where unquestioning obedience rather
than aloof detachment was constantly stressed. The whole idea of
being 'in the ranks' was that you were not isolated – least of all in
the British ranks of the Pals' Brigades where your morale was
boosted by being with men from your own town or even street. By
contrast, as Leutnant Rudolf Stark observed in June 1918 when he
was leading a German fighter squadron, *Jagdstaffel* 35,

We fliers live in fearful and splendid isolation. We cannot do
without this isolation and have no desire to. Isolation changes
a man's nature, and so many other things have changed for
us, too: battle, life and death. Nations wage war on one
another and down on the ground beneath us men tear each
other to pieces. We play a part in this war, and yet it seems
that everything that happens below is alien to us. We hover
between heaven and earth. We have not attained heaven, and
yet we no longer belong to the earth. We are alone.[92]

It is easy to see how this concept of the alienated loner could
later lead to its being over-romanticised for ideological reasons.

The groundwork for this had already been well laid by poets like Gabriele d'Annunzio and F. T. Marinetti in their pre-war celebration of Futurism and the idea of young warriors cleansed by the new violence conferred on them by machines. The writings of the French airman Antoine de Saint-Exupéry were later to tend in much the same direction. Mussolini himself proved susceptible to the twin spells of d'Annunzio and aircraft and in 1920 he took flying lessons near Milan under the instruction of Cesare Redaelli. In 1935 Guido Mattioli drew an explicit parallel between aviation and Fascism in an admiring book about the Italian dictator, who by then had his pilot's *brevetto*. In the book's jacket design the initial 'M' of Mussolini takes wing and is graphically transformed into a scarlet bird of prey. 'No machine requires so much human concentration of soul and willpower as an aircraft does to make it fly well. A pilot truly understands the meaning of the word "control". There therefore seems to be an intimate spiritual link between Fascism and flying. Every airman is a born Fascist.'[93]

This, however, was not yet the meaning any airman in the First World War would have attached to finding himself serenely remote at 15,000 feet above a world that was 'one map of wastening war unrolled'.[94] It was still too early in the history of aviation for the experience to have jelled into anything like an ideology, still less a political agenda. On the other hand it was quite distinctive enough to give airmen a profound sense of their collective identity, one that was clearly separated from that of the terrestrial army – the 'poor bloody infantry' or PBI. This was true even for men who had transferred from the trenches in order to fly. Only after the severe British troop losses of late autumn 1914 was there any attempted movement in the other direction, when some airmen applied to leave the RFC and return to their battalions because so many officers had been killed. Permission was refused because they were too valuable where they were. That was a time – not to be repeated until the Germans' *Kaiserschlacht*, the great Spring Offensive in 1918

– when the front was moving so fast it was possible to take off on a sortie and return after a couple of hours only to find your home airfield now in enemy hands.

Stuart Wortley became profoundly aware of the difference between the lives of airmen and those of the infantry when his CO gave him a rest from flying during the Battle of the Somme in July 1916. He had recently flown so many shows he was dog-tired. Curious to see how the other half lived and died he arranged to visit the trenches he had so often flown over and was given a guided tour by a battalion transport officer. One of the things about life in the British trenches that many visitors commented on was what sometimes looked like the troops' heroic light-heartedness in the face of unremitting death, rats, boredom, privation and danger. This was normally glossed over as evidence of the British Tommy's true fighting spirit and indomitable morale. It may well have been; but there was an additional possibility that visitors of the officer class preferred not to consider. This was that conditions in the trenches were often little worse – and in some respects actually better – than they were in an industrial slum back home. Plenty of Tommies had grown up with rats and privation; they were equally used to boredom with the possibility of maiming and even death while working in factories. Now, out of the blue had come the prospect of escape from slums, poverty and drudgery by means of foreign travel (however restricted) at government expense, plus regular free meals and medical treatment. This, together with excitement and youth's conviction of its own immortality, could for a while have made the experience something of a lark and explain the puzzling high spirits that visitors found so touching.

Stuart Wortley was alternately shocked, humbled and simply baffled by what he saw and heard on his own tour of the trenches, as also by his escort's casual acceptance of things.

Suddenly I felt we two were poles apart. We were both fight-ing the same enemy – he on the ground and I a few hundred feet above his head. But those few hundred feet constituted an abyss almost unbridgeable. We had not the remotest notion of each other's feelings. I wish it could be arranged that infantry officers should be attached to RFC units and vice versa...[95]

German pilots were naturally no different, and expressions of a complicated mixture of guilt, pity and wistfulness were common among those who had left the infantry to become airmen.

Many a man in the course of his duty up in the sky thought with shame of his own warm quarters as he watched those thin lines beneath him where our troops, beset by cold and rain, faced attack by forces ten times as strong, and longed to be with his old friends once more and join in their struggle.[96]

A recurring motif in airmen's memoirs is their consciousness of how infinitely more comfortable their lives were than those of the infantry in the trenches. Much of the time they were decently billeted on an airfield with proper sleeping accommodation and a mess with reasonable eating and drinking. Except when actually flying there was time off from the war each day – even for several days if dud weather kept the aircraft grounded. Depending on how near the airfield was to a village or town, and the opportunity to scrounge a lift, there were possibilities for visiting bars and restaurants and chatting up the owners' daughters. There are numerous descriptions of airmen in France spending languorous summer days swimming in a nearby river, writing letters or just horsing around, almost the only reminder of the war being the irritable dialogue of the big guns just over the horizon maintaining a rumble that could even be felt through the earth if one lay with one ear pressed to the ground.

Gradually, almost out of nowhere, a tradition assembled itself and grew. Because of the plurality of the men's origins it couldn't celebrate a particular county like an infantry regiment. Instead it emphasised the uniqueness of each squadron, together with its crest and motto. Since in the first two years of the war so many RFC officers were ex-public school men, much of the shape that squadron life and attitudes took was unconsciously modelled on the peculiar philistine ethos of Britain's fee-paying private schools. A school's honour morphed easily into the squadron's honour, the largely good-natured rivalries with neighbouring squadrons often being competitively based on sports fixtures as well as on combat successes, especially if they were flying the same type of aircraft. Squadrons in a particular sector might compete to see which would be the one to destroy an observation balloon that had recently appeared behind the enemy lines. It was a mission everybody knew was quite likely to be fatal but the challenge was, well, *sporting.* Cecil Lewis, who with a friend had defected from Oundle School in 1915 at the age of sixteen in order to join the RFC, wrote in 1936:

> The RFC attracted the adventurous spirits, the devil-may-care young bloods of England, the fast livers, the furious drivers – men who were not happy unless they were taking risks. This invested the Corps with a certain style (not always admirable): we had the sense of being the last word in warfare, the advance guard of wars to come, and felt, I suppose, that we could afford to be a little extravagant.[97]

If there is a suggestion here of arrogance it was surely not misplaced. 'Flying was still something of a miracle. We who practiced it were thought very brave, very daring, very gallant: we belonged to a world apart,' Lewis added. Identical sentiments were expressed in the RNAS and, come to that, in all the other combatants' air forces.

The RFC quickly acquired its own language that even trainee pilots soon picked up. A conversation between two such students was recorded by a *Daily Mail* correspondent identified as 'W.A.B', writing on 19th July 1917:

*First 'Hun':* Did you see old Cole's zoom on a Quirk this morning?

*Second 'Hun':* No, what happened?

*First 'Hun':* Oh, nothing to write home about... Stalled his bus and pancaked thirty feet... crashed completely... put a vertical gust up me... just as I was starting my solo flip in a Rumpty.

A 'Quirk' was standard slang for the despised B.E.2c. As always, the point of such jargon was to emphasise the exclusiveness of their world, while the nonchalance was a useful way of dealing with its mortal threat. It was all very much in the public school spirit. To describe oneself as having got the wind up was unthinkable; but to have a vertical gust up was permissible because ostensibly comic.

For young men from a world that was apart even back in Britain, having to sleep in a hut with four or six others on a damp airfield in France was nothing new after ten years of freezing school dormitories, and mostly no great hardship. By the time airmen from the Dominions arrived in numbers a regime of squadron life had been established with a unique flavour of its own, one that in many respects ran counter to many of the regular Army's most sacred tenets. Typical of this were matters of discipline and dress, for everyday life on an active squadron was often conducted in comparatively informal terms, depending on how much of a stickler the CO was for the proper military formalities. Visiting brass were often surprised and occasionally scandalised that RFC airmen might not only dispense with saluting but came and went on the airfield in a motley assortment of clothes. This commonly ranged from flying jackets black with the oil that rotary engines threw back to uniform trousers worn with tennis shoes. A visiting major from a cavalry regiment was reported to have almost fainted on discovering one of a squadron's pilots wearing pyjama bottoms beneath his flying suit, though exactly how he made this discovery is unfortunately not recorded.

★

The main locus of squadron life was undoubtedly the officers' mess, and getting it suitably furnished and civilised was something of a priority whenever the unit moved and was billeted somewhere new. Unlike in films, where squadrons seem always to wind up living in a château with a seductive young *comtesse* in the offing, most inherited a group of ramshackle farm huts and outhouses that the men made habitable in an amazingly short time, mainly by begging, borrowing or stealing some basic furnishings. Once the rats had been banished, the worst of the draughts plugged, the roof made rain-proof and the stove installed, things began to look more civilised. With chairs and tables and the odd flea-market picture bought in the local town, an unpromising barn became the squadron's mess, its walls hung with the familiar trophies brought from their previous station: shattered propellers and painted insignia on canvas cut from downed enemy machines.

Part of the filmic mythology surrounding the RFC involves riotous extroversion as though the mess was in a state of nightly mayhem. This was simply not so. In surviving memoirs there are plenty of vignettes of sudden flarings of temper over someone's unconsciously whistling the same tune over and over again in one corner of a brooding room. Many aircrew were far too exhausted or tense after the day's operations to stomach revelry. They would either go to bed, write a letter, or try to unwind in the armourer's hut by carrying out some useful but monotonous task like loading gun belts with their preferred mix of ammunition for a dreaded balloon-strafing sortie the next day. *One tracer, five ball, one Buckingham; one tracer, five ball, one Buckingham; one tracer...*

In its normal state the mess was a scene of endless card games such as poker, slippery Sam and Australian banker. Someone might have crafted a shove ha'penny board and had his mechanic grind down one face of the coins with valve seating paste until they had a mirror finish and 'floated' silkily on the chalk-dusted board. A scene, in fact, much like a junior common room at university, except for a certain dark undercurrent and the wind-up gramophone from whose ornate but battered horn music hall numbers would blare tinnily. It was an unwritten law that men returning from home leave should bring with them new records of songs from the latest London shows. As V. M. Yeates observed, the function of this constant background noise was to block 'the icy stare of eternity through chinks of silence'. Even so, the sound of aero engines being tested by mechanics in the sheds or someone taking off for gunnery practice or a patrol would regularly break in.

There were periods when squadron life became suspended: days of wash-out when bad weather made any flying out of the question. The men played desultory games in the mess or dutifully wrote home, their combat-tautened nerves unable to deal with enforced inertia. Now and then they itchily went outside to stand gazing upward in the chill gloom, cold mouths mumbling fog. Sounds of metal would come from the sheds as though through wool. The blood sang in their ears. Even the distant guns were silent, blinded as they were, their blank muzzles beaded with dew. It was as though all Europe held its breath, waiting for the cheerful sun to break through and announce that normal killing could resume.

Sometimes the squadron became subdued by loss, but more often tragedy was the signal for perverse celebration. Two American pilots who flew with French *escadrilles* described a mess dinner following the particularly grievous loss of a comrade:

> Dinner that evening was a very noisy one. Everyone talked at once; Golasse cracked his funniest jokes and the squadron phonograph was never allowed to stop for a moment. I have never seen a more gallant or a less successful attempt to drown the eloquence of one empty chair.[98]

However, when the squadron had reason to celebrate a particular victory, somebody's medal or simply a guest night, the celebratory 'binge' would usually be preceded by cocktails made by mixing together in a tureen as many of the local French drinks as possible, typically involving cognac, vermouth, cider, champagne, *pastis* and absinthe. Great quantities of wine would accompany the meal, after which there might be drunken speeches and a sing-song.

If there was a mess piano that had survived previous moves and dinners, and provided there was anyone left to play it, it might make a more or less harmonious contribution to the old favourites. These were often well-known tunes reset to cheerfully obscene or topical words. 'We are Fred Karno's army' was one, set to the hymn tune of 'The Church's one foundation'. (Fred Karno was the stage name of an immensely popular music hall comedian of the day.)

> We are Fred Karno's army,
> We are the RFC.
> We cannot fight, we cannot shoot,
> What blinking use are we?
> But when we get to Berlin,
> The Kaiser he will say:
> Hoch! Hoch! Mein Gott!
> What a jolly fine lot
> Are the boys of the RFC!

Or it might be a ditty of many verses sung to the tune of 'D'ye ken John Peel' and full of the pessimism that cheers:

> When you soar into the air in a Sopwith scout
> And you're scrapping with a Hun and your gun cuts out,
> Well you stuff down your nose till your plugs fall out,
> 'Cos you haven't got a hope in the morning.

*Chorus* –

For the batman woke me from my bed,
I'd had a thick night and a very sore head,
And I said to myself, to myself I said:
'Oh, we haven't got a hope in the morning!'

Perhaps the most famous home-grown song was the 'The Young Aviator'. This existed in many variants, much as rugger and drinking songs do. It emerged from RFC messes during the First World War in the way that folk songs start, almost by a process of osmosis when the pressure of sentiment filters through a semi-permeable membrane of alcohol. It varied from squadron to squadron and was still being sung in one form or another by a fresh generation of airmen in the Second World War. The first verse and the chorus were usually much the same:

The young aviator lay dying,
And as in the wreckage he lay,
To his comrades all gathered around him
These last parting words he did say:

*Chorus* –

Take the pistons out of my kidneys,
The gudgeon pins out of my brain, my brain,
From the small of my back take the crankshaft,
And assemble the engine again.

Many lugubrious verses followed. But by far the bleakest song the airmen roared was one to words written by the nineteenth-century Irish-born poet Bartholomew Dowling, who reportedly had in mind some Indian Army officers who had been victims of a tropical plague. It coincided perfectly with the nihilistic feelings of many airmen in the later years of the war. Half the faces in the mess might be new each time it was sung, and the ghosts of those no longer there clustered ever more thickly around the squadron's trophies. Two verses are enough to give the flavour:

> We meet 'neath the sounding rafter,
> And the walls around are bare:
> As they shout back our peals of laughter,
> It seems as the dead were there.
> Then stand to your glasses steady!
> We drink 'fore our comrades' eyes,
> One cup to the dead already:
> Hurrah for the next man that dies!
>
> Who dreads to the dust returning?
> Who shrinks from the sable shore
> Where the high and haughty yearning
> Of the soul can sting no more?
> No! Stand to your glasses steady!
> This world is a world of lies,
> One cup to the dead already:
> Hurrah for the next man that dies!

'This world is a world of lies' accorded perfectly with the conviction held by many airmen of all sides by 1918 that most of what they were told by officialdom was 'hot air', and almost everything said by politicians in Westminster, the Palais Bourbon or the Wilhelmstrasse was brazenly self-serving. It was in the spirit of such cynicism that the RFC's official communiqués were known throughout the force as 'Comic Cuts', after the popular cartoon weekly. By this stage in the evening no-one would know or care if the tears in many eyes were the overflow of drink or token of something deeper. The singing was often followed by horseplay that involved the smashing of furniture and general scrimmaging. Some semblance of order might be temporarily restored with a parody of army discipline in the form of a

subaltern's court martial. In this, an unlucky victim was charged
under Section 40 of the Army Act with 'conduct to the prejudice
of good order and military discipline'.

> The judgment of the Court was a foregone conclusion and
> the prisoner was condemned to be publicly de-bagged, and
> to be branded with the Censor's stamp upon either side of
> his posterior. His advocate, who was adjudged by the Tribunal
> to have given voice to subversive doctrines, was awarded the
> same penalty. The execution of the sentence was carried out
> after a terrific struggle…

Anything involving de-bagging was, of course, a throwback to
public schooldays in its purest form. The amazing thing is that,
drunk as these airmen were by the time they staggered or were
carried to their beds, they would be up again next morning after
'a thick night' and with 'a very sore head' to climb once more
into their machines and face the prospect of a hideous death
even before breakfast.

The question of drinking and flying evidently touched a raw
nerve at the time since it was often vehemently denied that any
airman would ever touch a drop. However, V. M. Yeates's character Tom Cundall takes it as axiomatic that 'no flying man could
live in France and remain sober', and gives a description of
going on morning patrol with his comrades after an entire
night's carousing:

> Climbed in all right, anyway. Felt better in cockpit.
> Comfortable. Couldn't fall out. It'd be damn funny doing a
> blotto patrol. Wouldn't be any Huns about so soon after rain.
> Contact. Giving her revs all right on the ground. Could see
> the rev-counter. Not so blotto. They were all pretty tight
> except Cross. Let's go. Could he taxi? Yes, easy. Open fine
> adjustment. Throttle. Off we go. Hold her nose down then
> zoom. Up, up. Pulling nicely. Roll. Left stick and rudder.

Throttle back. Here's the horizon coming straight. Stick and rudder central. Throttle open. God, trees. Just over. Near thing. What the hell, rolling at that height in formation. Bombs on too. Christ, he'd forgotten. No wonder he'd lost height. Tom, you're blotto. Sit tight, you loon. You know you're blotto, so don't play the fool.[99]

Others stoutly maintained, most implausibly, that they had never known any man fly under the influence, that airmen were far too responsible and had too great a respect for the effects of alcohol on airmanship. That is as may be; but a case study by Dr Graeme Anderson somewhat belies this since it describes

an accomplished aviator who after a few drinks at a friendly aerodrome did a series of stunts and then made off home, a distance of thirty miles. He felt content but sleepy, made up his mind to do no more stunts in the air, and remembered coming down to land at his own aerodrome. Later he woke up in the sick bay with a doctor stitching a scalp wound. Although he had made up his mind to do no more stunts, onlookers saw him loop and roll the machine a number of times when coming down to land. There seems little doubt that the action of alcohol is accentuated in the air...[100]

There are simply too many descriptions of pilots hitting the bottle, like those W. E. Johns gave, for there to be any doubt that it was a recognised problem. As Biggles's chum Mahoney told the station CO, Major Mullen:

Biggles is finished unless he takes a rest. He's drinking whisky for his breakfast and you know what that means – he's going fast. He drank half a bottle of whisky yesterday morning before daylight, and he walked up to the sheds as sober as I was. A fellow doesn't get drunk when he's in the state Biggles is in. ... It's a pity, but most of us go that way at the end I suppose.[101]

Plenty of pilots reached a stage of extreme stress when they could no longer fly sober. Like thousands of car drivers since, they were probably convinced they flew better that way and that their reactions were unimpaired. One or two of them may even have been right, but many more must have died without ever knowing how wrong they were.

Naturally, boisterous and boozy squadron guest nights were not peculiar to the RFC. It was the same in German *Staffeln* and French *escadrilles*, and to judge from letters and diaries left by American trainee pilots like John Grider and Elliott Springs who went on to fly in France, heavy drinking was practically a rite of passage. It is true that most of them were at that blessed age when bounce-back from a night's carousing is remarkably fast, but not all of them were and some of the older men probably needed to be cautious. Yet squadron revels were by no means confined to boozing, and there were often quite elaborate satirical pantomimes and fancy dress parties with the sort of cross-dressing many would have remembered from school plays. These home-grown entertainments, as well as the rough-housing, were encouraged by perceptive officers like the neurologist James Birley, who in 1918 was a lieutenant-colonel in the RFC and had marked views on the importance of keeping airmen's spirits up when on the ground. By that time he was not alone in this and other doctors had come to similar conclusions about the boys they were tending:

> When they have finished flying for the day their favourite amusements are theatres, music (chiefly ragtime), cards and dancing, and it appears necessary for the well-being of the average pilot that he should indulge in a really riotous evening at least once or twice a month.[102]

By late June that year the indestructible Louis Strange had once again been posted back to France, this time to command the 80th Wing. In the immediate aftermath of the German Spring

Offensive he often found morale sagging. It seemed to the men that at this rate the war might drag on until at least 1920 (for which the Entente's high commands were indeed making contingency plans). Strange quickly realised that a mess full of silently brooding men in armchairs listlessly reading three-week old copies of British newspapers was to be avoided at all costs. 'We could not afford to have any squadron's mess developing the atmosphere of, let us say, the Athenaeum Club,' he wrote. He took his cue from Lieutenant-Colonel Birley. 'Every pilot and observer was a patient and an object of interest in Birley's eyes. "When they are not working in earnest, keep them playing the fool," he told me. "Keep their tails up on the ground and they'll look after themselves in the air" was his very wise maxim.'[103]

By this time the RFC had become the RAF; but well before then the difference between the air services and the regular Army had become irrevocably marked. So long as a man's performance in the air was good a surprising degree of eccentricity could be tolerated on the ground. The young British ace Albert Ball was famously a loner who preferred to fly sorties on his own. He was allowed to live in a hut by himself where he planted a garden and played the violin in a brooding, Holmesian manner. Others acquired pets from neighbouring French farms. The Canadian ace Billy Bishop led many a local foraging raid and on one occasion he and his comrades returned with three ducks on whose wings they painted British-style red, white and blue roundels as though they were aircraft. They acquired more birds for their next experiment, which was to discover the effect of alcohol on the creatures. Bishop and his pals found that 'although they did not like the first drop of it, when they had been forced to swallow that they eagerly cried for more. Their return home was a ludicrous sight, sitting down on the ground every minute or two, and always walking in a "beaucoup" zig-zag course, as the French would say.'[104] They later captured a small pig and gave it the same treatment, Bishop for a while leading the animal everywhere on a rope as though it were a dog on a leash. Later, a large sow was named Baron von Richthofen, painted with German aircraft markings and a leader's streamer attached to her tail. Such adopted squadron mascots steadily came and went.

These men also played for hours with the farmer's baby rabbits but it was dogs that the airmen laid hold of with the greatest enthusiasm, picking up every stray they could find until the tally of animals made 60 Squadron something of a menagerie. Bishop's favourite was a black animal with Airedale in its ancestry that he adopted and called Nigger. Several other Niggers came and went on the station since this was the usual name for almost any dog that was black (and would most famously be that of Guy Gibson's own beloved Labrador when he was training at Scampton for the great Dams Raid in 1943). Fooling around with animals helped keep Bishop and his comrades sane in 1917, allowing them to show these stray victims of war a tenderness they dared not lavish on themselves and each other. There were enjoyable ratting parties with the dogs but the pursuit that gained the most official encouragement was shooting pigeons on the wing with a .22 rifle. This was, of course, extraordinarily difficult, which was perhaps as well since the farmer demanded compensation for each of his birds killed. One afternoon Bishop fired off 500 rounds and hit only a single pigeon, and that one a fluke. But as he said, 'It was the very best practice in the world for the eye of a man whose business it is to fight mechanical birds in the air.' On the occasional day off the airmen would spend it 'either sleeping all day or roaming about the orchard in silk pyjamas, or else one would go and visit friends who possibly were stationed near. It was a great thing, as it always left us keen for work the next day.'[105]

*

As the war went on and the toll of brothers and cousins and comrades grew, so undoubtedly did a general resentment of the enemy, compounded as always by the effects of constant patriotic exhortation, propaganda and the bitterness of men aware of missing out on the normality of a home life and career. The casual brutality of it all, of lives arbitrarily cut short or ruined, turned many men into unashamed killers, there being nothing like war for stripping things back to basics. There were indeed airmen like Richthofen who claimed to take deep satisfaction, even pleasure, in sending an enemy down in flames. Yet it is not always easy to tell how much of this was simply down to relief at being victorious in a fight that might so easily have gone the other way. Combat was a highly skilled sport, and to emerge from it as the winner would always be satisfying at a quite simple level. In most cases this would take precedence over worrying about the other man as a human being. That would come later – or not at all, depending on the person. The British ace James McCudden maintained a calm detachment most of the time, but occasionally this faltered:

> At 11,000 feet he engaged an Albatros and sent a burst into it. A small trickle of flame appeared, and the aeroplane began to go down. McCudden followed it. The flames enveloped the whole fuselage and tail assembly, and suddenly McCudden saw the doomed pilot writhing in agony as the fire reached him. He didn't sleep much that night, but the next morning he recovered his composure and confided to Rhys-Davids that a man had to ignore such incidents if he was 'to do his work properly.' 'Until yesterday I never looked upon a German plane as anything but a machine to be destroyed,' he said. 'But when I saw the flames touch that German pilot I felt sick for a minute and actually said to myself in horror: "There's a man in that plane." Now I realize we can't be squeamish about killing. After all, we're nothing but hired assassins.'[106]

Even so, he can't have been an over-imaginative man, given that his many previous victims had hardly been tin ducks in a funfair shooting gallery.

What is worth noting is how much fellow-feeling and even decency managed to survive between the airmen on both sides. Even to an ace like Billy Bishop, intent on racking up his score each time he went aloft, there were limits to what was considered fair game. In one sector of the front in 1917 a familiar sight was a large white German machine doing artillery spotting. It was very old, had a very bad pilot and a very poor observer to protect him, and was known as 'the flying pig'.

> It was a point of honour in the squadron that the decrepit old 'pig' should not actually be shot down. It was considered fair sport, however, to frighten it. Whenever our machines approached, the 'pig' would begin a series of clumsy turns and ludicrous manoeuvres and would open a frightened fire from ridiculously long ranges. The observer was a very bad shot and never succeeded in hitting any of our machines, so attacking this particular German was always regarded more as a joke than a serious part of warfare.[107]

In its way the 'flying pig' had become one with the barnyard animals the pilots petted or made a mock of but never deliberately harmed.

Enemy airmen who were downed were often treated to a mess lunch or dinner by the squadron to which they had fallen victim in a spirit of cameraderie that owed a great deal to the commonality of flying men everywhere. Their lives and skills were identical; only the uniforms differed. Just as the German pilot who shot down W. E. Johns and killed his observer intervened on the ground to prevent a crowd from lynching Johns, so Cecil Lewis and his comrades were called out one night when he was temporarily stationed at Rochford in Essex as part of Home Defence, to take charge of the German crew of a Gotha bomber. This big machine had developed engine trouble and its pilot crash-landed at Rochford airfield under the misapprehension that he was already back in German-occupied Belgium.

Next morning we went in to look at our prisoners. They were very quiet and rather sorry for themselves. I believe they feared victimization: raiders were not popular with the general public. However, whatever the public thought, we knew they were brave men and had a fellow-feeling for them. So we gave them a good breakfast and took them round the sheds. Then they were ordered an escort to take them to town. I accompanied them.

We had a reserved first-class compartment, locked, with the blinds down. But somehow the news had got about, and at every station there was an angry crowd. The officer in charge had to keep them off at the point of a revolver, otherwise we should all have been lynched. The Germans were anxious. We endeavoured to reassure them. One cut off the flying badges on his tunic and gave them to me. I suppose he thought they made him a little too conspicuous. At Liverpool Street there was a heavy armed escort, and the wretched men were marched away through a hostile mob to the safety of an internment camp.[108]

Rudolf Stark noted an exactly equivalent episode when he shot down a British machine in 1918, slightly wounding the pilot but leaving the observer unscathed.

Both look very unhappy, but their faces brighten up when they catch sight of me. It is rather an unpleasant business to fall into the hands of the troops. They are not very kindly disposed to enemy airmen, especially if they have just had a few bombs dropped on their huts. We greet one another almost like old acquaintances. We bear no malice. We fight each other, but both parties have a chance to win or lose. In a kind of way we are one big family, even if we scrap with one another and kill each other. We meet at the front, we get to know the respective badges of Staffel and squadron and are pleased to meet these old acquaintances in the flesh…[109]

There were even moments of pure farce, such as when a Sopwith Triplane from 8 Squadron RNAS and a Nieuport scout from 40 Squadron tackled a two-seater Aviatik in April 1917 and had a twenty-minute scrap at 12,000 feet that ended with the German machine's petrol tank being holed, forcing it to land in a field without further damage. The Triplane followed it down but made a bad landing on the rough field and turned 'ack tock' (absolutely turtle) at the end of its run. The pilot scrambled out unhurt in time to see the Nieuport pilot land and do precisely the same thing. Somewhat blushingly, the two Britons approached the Aviatik to take the German prisoner whereupon he saluted smartly and said sardonically in English: 'It looks more as if *I* have brought *you* down and not vice versa, doesn't it?'[110]

Once the war was over, Louis Strange went to Germany and got to know several of his old opponents well, including 'Leuzer' (Loerzer) mentioned earlier in the Weapons chapter, p.75. 'I have been lucky enough to meet quite a number of old German war pilots,' he was to write. 'They are the best of good fellows and marvellous hosts.'[111]

★

All this notwithstanding, it was hardly surprising that beneath the camaraderie of the squadron mess, conversations often held a savage undertow. A familiar topic concerned life when the war was over – on the off-chance that anyone present would still be alive. There was glum recognition that even if they did survive they would have lost their place on society's ladder; that in their absence others who had evaded being drafted or had managed to wangle a cushy job back home would have had first pick of the jobs going, the women, the housing, everything. It was a feeling almost of betrayal. They who were away bleeding and dying for their country would find themselves thereafter for ever pushed aside, having missed the bus at a crucial juncture. It was a widespread feeling and by no means confined to airmen. It found its way into popular adventure stories by authors like Percy F. Westerman (who was billed on a flyleaf in 1919 as 'Lieut. RAF', a non-existent rank). One of his characters mentions a bemedalled sergeant in France with a brother back in England, 'a hefty lout' who had managed to get exemption from military service by being an engineer – a reserved occupation.

> 'Lord! After the war, won't there be a gulf between men and slackers?'
>
> 'One will feel sorry for the slackers. They won't be able to hold their heads up,' remarked Derek.
>
> 'Not they,' corrected Kaye, giving his bootlace a vicious tug. 'They'll have whole skins and fat purses. The blighters who've done all the work and gone through all the danger will be back numbers when the war's over – if it's ever going to be over.'[112]

This was typical mess talk, even if the vocabulary of 'shirkers' and 'slackers' reeked of *Tom Brown's School Days*. It was yet another example of the chasm that marked off servicemen from civilians. Their day-to-day experiences had little or no counterpart back home, and they remained convinced that few civilians had any idea of what was really going on and who – if anyone – was taking responsibility for it. Worse still, aggrieved notions were frequently voiced of being actively betrayed back in Britain. 'We probably hate strikers at home, stabbing us in the back, far more than we hate the Huns we have to fight, who are risking their skins for their country just as we are – only they happen to have been born in Germany,'[113] as Arthur Gould Lee put it. In a squadron mess it was not unusual to hear politicians described as prolonging the war, whether by blundering ineptitude or from career motives of their own. Either way, they obviously preferred not to face up to the consequences of their actions. Such a cynical attitude could only be strengthened when an airman in France went to visit an injured comrade in hospital. Just such a visit was made by an American pilot who was flying with the

heroic volunteers who formed the Lafayette Squadron in the
days before US conscripts could join the RFC. He never forgot
the experience:

> The operating room was at the other end of the corridor, and
> the most serious cases were taken there mornings to have
> their wounds dressed. Their moans and cries, echoing and
> re-echoing along the hallway, froze my blood. There is a qual-
> ity scarcely human in the screams of a man crying out in
> sheer animal terror and pain ... Many a time I wished that
> politicians, munition makers, breeders and abettors of war of
> whatever sort, might be forced to make the rounds of such
> hospitals so that they might see with their own eyes the hor-
> rible suffering they had brought to pass.[114]

'You ask yourself,' went on Arthur Gould Lee, 'what are fellows
like these, and hundreds of thousands more, giving their lives
for? I hope it's not just to make England safe for bolt-holers,
profiteers, strikers, fake conchies, ponces and all the rest of the
indispensables.'

This conviction of a radical difference between two worlds
could even make home leave a very compromised experience for
a lot of men. Perhaps the best description of the alienation felt by
a man returning home from the front for a brief visit is still that
of Paul Bäumer in Erich Maria Remarque's classic *Im Westen nichts
Neues* (*All Quiet on the Western Front*); but even if most servicemen
were unable to express it so poignantly, the complex mixture of
emotions still leaked out from time to time. For months on end
nearly all men hugged an anxious yearning for home leave until
it became almost the only thing that kept them going: aching to
see again parents, girlfriends, wives and children, even the family
dog and the local pub. But when longing at last turned into the
reality of the khaki-packed cross-Channel steamer and train to
Victoria Station, a few might begin to feel something so awful they
dared not give it a name. The mere idea that home might after all

be an anticlimax was a kind of treason and could not be thought. The growing sense of disappointment gave rise to self-blame, later to baffled rage at being forced to acknowledge that it was not home that had changed but they themselves. Something in them had been destroyed. Stealthily, a malign restlessness had invaded to blight whatever was once so straightforwardly embracing. Familiar as it was in every detail, the bedroom with the boy's treasures and trophies seemed now to belong to someone else. The street, the town, the conversations overheard in the local pub – everything was oddly shallow and insubstantial. Even parents and girlfriends seemed different and uncomprehending. He alone had moved on while everyone else was nailed to the past, whingeing about shortages of this and that.

Gradually it became clear: only comrades who had lived daily and vividly with death understood the deal and were fit company; civilians had no idea and it was pointless trying to explain to them. And suddenly the squadron back in France seemed the only place left that didn't change, that alone made sense in its mad way. Rudolf Stark on leave sat drinking champagne with his fiancée and all he could think was that the upward streams of tiny bubbles in his glass reminded him of tracer bullets.

> Why must I always be thinking of the war? I sit here stuffing myself and ought to be happy, and away in the distance the front is roaring. I can't stay any longer, not even for your sake… The room is growing cold. When I say good-bye there is no return pressure from the hand that lies in mine. Home melts away into a cold night. The last emotion has fallen from me like a warm cloak. I understand nothing any more and have but a single longing – to return to the front.
>
> My leave is behind me. The train starts … At last it stops in Cambrai. A car from my *Staffel* is waiting at the station; two comrades have come to meet me. Somewhere a bomb crashes down. I sit in the car with a radiant smile and feel I have nothing left to wish for. My companions badger me to tell them

about my leave. 'It was good – but coming back is better. Best of all is getting back to the Staffel!'[115]

Stuart Wortley had similar feelings. 'I must honestly confess,' he wrote, 'that I am glad to be back again in France. The whole atmosphere is so different from that in England, especially so in the RFC. Everyone here is so cheerful and jolly, and there is none of that pompous militarism which distinguishes "the back of the front".'[116] Ultimately, of course, the experience of war was incommunicable to anyone who had not shared it. Rudolf Stark probably summed up the truth of the matter for them all: 'We are young; we want to live, and tomorrow we shall be dead. We have nothing but the war. No women await our return, for the *Staffel* is our home.'

If an RFC squadron seemed a home that was a world away from Blighty, it also felt increasingly divorced from the Army. By the time the RFC officially became the RAF in April 1918 most airmen felt utterly at odds with the military's khaki machine, as W. E. Johns experienced for himself:

> The war-time pilot fought the war in his own way. If the authorities wanted to drag a lot of infantry into the affair, well, that was nothing to do with him. He spoke a language of his own, understandable only to his own kind. If he was hurt, he complained solely because it meant leaving the Squadron; if he was killed his friends drank themselves unconscious and never mentioned his name again.[117]

Nevertheless, if Stuart Wortley found squadron life chummy and jolly by comparison with life back home, it remained for many airmen an oddly superficial comradeship. Life was too short to risk more:

> We seldom talk to each other about our private affairs. You seldom get to know much about a fellow's background. His

accent, education, bank account, don't matter, nor who his people are. You never ask. You don't even want to know. The only thing that counts is whether a chap has guts and can shoot straight. You share the same risks every day. Some get shot down on the other side, and that's the last you hear of them. Some go home and probably that's the last you hear of them, too. Yet here, in France, we're a sort of brotherhood. It's a rum life.[118]

# CHAPTER 7

# ACES

———

BY THE SPRING of 1915 the Western European battlefront had more or less stabilised into a line stretching unbroken from the Channel to Switzerland. The British troops were largely deployed northwards of Amiens on the Somme, the line to the south being defended by the French. Since the British sector was mainly open farmland interspersed with woods and villages, airfields were quite easily established and vacated. Aircraft of that period needed no concrete runways so there were none to lay. Even a grass airstrip was inappropriate because it was directional. The whole point of an airfield or aerodrome was that aircraft could land and take off in any direction according to the wind. Nor were there any permanent metal hangars to erect. The French Bessonneau wood-framed canvas hangars (always known as 'the sheds') were portable and adequate for much of the time although vulnerable to fire and gales and offering little protection in winter.

> Sometimes the conditions under which our mechanics had to work were deplorable. Imagine nine inches of snow on the ground, with icy wind blowing through many holes in the canvas walls, the feel of cold spanners and frozen oil, the making of delicate adjustments with hands numbed to the bone...[119]

A typical RFC or RNAS squadron required an array of professional specialists. Riggers and fitters, mechanics, armourers, blacksmiths, carpenters, drivers, clerks and cooks: they all needed places to work, eat and sleep. Typically, the squadron's administration offices, medical bay, armourer's hut, officers' mess, cookhouse and accommodation were draughty wooden sheds, but sometimes the men and even the officers were housed in tents in a temporary measure that could drag on for months of mud and damp. Not until August 1916 did the first Nissen huts begin to appear, the utility buildings designed by a Royal Engineer that were essentially a tunnel of corrugated iron with a semicircular brick wall at either end and made habitable by efficient Canadian stoves. Sometimes personnel were farmed out in 'digs' in the local village. Failing that, it was a lucky unit that was billeted somewhere with brick buildings, let alone in a requisitioned château with extensive grounds (as did occasionally happen). All that was needed then was to stick up a pole with a wind sock on it – jocularly known in the RFC as the 'effel' from the initials of 'French letter' – and they were in business.

It was from such lumpy fields, often dangerously ringed with trees, that aircraft on both sides took to the skies to do their armies' bidding. Perhaps because the RFC's commander Hugh Trenchard was himself a pilot and had so early been convinced that aircraft had a potential far beyond that of simple observation, he formulated his strategy of using the RFC to wage an aggressive war from the first. (Maybe after all he had read Douhet.) One consequence of this soon became apparent. Because of the prevailing westerlies it was easier for the British and the French to fly into German territory than it was for German airmen to cross the Allied front – itself an indication of how weak the early aircraft were, even in the autumn of 1917:

> The Wing ordered a patrol this morning: at which I protested that the wind was too high, and that if we got mixed up in a fight over the lines we ran an excellent chance of losing the lot. GHQ insisted, so I took the patrol myself. I climbed to 15,000 feet dead into the eye of the wind (blowing from the

west, of course). The air speed indicator showed a steady 90 m.p.h., and I remained perfectly stationary over the hangars! Turned east and reached Arras in five minutes. Turned back at once and took 2½ hours to get home! Rang up the Wing to tell them all about it. They replied that they had since received a message from GHQ cancelling my patrol...[120]

Because of the prevailing winds Allied pilots, once over the lines, felt particularly vulnerable to damage, engine failure or simply running out of fuel. Being forced down on the wrong side would at best lead to internment for the duration and at worst to being attacked and even killed by angry civilians in retaliation for injuries the airman (or anybody else) had previously inflicted. Many RFC and RNAS pilots and observers flew with a pistol but also with a small pack containing a razor, a toothbrush, some money and, in the pre-Sidcot suit days (see page 212) of thigh-length sheepskin 'fugs', a pair of ordinary shoes. This practice was often frowned on by commanding officers (by Robert Smith-Barry, for example) because to the faithless military mind it looked as though airmen might be making preparations to fake a forced landing behind the lines in order to be safely interned for the remainder of the war.

Where Trenchard's policy was one of taking the fight to the enemy, German pilots were more constrained. This was certainly true in 1915 with the introduction of Fokker's new E.I monoplanes. As already noted, the fear was that they might be shot down on the wrong side of the lines and the secret of their synchronised machine guns be discovered. Thereafter this turned into something of a habit and in general German aircraft ventured over the lines comparatively rarely except for the odd raid and to attack observation balloons. Later in the war they would also night-bomb the occasional airfield. (The big bombers that blitzed London were based safely in German-occupied Belgium.) German pilots understood only too well how the prevailing wind usually made it harder for Allied aircraft to get back home. So did their anti-aircraft gunners, who often craftily conserved their ammunition and disdained to fire at RFC machines crossing their lines when setting out on a sortie, preferring to wait for the machines' return when they would be low on fuel and labouring against the wind. In general, German pilots were freer to choose when to attack, safe in the knowledge that if they were forced down it would usually be in friendly territory.

Obviously Trenchard knew this too, but as the war went on it did not deter him from sending his aircraft on varied missions ever deeper into hostile territory. His pilots mostly spent these lengthy shows in a state of high anxiety, their senses attuned more than ever to their engine's note, alert for the faintest sign of trouble that might leave them stranded forty miles on the wrong side of the lines with a dud magneto. Since this strategy of carrying the war to the enemy involved greater risk, it naturally resulted in much higher casualties than if the RFC had just been deployed defensively. From time to time it was denounced in the House of Commons and by newspapers as a 'murderous' policy, but for all his genuine sympathy for his fellow pilots Trenchard knew what he was doing. Besides, he had the backing of Army generals who probably felt that if his nasty smelly machines had presumed to usurp the role of the cavalry then they ought also to emulate those gallant, pulse-quickening horseback recces deep into enemy territory that had gained so much useful information in previous wars. The strategy was vindicated by the fact that ever since, air power has primarily been used aggressively rather than defensively. It is the nature of the beast and Trenchard was among the first fully to understand and act on it.

★

For all the political rhetoric in Westminster about the 'Fokker Scourge' of late 1915, the skies above the battlefields of Belgium and France were often remarkably empty of aircraft for the first two years of the war. Until the first Battle of the Somme in the

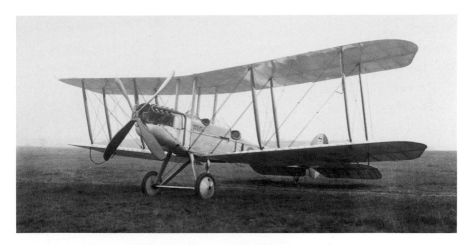

1. An early B.E.2c. A remarkably stable British machine designed in 1912 expressly for reconnaissance and photography, it later acquired unfair notoriety by being pressed into combat situations such as artillery spotting in which it was virtually defenceless.

2. A photo by Stephen Slater of Matthew Boddington flying their replica B.E.2c. Unlike the earliest versions of the type this has staggered wings and ailerons instead of using wing-warping. The skid undercarriage was authentic until spring 1915.

3. A 'Rumpity' or Maurice Farman MF.11 'Shorthorn'. The flares throw into relief the birdcage construction that so baffled trainee RFC pilots like W.E. Johns when first they tried to climb into the exposed nacelle of this prewar 'pusher' design.

4. The Fokker E.III, the world's first warplane with a synchronised machine gun. It was primarily responsible for the 'Fokker scourge' of winter 1915–16 and was much feared despite its poor handling due to using wing-warping rather than ailerons. It also had a tendency to shed its wings in a dive.

5. Anton 'Anthony' Fokker (1890–1939) the Dutch pioneer aviator and designer. He went to work in Berlin before the war and produced several of Germany's best fighter aircraft. The unarmed prototype M.18 seen here never became one of them. He is also credited with designing the first reliable synchronisation gear in 1915.

6. A pre-war flight instructor and test pilot for Louis Blériot, Adolphe Pégoud was the second man ever to loop the loop and the first pilot to parachute from his aircraft. In 1915 he became the world's first air ace and was known in France as le roi du ciel.

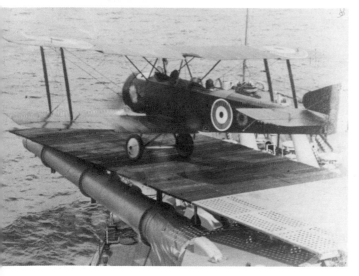

7. (*left*) The king lies dead. Pégoud was shot down in late August 1915 by one of his ex-students, Walter Kandulski. When he learned who his victim was, Kandulski reportedly burst into tears.

8. An RNAS Sopwith 1½-Strutter taking off from a platform built over the forward turret of a battle cruiser, probably in 1917. This was the first British aircraft with a synchronised machine gun, although the aircraft on test here is plainly unarmed.

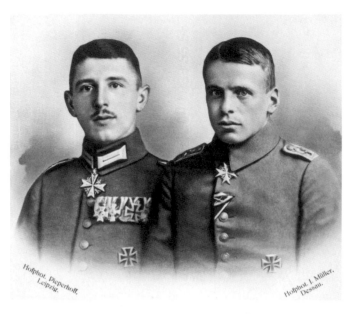

Hofphot. Pieperhoff, Leipzig.

Hofphot. J. Müller, Dessau.

9. German aces Max Immelmann (l.) and Oswald Boelcke (r.), arguably the joint founders of aerial combat as combining technique in the air with organisation on the ground. Both were killed in 1916 leaving a legacy that long outlived them.

10. French ace Georges Guynemer pictured days before he went missing in September 1917 with 54 victories. His body was never found. The stick-thin legs and thousand-yard stare betray the true cost of becoming a national hero. He was 22.

11. A recruitment poster of 1915 in response to the early Zeppelin air raids on London. The admonishing, homiletic tone cloaked the reality that the military authorities were utterly unable to protect the capital or organise its citizens' defence.

IT IS FAR BETTER TO FACE THE BULLETS THAN TO BE KILLED AT HOME BY A BOMB

JOIN THE ARMY AT ONCE & HELP TO STOP AN AIR RAID

GOD SAVE THE KING

12. Women workers applying dope to aircraft wings. The complete absence of protective clothing – not even gloves  is striking. Such workers were frequently overcome by toxic fumes. Chronic poisoning and even death were not uncommon.

13. A downed German aircraft near Verdun in 1916. French soldiers shield their faces from the intense heat while one appears to be going through the airman's papers to identify him. Such papers in a wallet often miraculously survived.

14. Curious German soldiers contemplate their fallen enemy. From the proximity to his body of the barbette ring it is possible the dead British airman was the observer/gunner. He is wearing the thigh-length sheepskin-lined boots known as 'fugs'.

15. This famous image of a falling German airman was revealed as a hoax in the early 1980s. Wesley D. Archer, an American pilot who had served in the RFC, faked this and sundry images of dogfights in a studio and published them anonymously in 1933.

16. An RNAS Sopwith Pup armed with Le Prieur incendiary rockets for attacking observation balloons. The much-loved Pup charmed all who flew it. The notoriously inaccurate rockets were much less popular, needing to be fired in a steep dive at a maximum range of 100 yards through a barrage of defensive fire.

17. The Siemens-Schuckert R.VIII was the last of the 'Giant' series of German bombers. Designed in 1916, it was the world's largest bomber by far, with six engines and a wingspan of 157 feet: greater than that of the Second World War's Boeing B-29 Superfortress.

18. Manfred von Richthofen wearing his 'Blue Max' in Cologne on 17th June 1917. Fresh from the recent 'Bloody April' he now had nearly 60 Entente victories. The Albatros C.III behind him was not his: he was probably ferrying it back to Jasta 11 in Courtrai.

19. The Nieuport 11 or 'Bébé' did much to end the 'Fokker scourge' in 1916. For many months RFC aces like Bishop and Ball preferred this superb French fighter despite its lack of a synchronised machine gun. Note the narrow lower wings of its 'sesquiplane' design.

20. No. 1 Squadron RAF's officers, ground crew and at least two canine mascots drawn up on Clairmarais aerodrome near Ypres in July 1918. The aircraft are S.E.5a scouts. The men at either end of the front group are two American pilots who served with this British squadron.

21. Billy Bishop in the cockpit of his Nieuport 17 in late summer 1917. With 72 victories he was not only the top scoring Canadian ace but that of the British Empire as well. His very dangerous 'lone wolf' tactics led to controversy over unverifiable claims and especially over his Victoria Cross.

22. The observer in an F.E.2d's nacelle demonstrates firing back over the top wing. With no parachute or safety belt he might have to balance on the cockpit rim during violent manoeuvres. He also manned the front Lewis gun and the camera visible on the right.

23. Ernst Udet standing beside his Albatros D.III. Udet became Germany's second-highest scoring ace of the war with 62 victories and survived to become a playboy alcoholic. He shot himself in 1941, exasperated by Hitler's mishandling of the Luftwaffe

24. The SPAD S.XIII: another excellent French fighter, with a top speed of 135 mph and a ceiling of 22,000 ft. It was flown to brilliant effect by Guynemer, Fonck and Baracca as well as by the Americans Luke and Rickenbacker (whose insignia this aircraft bears).

25. The Sopwith Triplane was a revolutionary design flown by the RNAS. In its short career it showed superiority over the Albatros D.III and triggered a triplane fashion among the Central Powers that produced Fokker's Dr.I and thirteen other lookalikes.

26. The Fokker Dr.I was a quite different aircraft to the Sopwith, highly manoeuvrable but prone to wing failures. Although he only scored 19 of his 80 victories in the triplane Richthofen is indelibly associated with this type in which he died.

27. W. O. Bentley's magnificent B.R.2, perhaps the apotheosis of the rotary engine and the last of its kind to be used by the RAF (in the post-war Sopwith Snipe). It also powered some Camels. With a displacement of nearly 25 litres it was rated at 250 h.p.

28. The highest-scoring of all WWI fighters, the Sopwith Camel was also a serial killer of incautious and trainee pilots. Engine, gun, fuel tanks and pilot were all contained in the aircraft's first six feet. Those who mastered it swore by it. Those who didn't swore at it.

29. This S.E.5E was a version of the S.E.5 built in America after the war as a trainer. It lacks armament but is otherwise the same aircraft that in sheer strength and speed outdid the Camel. Many pilots thought it the most successful British design of the war.

30. A replica of the Fokker D.VII, the aircraft reputed to 'turn a mediocre pilot into a good one and a good pilot into an ace.' Its reputation led to the Allies' near-superstitious confiscation of hundreds of these capable but outmoded aircraft after the Armistice.

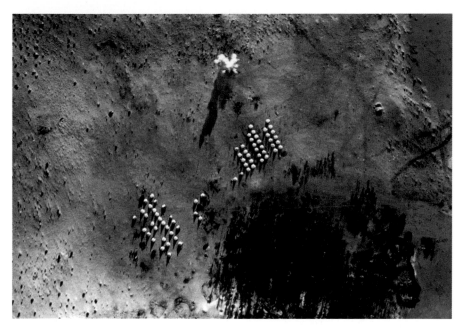

31. A German aerial shot of a bombing raid on a British camp near the Suez Canal. The sun was low, making the uncamouflaged bell tents look like ice cream cones. Given such air attacks, pitching them together in neat ranks displayed little military acumen.

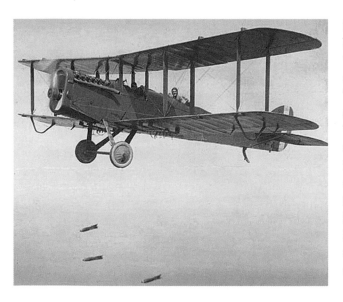

32. A D.H.4 day-bomber drops its 'pills' some time after May 1918. This outstanding aircraft is the type W.E. Johns flew and was shot down in. The machine depicted is one of the 3,227 D.H.4s built in America for the RAF and has the US-designed Liberty 12 engine.

33. This archive photo is captioned 'An Italian aeroplane chases an Austrian Albatros in the Alps.' Its main value is to show the forbidding terrain such airmen constantly overflew outside Western Europe and in which they frequently disappeared.

34. A German ground crewman holds the eight-foot static line of his pilot's Heinecke parachute. The Heinecke saved many German and Austrian lives in the last six months of the war. By contrast, no Allies' aircrew were ever issued with parachutes.

late summer of 1916 it was perfectly possible for a two-seater observation machine to go up for three hours over certain sectors of the front without ever seeing another aircraft, whether hostile or friendly. Obviously, most would tend to congregate in the neighbourhood of features of immediate military interest on the ground; but the vastness of the area that could usefully be overflown at heights of up to 10,000 feet further diluted the small number of aircraft in the sky at any one time.

As we know, Roland Garros's victory on 1st April 1915 in his Morane was the first ever by an aircraft using a fixed machine-gun firing through the propeller, and the autumn and winter of that year saw the worst of the Germans' answer: the Fokker monoplanes' supremacy against which the British and French had no real defence for some months. The truth is, however, that the Entente's casualty figures were by no means as enormous as the impassioned rhetoric in the debates back home suggested, and vanishingly tiny when compared to the slaughter taking place on the ground. In the sixteen months between August 1914 and December 1915 153 British aircrew are listed as being killed – a figure that includes training fatalities.[121] By the end of 1915 there were some 107 Fokker and Pfalz monoplanes operating on the whole of the Western Front, and the Germans' official published list of their victories showed a grand total of twenty-eight.[122] Even had these victims all been two-seaters and their crews killed or captured, the loss of fifty-six men over five months would scarcely have constituted a 'scourge' at a time when the infantry might easily lose 4,000 men in a single day. The real loss to the Army was that the downing of its few observation machines effectively blinded the commanders on the ground. The rhetoric reflected an impotent anger that the RFC was not yet equipped to meet the German aircraft on an equal footing. It was crafted for public consumption and to shame the government into leaning harder on the Royal Aircraft Factory and others to come up with an appropriate answer. A new generation of French and British aircraft did indeed begin to appear in early 1916 but the German monoplanes did not disappear completely until that summer, by which time the tables were turned and they themselves had become obsolete fodder. However, their real significance in the twelve months from mid-1915 to mid-1916 was to mark the moment when the idea as well as the science of modern aerial combat was invented and certain pilots became 'aces': celebrities whose names are famous to this day.

The comparative lack of aircraft in the skies of that early period of the war is part of the reason why the total scores of the early French and German aces were so much smaller than those of their later counterparts. At the time, too, air-to-air fighting was simpler in terms of the evolutions pilots could perform, and the majority of combat was not in the form of 'dogfights' but simple diving attacks on unwary victims. As previously indicated, Fokker's 'E' series of monoplanes (and the Pfalz lookalikes) were not in themselves such distinguished aircraft; they were merely superior to most of the Entente aircraft they met at the time, and that largely on account of their forward-firing machine guns. Many of the machines they shot down were antiques such as Farman 'Longhorns' and Caudron G.3s, wire and canvas bird-cages dawdling along at fifty or sixty miles an hour, or the more advanced but still defenceless B.E.2cs.

One of the skills of air-to-air combat the German pilots were acquiring was knowing how to take advantage of the wind and the sun's position. For their part the RFC pilots were keenly aware of the disadvantages of nature under which they flew. The Canadian ace Billy Bishop later spoke for them all when he described the drawbacks of an early show, typically on a morning when, having gone to bed past midnight, pilots were woken at 4 a.m. by an orderly.

> After a cup of hot tea and a biscuit, four of us left the ground shortly after five. The sun in the early mornings, shining in such direct rays from the east, makes it practically impossible

to see in that direction, so that these dawn adventures were not much of a pleasure. It meant that danger from surprise attack was very great, for the Huns coming from the east with the sun at their back could see us when we couldn't see them. In any case one doesn't feel one's best at dawn, especially when one has had only four hours' sleep. This was the case on this bright May morning, and to make matters worse there was quite a ground mist. The sun, reflecting off this, made seeing in any direction very difficult.[123]

'Beware the Hun in the sun' was the warning repeated to every RFC airman who came to France. Bishop must have taken the adage to heart and learned how to use it to his own advantage since he was to become the war's third- highest-scoring ace after Manfred von Richthofen and France's René Fonck, which made him the top-scoring RFC, Canadian and British Empire pilot. Strangely, the flying aces remain almost the sole aspect of the first air war of which most people today have even the faintest knowledge, much of that being incorrect.

The system was largely invented by the French press, which first awarded the appellation of 'As' to Adolphe Pégoud. As mentioned in Chapter 5, Pégoud had achieved great fame in France and Europe in 1913 when he was acclaimed as the first to loop the loop, although in fact the Russian Pyotr Nesterov had done it a few days earlier in a Nieuport IV. That same year Pégoud became the first pilot (rather than passenger) to make a successful parachute jump, abandoning his single-seat aircraft, an old Blériot, to find its own way back to earth. Once the war had begun his combat career was brief. On 5th February 1915 he shot down two German aircraft and forced a third to land in French territory. In those early days this was dramatic stuff and thereafter the French press blazoned his every move. On 18th July when he had shot down his sixth German victim he was awarded 'ace' status. On 31st August he was himself downed in combat, shot through the heart. All France mourned.

The propaganda effect of Pégoud's example was not lost on the Germans. It had great patriotic significance while also trading on the romantic aura that flying already held for most people. His death came just before the autumn battles of Loos and Artois, and amid the general slaughter it was clear the French Army was taking many more casualties than the Germans. Flying aces like Pégoud acquired an additional sheen of glamour because they were named individuals, and as such the very antithesis of the anonymous carnage of the battlefields. Something gallant and heroic could be retained in the idea of aerial knights jousting in encounters high above the mud and smoke. Although the ace system itself was no more than the glorified equivalent of the notches on a gunfighter's gun, it partook of the same mystique of the lone champion. The German press was quick to follow suit by publicising the exploits of *Fliegerasse* like Oswald Boelcke and Max Immelmann flying Fokker's new monoplane. The newspapers soon developed the pilots' friendly rivalry into a competition, with one man now ahead in the scoring and then the other, with the readership of all Germany following it as though the two were Olympic sportsmen representing their country rather than 'hired assassins'.

However, it must be emphasised that it is often misleading to compare different pilots' valour and skill solely by reference to 'league tables' of their scores. At the outset it seems to have been unofficially agreed that a minimum of five victories was required before a pilot could officially become an ace. This minimum crept upwards over the remaining three years and four months of the war, partly because by the end there were many more aircraft in the sky compared to 1915 and total scores tended to be higher. Secondly, in the beginning both German and British 'victories' would often include aircraft that were merely forced down rather than destroyed, and sometimes even those that were merely driven away from an observation task. In the RFC this practice of crediting so-called 'OOC' (Out Of Control) claims was only stopped on 19th May 1918.[124] But thirdly and most crucially, records did not always tally. A pilot might have believed he had shot down an aircraft and watched it fall, but the only way of being certain was to follow it down and see it crash. Yet this was often impossible because he was being harried by another machine. So back at his airfield he might report a victory with a reasonably clear conscience, and efforts would be made on the ground to confirm the crash. If none could be found it might be because the aircraft had fallen in no-man's-land in the middle of an artillery barrage, in which case nobody might have noticed, or it could mean that the enemy pilot had merely faked being mortally hit in order to escape. Furthermore, as the war progressed and the front line was hurriedly redrawn here and there, many airfields had to be abandoned at short notice and squadron records were very easily lost in the general panic and turmoil. Even after the war was long over and military historians from opposing sides could examine each other's operations books, certain 'victories' were exposed as enigmatic, unlikely, or almost certainly imaginary – for airmen everywhere could hardly help being drawn into the competitive nature of their trade, occasionally making claims for themselves or their squadron that were wishful thinking or even downright false. All that being said, the offices of the Kofl and then the Kogenluft* soon insisted on rigorous standards for German pilots reporting victories, and claims were frequently disallowed. But in the heat of battle, and with rivalries between individual pilots and squadrons being keen, factual accuracy must often have been a fairly flexible concept.

With the immense newspaper publicity given to Germany's most successful combat aces of that early period, Immelmann and Boelcke, it was clear that medals would have to follow. Prussia's highest award for valour, the Orden Pour le Mérite (which from the colour of its enamel was popularly known as the Blue Max) was very roughly the equivalent of Britain's Victoria Cross; but unlike the VC it had to be worked towards via a strict

---

* *see* Glossary on p.321 for an explanation of these terms.

precedence of other medals such as all three classes of the Iron Cross. By November 1915 only three Blue Maxes had been awarded to the German military, two to navy men and one to a soldier. In that month Boelcke and Immelmann were given the next highest award. Two months later in January 1916 both pilots had scored eight victories each and became the first two airmen to be awarded the Blue Max. It is interesting to compare this with the case of Manfred von Richthofen, who was to receive his own Blue Max exactly a year later but had needed twice as many victories to get it. By May 1918 his protégé Erich Löwenhardt needed twenty-four, and at the end of 1918 the last-ever recipient of a Blue Max, Carl Degelow, had thirty to his credit. This apparent inflation reflected less an effort to prevent depreciation in the medal's value than recognition that with many more pilots in the sky the opportunities for victory had become more plentiful, if not necessarily easier. In any case a Blue Max man became a publicly lionised hero, and even the military often granted him a remarkable degree of autonomy in how he chose to fight.

From its inception the German ace system also offered a valuable practical advantage to its pilots. As they became national celebrities they were eagerly sought after by representatives of the aircraft industry, who listened attentively to what they wanted from an aircraft.

> German aircraft and engine manufacturers were in sharp competition. To a great extent the orders they received depended upon what the pilots themselves thought of their engines and their machines. Each manufacturer rented rooms in Berlin's best hotels, and a pilot on leave could bask in luxury at the expense of those who made the aircraft they flew. There was no word in German for 'lobbyist' then, but the industrialists of 1915 anticipated the manufacturers and pressure groups of today by providing everything in the way of alcoholic and feminine charms for the customer. And the pilot was the customer.[125]

The value of such a system in ensuring feedback between pilot and the industry, especially when aviation was developing so fast, can hardly be exaggerated. It can also hardly be imagined in a stolidly British context in 1915. The idea of the Royal Aircraft Factory renting suites in the Ritz or the Savoy and liberally stocking them with champagne and floozies for the benefit of RFC pilots on leave is comic in its implausibility. And yet a Flight Lieutenant Mackenzie, who was killed early in 1917 while flying with the RNAS, could write with some ruefulness:

> If a designer while designing, building and testing a machine had the constant advice of a thoroughly experienced war pilot, a much more efficient and satisfactory machine could be turned out. This would also avoid endless work in the flights, under the difficult conditions of active service, and would avoid such simple mistakes as not putting the trigger on the joystick. The experience of this pilot must not be more than one month old. This would also give a good opportunity of resting a pilot after a strenuous time.[126]

However, this idea of pilots' feedback was evidently too common-sensical for the British to adopt, just as their initial attitude towards the ace system was that it was all a lot of foreign flapdoodle, failing to see how it might actually have advantageous practical and even political effects. As far as the RFC was concerned the Expeditionary Force's airmen were simply soldiers doing their duty as required by God and the King, and heroism was only to be expected. That was what medals like the Military Cross were for. Any suggestion of a cult of individualism tended to be frowned on as basically unBritish and immodest, unless perhaps a VC was awarded. 'A bit of a star turn,' senior officers might allow of a particular pilot, as though he were playing the lead in a panto or music hall show. In the summer of 1917 the anonymous author of an article in *Flying* entitled 'The Flying Corps Spirit' explained this policy as embodying a quintessentially British virtue:

The Royal Flying Corps is coldly impersonal in its official reports. It is in this aspect splendidly unique. It alone among the belligerents steadily refuses the limelight of publicity so far as its personnel is concerned. In its bulletins aeroplanes, not men, are mentioned. The names of its flying officers and observers are recorded only in the Roll of Honour or in the list of awards. 'Baron von Richthofen,' says the German bulletin, 'yesterday secured his sixtieth victim.' Doubtless the Germans have some good reason for booming their Richthofens at the expense of their [lesser] comrades. It is their considered policy, and it has its advantages as well as its drawbacks. On the whole, our policy is peculiarly British, and it is based upon British traditions. It springs partly from the regimental spirit, partly from the public-school spirit, and partly from the sporting spirit which is found in the British wherever they are...[127]

Such cultural differences aside, Trenchard initially thought it unfair to laud one man for his bravery while every day equal bravery was being shown by the pilots and observers of humbler types of aircraft, especially two-seaters doing artillery spotting and the like. Nor was it clear who might claim the victory in such a case: the pilot or the observer with the machine gun who actually did the shooting. It was equally problematic when two or more British machines joined forces to down an enemy aircraft. At first each pilot was credited with a kill, but later on a more scrupulous system of awarding fractions was adopted, so an individual score like 12½ became the norm.

The award of the third wartime VC to an RFC airman, Captain Lanoe Hawker, for shooting down three enemy aircraft on a single day in July 1915, was the exception that proved the British rule. By the end of the year Hawker had seven victories, which put him almost on a par with the German aces, and the newspapers back home were already acclaiming him as an ace. To his further credit Hawker had managed this feat against opponents armed with machine guns while flying a Bristol Scout on which he had fixed a mounting for his single-shot cavalry carbine to fire obliquely past the propeller. Hawker was already an outstanding rifle shot and became expert with this idiosyncratic arrangement that a few other pilots copied but never mastered as he did. When after a tremendous twenty-minute aerial battle in November 1916 he became Manfred von Richthofen's eleventh victim, his passing was mourned throughout Britain and particularly by the RFC, for whom by then he had become the grand old archetype of a fighter pilot. He was twenty-five.

Immelmann and Boelcke were also killed that same year – Immelmann in June and Boelcke in October. Both were mourned nationally and the RFC dropped notes of regret and respect for such worthy opponents. Of the two, Boelcke was perhaps the more whole-heartedly lamented. By all accounts he was an outstandingly decent man who, whenever he could, landed next to his victims to shake them by the hand, invite them back to his Staffel's *Kasino* (mess) for lunch, ensure their swift transfer to hospital or salute their cadavers. More than that, he was a superb tactician who did much to bring about the organising of the German *Jagdstaffeln* or Jastas – the hunting squadrons that later formed the 'flying circuses' that would serve aces like Richthofen so well. The immense prestige Boelcke had won for himself in Germany – not to mention the Blue Max – enabled him to exert considerable influence on the military authorities, who were happy to defer to him in the field in which he was so clearly expert.

Boelcke lived to see the end of the *Fliegertruppen*'s monoplane supremacy at the hands of the now better-organised fighter squadrons of the RFC and the Aéronautique Militaire. These were principally flying the D.H.2 and the Nieuport 'Bébé', although rather earlier in 1916 the RNAS had already begun making inroads into the German monoplanes with the new Sopwith Scout, usually known as the 'Pup'. Had the RFC been given the vastly superior Pups at the same time as the Navy, the Fokkers would have been finished months earlier; but of course the Sopwith company was contracted to the Admiralty and not to the Army, a good example of the absurd inefficiency of the British system.

Since the new category and role of the dedicated single-seat fighter was by now firmly established, the German Army let Boelcke undertake far-reaching reorganisation of the *Fliegertruppen*'s fighters. The first of the new 'hunting squadrons' was Jasta 2, and in September 1916 it began taking delivery of the Albatros D.1 fighter. Although not outstandingly manoeuvrable, the Albatros was faster and had better firepower than anything the Allies were flying, and even the lighter Pups had to rely on their agility and eventually on sheer altitude to defeat it. In its subsequent marques the Albatros became the main German fighter for the rest of the war. Boelcke was also responsible for instituting the systematic tuition of combat flying. He would accompany formations of new Jasta pilots and assess the performance of each. Using his own hard-won principles, he was probably the first to realise that where combat was concerned, being able to fly and even to perform aerobatics was not enough. Combat was a separate art; and thanks to him the German air force was the first to institutionalise it as something needing to be properly taught.

On 8th October 1916 the German Army's *Fliegertruppen* officially became the *Luftstreitkräfte*: the first of all the air forces to acquire a degree of administrative independence from the army. Much of the credit for this change was down to Boelcke and the highly effective Jasta system he had planned. Twenty days later, in a grievous blow to the German Air Force, he was dead. Boelcke was killed in combat, not by being shot down but in collision with a colleague when both were attacking the same enemy aircraft. He had nineteen official victories but also many others that he hadn't claimed in his scrupulously honest and modest fashion and with which he was later to be credited. Of all the

German aces Oswald Boelcke was probably the one whom his admiring RFC opponents would most have wanted to shake by the hand and stand a drink. They felt he was one of them, more a fellow airman than a Hun.

His legacy was considerable. By early 1917 the Albatri (the RFC's own whimsical plural of Albatros) D.IIIs of the now thirty-seven Jastas that Boelcke had projected had once more restored German air superiority and precipitated the 'Bloody April' that even today is still regarded as one of the most disastrous periods in British military aviation history. In that single month 316 pilots and observers out of 912 aircrew in 50 squadrons were killed or captured,[128,129] and German aircraft shot down Allied machines in a ratio of five to one. The life expectancy of a newly arrived RFC pilot was eleven days.* Oswald Boelcke also left behind his *Dicta*: basic rules for combat flying that became the bible of all German pilots, much as Mick Mannock's *Rules* did in the RFC. Finally, he had acted as tutor and mentor to the young Manfred von Richthofen, who was about to make history of his own.

Boelcke's code of correct behaviour had much to do with his personal sense of honour. To an extent this same code permeated all the combatants' air forces although the pressures of war could render it capricious. On 1st July 1916 Lieutenant W. O. Tudor-Hart and Capt. G. W. Webb were shot down in their F.E. Webb was killed outright but Tudor-Hart managed to crash-land the aircraft and survive, later writing home from internment describing the incident and adding that the German pilots had acted 'like sportsmen and gentlemen'.[130] This probably meant he was grateful they had not machine-gunned him on the ground, a practice that by then was not unknown on both sides, usually camouflaged as an attempt to

---

* 'Between March and May 1,270 RFC aeroplanes were destroyed or failed to return; and during one five-day period in April 75 were shot down, of whose 105 occupants 86 were killed or missing' (Arthur Gould Lee, *No Parachute*, p.21).

destroy the aircraft. The young Blue Max holder Werner Voss was several times accused of deliberately shooting up his crashed victims on the ground.

By Bloody April in 1917 the original glamour of flying aces as stainless knights of the air was definitely tarnished. The steady proliferation of aircraft combined with the various armies' increasing demands on their airmen was taking its toll. The gallantry of pilots like Boelcke gave way to a colder and more businesslike ethos of racking up scores by whatever means. This was probably inevitable by this stage in the war, when mass slaughter on the ground was commonplace and a spirit of cynicism and even nihilism was replacing the naïve patriotism of 1914. To many a combatant it must have felt as though everyone in uniform was an automaton on a treadmill of obligatory killing that might eventually lead to the ending of the war, although how the one might bring about the other seemed beyond conjecture. From Bloody April onwards not much quarter was given in air operations and inter-squadron rivalries over combat scores did little to improve things. Even so, a comradeship among fliers did still exist patchily, and there were shining examples of gallantry on all sides right through to the war's end.

Manfred von Richthofen probably supplied precious few of these. Although no doubt honourable enough in private life, he was too dedicated a professional fighter in a late period of the war to waste time on gestures. He was never a born pilot but he was a superb tactician and an excellent shot (this last ability being shown time and time again as more valuable than any capacity for brilliant aerobatics). In January 1917, when he was awarded the Blue Max for his eighteen victories, he took charge of Jasta 11 and thereafter laid the foundations of his reputation as the only pilot of the First World War famous enough for his name to appear in cartoon strips a century later. Until 21st April 1918 Richthofen went on steadily increasing his score and his fame. It is interesting that instructors at the German Fighter

Pilot Training School would tell their students: 'Aim for the aeroplane, not the man. When you put the aeroplane out of action, you will take care of the man.'[131] This was the exact opposite of Richthofen's own advice: 'Aim for the man and don't miss. If you're fighting a two-seater, get the observer first; until you have silenced the gun, don't bother about the pilot.'[132] This sounds as sensible as it is ruthless and was probably the policy adopted by most pilots of all sides including Mick Mannock, although he always said 'Aim for the pilot.' Still, many spoke privately of the instinctive reluctance they had to overcome in order to deliberately fire a stream of machine gun and tracer rounds into the back of a fellow aviator from thirty yards away. At that range you could actually see the tracers' grey smoke trails converging on his sheepskin jacket, watch his body jerk and the nose of his aircraft pitch upwards as he convulsively clutched the stick. Sometimes if you were close enough your goggles might be misted by his blood or brains. The one thing all the aces agreed on was that it was absolutely essential to get really close to your target. As Carl Degelow was to put it, this really separated the men from the boys in aerial combat. The closer you flew to your target, the more nerve it required but the more certain you were of scoring. Nothing so betrayed the nervous airman or the beginner as did opening fire from 300 yards; at that point an experienced combat pilot rejoiced, knowing he had a potential 'kill' awaiting him.

Whatever Richthofen's tactics, they were extraordinarily successful. In that single month of April 1917 he claimed twenty-two victories in his Albatros D.III, once shooting down four Allied aircraft on a single day. His official score was now fifty-two. His preferred method was to attack out of the sun, and he generally did so with other members of his Jasta covering him. He seldom was the 'lone hunter' of combat myth; he couldn't see the point in taking unnecessary risks. If he didn't think the odds were good enough he wouldn't engage. Instead, he became a well-organised and efficient killing machine, which was simply what he interpreted his job to be. As his total climbed, so did his reputation until the name of Richthofen was accorded national hero-worship, although it must have helped that his younger brother Lothar – a much more flamboyant pilot – had forty kills of his own.

Manfred von Richthofen's 'Red Baron' nickname was given him by his squadron comrades and swiftly taken up by newspapers everywhere. It derived from his family title of 'Freiherr', which translates more or less as 'baron' in English and accounts for the 'von', and his habit – acquired as a squadron leader – of painting the various aircraft he flew red. Here was a curious contrast with the RFC, nearly all of whose aircraft were a uniform khaki colour, which was good camouflage when viewed from above but less good for quick identification in a fight. James McCudden asked for the underside of his Sopwith Pup to be sprayed light blue so it would be less easy to see from beneath when he was flying high. Later, some colour did begin creeping into the RFC's aircraft, such as the ace Albert Ball's red propeller boss, but these were exceptions. The British had long tended to view the Germans as rigid conformists (much as most Germans viewed the Prussians); yet it was the German Army and not the British that allowed its Staffeln and individual pilots to paint their aircraft according to whim. This was fighting machinery gaily decked out. There were black aircraft and white, yellow and green, orange and brown, speckled and striped. However, after Richthofen's rise to fame there was only one all-red aircraft, although others in his Jasta might have parts of their machines painted red for identification in the air.

The 'flying circus' appellation derived from Richthofen's leadership of *Jagdgeschwader* 1. The *Jagdgeschwader* were something like the RFC's 'wings': groups of squadrons convened for a particular purpose. In this case they were groups of Jastas that were highly mobile and could be deployed up and down the front to trouble spots as required. With their gaudily painted aircraft and habit of travelling around, they quickly acquired the nickname of flying circuses. Inevitably, the one led by the Red Baron acquired the most notoriety among Allied squadrons, as well it might since Richthofen cherry-picked the best combat pilots from the Jastas for his own Jagdgeschwader 1: first-rate men like Ernst Udet and his young friend Werner Voss. He would also dump inferior pilots on other Jagdgeschwader, with the unsurprising result that no other flying circus was as successful as his.

Not that any of Richthofen's men was invincible, not even Voss, whom some later reckoned to be the single finest pilot of the war. By 11th September 1917 and barely out of his teens Voss had forty-seven confirmed victories (and Richthofen sixty-one), but he was in severe need of a rest. On 23rd September, flying his new Fokker F.I Triplane (the prototype of the Dr.I), he became embroiled in what was to be one of the most celebrated dogfights of the war in which he found himself effectively alone facing no fewer than eight British aces flying S.E.5a's. These were from 56 Squadron and included James McCudden and Arthur Rhys-Davids, all of whose aircraft Voss riddled with bullets in a ten-minute exhibition of virtuoso combat flying before he was at last shot through the chest and stomach. He probably died in the air, but in any case his Fokker smashed into the ground so violently it appeared to the watchers overhead that it 'went into powder'.

His victors landed their shot-up machines one by one back at their station, shattered by the sheer tension of the encounter, one of them bursting into a fit of weeping and Rhys-Davids (who had fired the shots that killed Voss) still hyperventilating. At that point they none of them knew who their defeated foe was and wondered whether it could have been Richthofen himself. They all recognised him as a superlative airman and the most courageous opponent any of them had ever fought. That night they solemnly drank a standing toast to him in the mess. What was left of Voss's body was retrieved by a British patrol the following day, identified, and buried in a shell crater that soon vanished beneath fresh artillery barrages. He was twenty years old.

Mention of Voss's Fokker F.I (then so new that one of the British pilots misidentified it as a Nieuport) is a reminder that nowadays the commonest depiction of the Red Baron is of him flying an all-red Fokker Triplane. It is not clear why this association should have become so indelible. As already noted, this aircraft was not especially Germanic since it and all other triplane fighters had been directly influenced by the revolutionary Sopwith Triplane whose rate of climb and manoeuvrability had made it so lethal in the hands of its RNAS pilots when it was new in the first half of 1917. (Indeed, had it not been for the small numbers of this new fighter in the hands of Navy pilots, the RFC's 'Bloody April' would have been still bloodier.) Secondly, Richthofen flew several different kinds of aircraft, only piloting his Triplane for a limited period when it accounted for a mere nineteen of his eighty victories. The type he most favoured was the Albatros D.III, although he would almost certainly have switched to the formidable new Fokker D.VII when it came into squadron service in May 1918. However, that aircraft arrived too late for the Red Baron, who was himself finally downed on 23rd April that year in circumstances that will probably be argued over for as long as air historians continue to enjoy an utterly pointless dispute that has already lasted nearly a century. In trying to shoot down a Sopwith Camel at very low level Richthofen was attacked by a second Camel and fatally wounded in the chest by a .303 bullet. He just managed to land his aircraft before dying in his seat. Thereafter argument has raged over whether the bullet was fired from the air or by troops on the ground. It hardly seems to matter now that everybody involved is long dead.

The twenty-five year-old German who was destined to become the most famous flying ace of all time – a status that will surely now never be eclipsed – was given a burial with full military honours by the Australians of 3 Squadron in whose sector he fell. Units from all over the newly formed RAF sent wreaths in homage to their most redoubtable foe, and messages of commiseration were dropped over the German lines. In Germany itself Richthofen's death came as a savage blow: the inevitable outcome of elevating anyone to the point of myth where he is believed to enshrine a portion of a nation's soul. Certainly the whole Luftstreitkräfte felt its morale shattered. Had the Red Baron not been immortal? Well yes, so he was in a historical sense; but as flesh and blood he had proved just as vulnerable as the merest novice to a small copper-jacketed bullet travelling at 2,400 feet per second.

As with so many other German aces, death had at least spared Richthofen from having to witness his nation's total collapse of morale in the last weeks of the war and afterwards. Towards the end of 1918 the streets of cities like Hamburg became full of marauding gangs of communists inspired by the Russian Revolution, anarchists or just half-starved citizens desperately looking for food, fuel and warm clothing for the coming winter. As usual after a lost war, returning soldiers were no longer regarded as heroes. As Carl Degelow put it, 'I realised that my officer's epaulettes and Pour le Mérite [Blue Max] were not looked upon with favour by people wearing red armbands. A thick briefcase and an official-looking bearing was the preferred style of appearance.'[133] Degelow was to survive until 1970. His fellow-ace, Hauptmann Rudolf Berthold, was not so lucky. He had ended the war with forty-four victories in the air, only to fall foul of a street gang of his own countrymen in Hamburg. One of the mob got behind him and strangled him to death with the ribbon of his Blue Max.

★

As Hugh Trenchard had maintained from the first, the 'flying aces' system would always entail a degree of injustice, not least by implying a monopoly of bravery and skill in the hands of a comparative few. Also, of course, the competitive sports mentality it fostered (which included the amassing of medals) led to endless disputes about the true scores of the 'winners', a few of which persist even to this day, fuelled as they sometimes are by ill-concealed nationalist motives. Probably the main figure here is that of the Canadian ace, Billy Bishop, whose total score of seventy-two has been much questioned in the last thirty years, one official historian of the Royal Canadian Air Force, Brereton Greenhous, saying that his true total might actually be twenty-seven.[134] This allegation is founded on the fact that many of Bishop's victory claims cannot be matched with German records, which are admittedly patchy and not always reliable. Despite many crucially missing documents, surviving British casualty records are generally more complete and accurate than their German counterparts. Above all, the famous engagement for which Bishop won the VC cannot be corroborated from the German side. This action took place at 4.30 in the morning of 2nd June 1917. His award citation, as it appeared in the *London Gazette* for 11th August, read as follows:

> For most conspicuous bravery, determination and skill. Captain Bishop, who had been sent out to work independently, flew first of all to an enemy aerodrome; finding no machines about, he flew on to another aerodrome about 3 miles southeast, which was at least 12 miles the other side of the line. Seven machines, some with their engines running, were on the ground. He attacked these from about fifty feet and a mechanic, who was starting one of the engines, was seen to fall. One of the machines got off the ground, but at a height of 60 feet Captain Bishop fired 15 rounds into it at very close range, and it crashed to the ground. A second machine got off the ground, into which he fired 30 rounds at 150 yards' range, and it fell into a tree. Two more machines then rose from the aerodrome. One of these he engaged at a height of 1,000 feet, emptying the rest of his drum of ammunition. This machine crashed 300 yards from the

aerodrome, after which Captain Bishop emptied a whole drum of ammunition into the fourth hostile machine, and then flew back to his station. Four hostile scouts were about 1,000 feet above him for about a mile of his return journey, but they would not attack. His machine was very badly shot about by machine-gun fire from the ground.[135]

The problem here is that in theory, at least, it is an inviolable rule that a Victoria Cross is *never* awarded without the corroborative evidence of independent witnesses (except in the sole case of the Unknown Warrior), and it is sometimes claimed that Bishop's remains the only VC ever to have been awarded entirely on the recipient's testimony. It is true that his award citation is essentially identical to the report he himself gave on returning to his airfield. One investigator claims that 'the evidence, from both British and German sources, shows that there were no aircraft losses in the Jastas of 2 or 6 Armée on 2nd June 1917, and indicates very clearly that the aerodrome attack never took place. There is not a shred of evidence to support Bishop's claims.'[136] By contrast the respected American scholar Peter Kilduff, in a definitive and exhaustive new investigation of each of Bishop's 72 victories published in 2014,[137] sees no reason to doubt that this early morning attack took place precisely as Bishop said it did. Furthermore, he believes that the rest of Bishop's victories should stand – with exactly the same proviso that attaches to every other top-scoring pilot's claims, viz. that they would inevitably have been subject to a young man's occasional economy with the truth and wishful thinking, as well as to the pressures of national propaganda and the inter-unit rivalries of the day. No-one's scores can ever now be proved with absolute certainty.

But there is another aspect. Unlike Richthofen, Bishop was one of the aces who acted as 'lone wolves'. Such men of exalted reputation were often pretty much free to come and go as they chose, preferring to hunt alone, and this inevitably made corroborating their victories more difficult even at the time. The implication that anyone whose score is doubtful was probably a liar is an easy cynicism. Bishop and others like him typically flew far more sorties in a given period than the average airman – often twice as many - and there is every reason to suppose that this level of obsessive searching for quarry would have paid off in higher scores. At the very least the sheer courage in spending twice as much time in the air, thereby doubling the chances of disaster, is undeniable.

However, the lingering doubt about Bishop's award of the VC for his 2nd June sortie remains awkward, and even Kilduff skirts the issue. The awarding of the most prestigious British medal in these anomalous circumstances must naturally prompt the question of whether there might not have been political motives at work here. First it must be said that the awarding of *any* medal has a political component since the recommendation has to be passed from the unit commander up through the chain of higher command until it is officially ratified, rejected or modified. Some sort of attempt at even-handedness has always to be made: it would be injudicious to allow one particular service, regiment or squadron to receive far more awards than any other. It was yet another of the drawbacks of the 'ace' system that once its laurelled heroes had entered a kind of national pantheon, they themselves acquired political significance willy-nilly. It so happens that in Canada by April 1917 popular backing for the war was evaporating. In that month the Canadian House of Commons passed a conscription act that was bitterly divisive. For one thing French Canadians in Québec were stolidly opposed to being forced to fight in yet another European war. Canada had already sacrificed large numbers of its bravest young men on a muddy altar thousands of miles away with no sign of an end in sight. And while British Canada continued to support the Canadian Corps, which had racked up brilliant victories as well as catastrophic casualties, many Canadians were privately opposed to conscription – above all farmers who stood to lose their young farm hands. Thus it is not at all beyond conjecture that a decision was taken at the most senior British level, and almost certainly with the agreement of the King himself, that the Empire's highest award for bravery would be a very timely morale booster for Canada and make it that much more difficult for the Dominion to slacken its efforts.

The fact is that by 1917 (and regardless of disdainful leading articles in *Flying* about foreign practices) no military was above using its heroes to its own internal advantage, especially when it came to the various services competing to prise more money out of dwindling national treasuries. This writer has no desire to enter the lists in disputes about any of the aces' scores. Even if it turned out that none had ever made more than thirty kills they would still be revealed as men of quite outstanding valour and skill, and Billy Bishop is no exception to this. It would just have been far better for his posthumous reputation had he been awarded the medal for cumulative bravery, like Albert Ball. God knows he'd earned it. It was a shame they chose that particular morning's unwitnessed action for the citation. In any case the VC Bishop was awarded in 1917 turned him overnight into a national hero, to be fêted and celebrated for the rest of his life. Perhaps the most famous Canadian of his generation, he went on to become Air Marshal of the RCAF on the outbreak of the Second World War and died in 1956 at the age of sixty-two, a national hero to the last. Nevertheless, the scholarly wrangles continue to this day over the deeds of his younger self in the skies above France almost a hundred years ago, as they do over those of his peers on both sides.

There are 188 known First World War flying aces listed with twenty and more kills, which of course excludes virtually all the earliest aces like Pégoud with five and over, as well as one of the two greatest pioneers of aerial combat, Max Immelmann, with his fifteen victories – a good example of the inherent bias of a system that only counts gun-notches. Justice has since been done to Oswald Boelcke, who at the time of his death was credited with nineteen victories but has now been granted forty, scholarship having posthumously overcome his modesty. Even among the highest-scoring men some names are more familiar than others, perhaps a reflection of the attention paid to them by the newspapers of the day according to the relative attractiveness of their personalities. Thus the second-ranking ace of the war, René Fonck with seventy-five victories, is arguably less well known outside France than his more sympathetic compatriot Georges Guynemer with fifty-three. Similarly, while many Britons have heard of the RFC's second, third and fifth highest scorers – respectively Mick Mannock, James McCudden and Albert Ball – fewer are familiar with George McElroy, in the UK's fourth position with forty-seven victories. But why? Was it because he was Irish-born?

At all events the relative absurdity of the ace system rests in its never making quite clear what was being rewarded other than notches. True, there was always going to be an unusually high standard of airmanship, marksmanship and courage. But as any pilot of the day would have attested, an awful lot depended on sheer luck: on being in the right place at the right time, on a gun not jamming or an engine conking out, on the wind suddenly dropping or a chance hazard like a bird-strike on an opponent's aircraft at a critical juncture. In addition, as Trenchard rightly thought, the 'sports' nature of competitive scoring heavily discounted the astounding daily bravery of men in two-seaters who had to loiter in the sky for hours on end as targets while observing for artillery or taking photographs of enemy positions; of those who ventured far over the lines to the limit of their fuel to drop a few small bombs on a factory or railway junction; or of those sent to fly low-level 'trench-strafing' missions in unarmoured machines of wood and canvas with every man on the ground focussing a withering barrage of lead and steel at them from close range. And not only this, but these men did it over and over again, day after day after day until their luck or nerve ran out. The more one reads the histories and accounts and memoirs, the more one realises that, admirable though the aces were, they were emphatically not the only flying heroes. What is more, in terms of the war's outcome they were a complete irrelevance.

## CHAPTER 8

# AIRMEN AND MEDICS

I N THE EARLIEST days of flight there was little reason to think that the new science might also require new medical expertise. However, as soon as aircraft performance improved an entirely novel range of aviators' symptoms presented that needed to be addressed. Among them were the effects of altitude, disorientation, vertigo, air-sickness and even g-forces. Furthermore, once war had broken out and the various armies needed to recruit aircrew by the hundred, the question of how best to select suitable trainees became urgent. Should they be different from ordinary soldiers? What qualities – both physical and mental – made a good airman? Having a private income and being able to drive a motor car might not, after all, be enough. Being fit and healthy was surely a good start, but even the fittest human body had its limitations when faced with conditions for which no terrestrial creature had evolved. Of these, the ill-effects of altitude had at least been long recognised.

The early balloonists had been much admired and even lionised for their daring, and few did more to earn their accolades than Victorian scientists like James Glaisher and Henry Coxwell. On 5th September 1862 these two gentlemen, clad in ordinary street clothes with tweed jackets, ascended in their basket without oxygen to some 32,000 feet or six miles (nearly 10,000 metres). This was as high as today's transatlantic jetliners grazing the stratosphere and leaving their white contrails. At 29,000 feet the temperature had sunk below minus 21°C. Quite apart from the cold, both men had for some time been suffering the increasing effects of hypoxia. Their hands had turned black and now their vision was too blurred to take further readings from the barometer that was effectively their altimeter. Both men were losing control of their limbs and drifting in and out of consciousness, and the balloon was still rising. One of the pigeons they had brought with them was already dead. They would undoubtedly have died as well had not Coxwell somehow willed himself to climb up, seize the rope attached to the gas-release valve in his teeth and pull it open before slumping down beside his insensible companion. Once the balloon had descended and the temperature risen the men, like their remaining pigeons, recovered quickly. This was just as well because on finally landing they had to tramp several miles to the nearest house. It was not for nothing that such pioneers inevitably became known as 'balloonatics'.

Elsewhere in Europe, and particularly in France, scientific studies were being carried out to discover the precise effects of high altitude on the body. Increased heart rate and respiration, headaches, blurred vision, intense weakness and finally unconsciousness: were these caused by the low pressure or lack of oxygen or by something else as well, such as changed blood chemistry? And were such symptoms made worse by subzero temperatures? A tough breed of scientists began setting up some very stark laboratory huts at remote sites on Europe's highest mountains. Not only must they have been competent mountaineers but unafraid of sheer physical hardship as well. The French climber and natural scientist Joseph Vallot was the first, constructing his hut 14,320 feet up Mont Blanc in 1890. Three years later the Italian neurophysiologist Angelo Mosso built a similar hut 650 feet higher on Monte Rosa. In 1910 the German physiologist Nathan Zunz led an expedition to Tenerife, setting up his laboratory at 10,695 feet in the Rifugio Altavista del Tiede the Scottish astronomer Charles Piazzi Smyth had first built there in 1856.

It was not until 1911 that there was a fully scientific anglophone high altitude research trip. This was the celebrated Pike's

Peak expedition to the mountain in Colorado where there was already a comfortable hotel at 14,100 feet and, better still, a rack and pinion railway to reach it. Two leading British physiologists, J. S. Haldane and C. G. Douglas, together with two equally distinguished American colleagues, Yandell Henderson and E. C. Schneider, spent five productive weeks at the hotel. With classical thoroughness they had earlier taken their bodily measurements at sea level. They then did the same at altitude for over a month plus a final set of data back at sea level. Their findings were of unprecedented accuracy.

Even so, the French scientist Paul Bert had long been granted the honorary title of 'the father of high-altitude physiology' since the publication of his great treatise *La Pression Barométrique* in 1878. He had used animals in low-pressure chambers at his laboratory in the Sorbonne and established once and for all that the ill-effects of high altitude were caused by low concentrations of oxygen in the atmosphere. Given this finding, which was fully corroborated by all subsequent research, it is surely very odd that forty years later pilots flying above 12,000 feet or so did not automatically carry an oxygen supply once aircraft were powerful enough to manage the extra weight of the cylinder. RFC pilots flying Sopwith Pups in 1917, for example, quite frequently went to 20,000 feet for lengthy patrols. The main reason for flying so high was that by then the Pup was obsolescent and the only way it could defend itself against the German Albatros D.III was by its sole advantage of superior manoeuvrability at extreme height. But the effects of flying at that altitude for extended periods without oxygen were very severe, especially if the least effort was required. Arthur Gould Lee left a vivid description of having to answer a call of nature in his Pup at 20,000 feet:

> I give my reluctant attention to a difficult expedient, with the hope that no Hun will come along at an inconvenient moment. My hands are completely numb, but I pull off my right gauntlet and fumble interminably at opening buttons,

which takes quite a time because my fingers have no sense of touch. Then comes the task of finding the way through a barrier of obstinate underclothes. This achieved, there is the problem of where? The refined procedure is to have a funnel with a rubber tube running to a container on the floor of the cockpit, but most of us just aim at the joystick and hope for the best, the hope being strongest over Hun territory. Then comes the job of getting things back as they were. When it is all over and the gauntlet is replaced, the effort has exhausted me and I flop back in my seat panting for several minutes.[138]

It might have been even worse. Diarrhoea was a well-known affliction of those who flew aircraft – like the Pup – with a rotary engine that spewed out quantities of castor oil whose laxative mist airmen constantly inhaled. Supposed remedies included blackberry juice and brandy, flasks of which pilots sometimes carried. After a while many men acquired an immunity to castor oil and quite probably to brandy as well.

Almost as bad were the agonising pins and needles in the hands and feet when descending quickly to lower altitude, not to mention the splitting headache that would sometimes linger for days. The Germans, too, had long experience of these symptoms in their airships, and during the war Zeppelin bomber crews were often badly affected. The hours of slow flight by night to the English coast against the prevailing wind, temperatures of forty degrees of frost and a lack of oxygen rendered many men useless. They were obliged to give up flying altogether and return to the trenches. A German officer later recorded the example of one such Zeppelin, the L.44, making a raid on Harwich in May 1917. The crew were so incapacitated by hypoxia that 'the ship drifted over the town completely out of control, and without a single engine running. It was not until they were well out in the middle of the North Sea that two of the engines were restarted, and the ship was able to return to its base.'[139]

What is strange about these examples is that despite all that had long been known to science about oxygen deficiency impairing performance, the various militaries were so slow to do something to alleviate it even though their airmen were being incapacitated as fighting men. Certainly the slight extra weight of oxygen cylinders would have been insignificant in an airship. Nor was it for lack of suitable equipment. Back in October 1904 *Scientific American* had carried an article on 'The Guglielminctti–Draeger Respiratory Apparatus' and it was clear that some medics with an interest in aviation were aware of this piece of equipment because in 1914 the British surgeon J. Elrick Alder wrote about its advantages. Among these was the pilot's ability to control the flow of oxygen according to need. He simply wore 'a mask communicating by a pipe with the vessel. This caused the aeronaut to avoid all effort in carrying to his mouth the vivifying gas.'[140] Mr Alder knew all about the effects of altitude and had observed 'cyanosis of the extremities: the fingers become purple. Wynmalem [the Dutch flyer and altitude record holder, Wyn Malem] who reached a height of 8,340 feet felt the blood pour from his nails into his fur gloves, and red pearls were on his lips.' (This last phrase is pure Oscar Wilde.)

The particular example he quotes picked up yet another important characteristic of altitude sickness that any mountaineer recognised: that different people reacted very differently to it, and it was not just a matter of fitness. There seemed no way of knowing in advance who would be better able to resist hypoxia without subjecting each man to tests in a barometric chamber. A British aviation doctor who had studied under Haldane, Captain Martin Flack, recorded a series of thirty-five pilots he had examined while consultant to the Air Board in 1917. He listed them (together with the number of flying hours in their log books) to show the variation in their reactions to altitude:

No. 1 (28 hrs): Giddy above 4,000 feet.

No. 2 (10½ hrs): Giddiness and blurring of vision when flying at 6,000 feet.

No. 3 (140 hrs): Fainted twice in air above 8,000 feet.

No. 11 (300 hrs): Since crash, fainted twice in air at 8,000 feet and 10,000 feet.

No. 31 (400 hrs): At first all right, then on 3 occasions faint at 7,000 feet.[141]

Quite often pilots seemed to have no idea that they were affected by altitude. This is a familiar syndrome, which explains the later testing of military aircrew in decompression chambers to teach them how to spot the symptoms of hypoxia. Despite their own blue fingertips subjects may gradually lose consciousness without the least awareness of its happening. In the first air war men carrying out high observation recces over 15,000 feet would often return to earth quite unable to remember what they had seen, their reports sketchy or useless. Many had failed to take notes at the time because, either through hypoxia or cold, they couldn't hold a pencil. Once back on the ground the effects of amnesia became obvious. The military doctor Lieutenant-Colonel J. L. Birley RAMC recorded how 'One observer returned from a high photographic reconnaissance well pleased with his effort until it was discovered that he had taken 18 photographs on the same plate...'[142] After the war Birley, who had co-authored reports for the new Air Ministry, confided to *The Lancet*: 'It has always been my opinion that the paralyzing and insidious effects of oxygen-want had a far greater influence in determining the course of aerial operations than has yet been realized.'[143]

If it was odd that no air force did much to deal with this phenomenon until quite late in the war, stranger still was the resistance by many pilots themselves to the very idea of carrying oxygen. In fact, some British squadrons luckier than Arthur Gould Lee's were being supplied – albeit patchily – with oxygen equipment at the exact moment he was describing. The chronicles of W. E. Johns's own squadron, No. 55, mention it in July 1917 (exactly a year before Johns was posted to France), but the

tone of the entry makes it clear that the crews were initially sceptical of its value. '[T]hough opinions differed at the time as to
the real usefulness of this additional "gadget", it proved that
ultimately the pilot and observer who dispensed with it felt the
effects of altitude flying very much more than they who had
consistently used it, and also that the former were liable to a
sudden breakdown, possibly in the air.'[144] In a leading medical
journal nine months later in 1918 an exasperated M.O. noted a
continued resistance to oxygen: 'Unfortunately, some pilots
have an unreasonable prejudice against the use of oxygen, possibly bred of some irresponsible scoffer, and medical officers
should therefore patiently explain in the mess or in individual
talks the value of oxygen at high altitudes in preventing drowsiness and loss of rapid judgement...'[145] The obvious assumption
has to be that of sheer ignorance: many British aircrew must
have understood so little of basic science and human physiology
that they didn't realise oxygen's importance. This seems all the
more extraordinary given that nearly every pilot who had flown
high for any length of time had personal experience of the
deadly effects of hypoxia and dreaded being caught by an enemy
aircraft when his reactions were slow and his energy depleted,
like this German:

> Many a poor fellow who had carried out a long and successful
> flight far behind the enemy's lines lost his strength before his
> sortie was over. Weakened and unable to concentrate, he
> would fall easy prey to some enemy fighter on his return
> flight. Others could not use their machine guns on account
> of frostbite. Defenceless, they succumbed to the enemy's
> relentless attacks.[146]

What was more, pilots dreaded being injured at altitude because
they knew that with increased heart rate and low barometric
pressure bleeding was often severe despite the cold. This syndrome had been known about since at least 1812 when the

French solo balloonist Sophie Blanchard suffered a severe and unstaunchable nosebleed at 22,800 feet. The pilot of one German two-seater, seeing his wounded observer was losing blood at a great rate, broke off a fight at altitude and dived as steeply as he dared to land beside a hospital.[147] In a British squadron, leaving a combat because your observer was wounded could have looked suspiciously like 'blue funk' or a lack of 'fighting spirit'. But since in a German two-seater the observer was usually also the officer in command, it may be that this particular pilot was simply obeying orders bellowed imperiously from the back seat.

★

Even without the problem of oxygen deficiency, the sheer cold in an open cockpit with nothing but a minuscule windshield for protection from the slipstream's freezing gale was an agony in itself. No-one was impervious to it, not even fit young men with excellent circulation. Despite leather garments with layers of clothing underneath, their legs enclosed in thigh-length sheepskin 'fug boots', exposed areas of the face smeared with foul-smelling whale oil and with a sinister-looking dogskin mask and goggles, the cold always got through. An inventive Australian pilot with the RNAS, Sidney Cotton, designed a one-piece suit he proudly named the 'Sidcot'. It became officially adopted by the RFC at the end of 1917 and went on being used by the RAF until well after the Second World War.[148] But good though it was, the Sidcot could do little to warm the extremities. Being roused by a batman at 4 a.m. on a dark and frosty winter morning in France to fly a dawn patrol clad in stiff and freezing leather in an open-cockpit aircraft – and usually on nothing more than a cup of tea and a slice of toast – must have demanded quite exceptional fortitude. Life in the trenches in winter with snow on the ground was no picnic; but the appalling cold at 15,000 feet or higher was another matter – further exacerbated as it was by the wind-chill of the slipstream, especially for the observer who had to stand up to man his gun. Even in summer, temperatures of minus 40°C were not unknown at altitude. Even the alcohol in the aircraft's compass could freeze. Supposedly cold-resistant gun oil thickened to the point where weapons jammed and became unusable. Aircrew sometimes arrived back on the ground unable to climb out of their machines and in no fit state to fly again that day or even for weeks. 'My face feels like one big bruise after the cold yester-day,' admitted Lieutenant-Colonel H. Wyllie to his diary. 'Mowatt rather badly frost bitten.'[149]

> CASE 2 – Flight Sub-Lieut. M., aet 27. Returned from bomb-ing raid of about two and a half hours' duration. Face very swollen though not particularly painful. Next day the face was enormously swollen, the cheeks being almost in line with the tips of the shoulders, and in addition there was much redness and some vesication of the skin below the right angle of the mouth. This latter developed into a fairly superficial necrotic patch about the size of a crown piece.
>
> Treatment consisted of keeping the face warm by wool and bandage, and dusting powder to the necrotic patch. Later a zinc oxide ointment dressing was applied to this latter. The swelling gradually decreased, and the slough turned black and separated, leaving a healthy base about the fifteenth day. The face was very painful for some weeks after this whenever exposed to the cold.[150]

Yet just as with oxygen, there was resistance on the part of some pilots and observers to the issuing of electrically heated cloth-ing, some versions of which were introduced in early 1918. Like the electrical supply for wireless sets, the power came from a generator attached to a strut and driven by a small propeller that turned in the slipstream. One pilot noted the case of an Australian who refused both these aids to his well-being on the grounds that the small extra weight plus wind resistance 'added to the burden put upon the engine, and so tended to deprive him of just that last ounce of power which makes all the difference when manoeuvring against the Hun'.[151]

\*

By now military doctors serving with all the combatants realised that a significant proportion of their aircraft accidents and losses was caused by the aircrews' physical state rather than by enemy action. An example of this was recorded of a new officer who joined 20 Squadron in France in 1917:

> He was a quiet and delightful man who had just been elected to the Fellowship of his college. A week or so later, he was under arrest for cowardice. On each of three occasions when his flight had been on reconnaissance patrol, he had joined the flight above the airfield, had begun to move off with them and then broke off and returned alone. He did not know why he had done this and did not even realize that he had until after he had landed. Heald [an RAMC captain, the squadron's Medical Officer] examined him and found a chronic suppurating otitis media [middle ear infection] and a history of his having been awarded his wings without ever exceeding 1,000 feet. As he had to rendezvous at about 2,500 feet for his sorties he had obviously become dizzy and disorientated. Heald made a full report in writing and in person to the brigadier and the court martial was cancelled. The officer returned to his regiment with his honour unsullied.[152]

This reveals much about the standards of aircrews' medical selection and training in the RFC at the time. It seems incredible now: a highly articulate young man with a chronic weeping ear infection and no experience of going above 1,000 feet who was nonetheless passed as suitable for combat flying in a war zone. Behind such cases lay an administrative absurdity: that despite all that was being recognised by aviation medics, RFC recruits were still given the standard army medical inspection designed to weed out obvious physical deficiencies such as bad eyesight or lameness, as well as infectious diseases like TB and VD. One army doctor wrote candidly of the inspection he was required to carry out as 'a perfunctory examination calculated to exclude the one-legged, the hunch-backed, the man moribund of cardiac disease, and the blind'.[153] To be fair, he was speaking of coping with the great rush of volunteers in the autumn of 1914. All the same, standards of public health in Britain were often so bad that in some units upwards of 20 per cent of men were found unfit for military service.

> The 42nd Territorial Division was nearly at full establishment when it left Britain, but when it arrived in Egypt in September 1914 the GOC, Sir John Maxwell, found 100 men technically blind, 1,500 riddled with vermin, one dying of Bright's disease and 'hundreds so badly vaccinated they could hardly move'. One officer concluded that the division had 'picked up any loafer or corner boy they could find to make up the numbers'.[154]

For all that these men had volunteered, the result was like press-ganging all over again; and it scarcely helped that until May 1915 doctors were paid half a crown for every man they passed as fit: a system that practically guaranteed abuse. Both the French and the Germans were well aware of deficiencies in the health of their own potential recruits, but all evidence suggests that they were generally more thorough, and at an earlier date, than were the British, certainly when medically vetting their future airmen. Once he had passed the standard Army inspection a man applying for the RFC was usually deemed by implication to be fit to fly. Indeed, there were documented cases of men diagnosed as unfit for the trenches being recommended for transfer to the RFC, although it is probably safe to assume a degree of Army ill-will was operating here, and not just medical incompetence. This being noted, 1917 was also the year when the RFC formed its Special Medical Boards – much to the scepticism of the existing Army medical services. This was in direct response to casualty figures that had become quite unsustainable. In that year of Bloody April the air arm's reinforcement demands were running at roughly 500 per cent per annum – a rate that implied a complete turnover of RFC personnel every ten weeks or so. More than half these casualties occurred in the first six weeks of training. The Special Medical Air Boards began applying much more rigorous selection standards and by autumn these were showing dividends. They halved the wastage of men and machines by weeding out early the obviously unfit, and disqualifying certain prospective flyers from even basic training. Even so, a further 10 per cent of recruits were eliminated during training as 'unlikely to become efficient flyers'. It was yet another sign of the impending break of the Royal Flying Corps from the Army, which formally took place on 1ˢᵗ April the following year with the creation of the RAF. By now it had become evident that a particular sort of man was needed in the air, with quite different attributes to those of an infantryman. Inevitably, he would also be prone to a different set of ailments and injuries.

★

The question of the best flying temperament had long been moot. It was all very well bluff types in flying club bars booming that anyone who could drive a motor car could learn to fly; but since at least the days of Blériot and his flying schools the question of whether there was a particular 'type' of person who made an ideal aeronaut had been much debated. The war only made this both more urgent and more problematic because men were no longer required just to be skilled aviators. They also had to be warriors; and 'fighting spirit' seemed to demand yet another kind of character. The idea was common then (and persisted into the 1930s among older officers in the RAF) that a good horseman made the best aviator. Sensitive hands, a good seat and an eye for country were thought to be essential requirements. It is perhaps too easy to scoff at this today. In fact, the light biplanes of the early days of flying never responded well to heavy-handed treatment and nor, for that matter, do modern aircraft. Once stable machines like the B.E.2c had been superseded by fighting aircraft deliberately designed to fly on the very edge of stability like the Sopwith Camel, it was not hard for an unwary pilot who was a little rough on the controls to tip his machine into a spin or a stall – either of which could easily prove fatal, as training airfields witnessed almost daily throughout the war.

A further reason for not scoffing at the perceived connection with riding has to do with class. In 1914 horses were ubiquitous and most well-to-do young men could ride, if only after a fashion. Such youngsters constituted the pool from which the British Army mainly drew its pilots in the early part of the war because by and large they were the middle-class men who had already learned to fly at their own expense in private aero clubs. Particularly in Britain, the type of man the military chose tended to self-select in conformity with the Army's preconceptions. Yet the pressures of war soon obliged the RFC's recruiting officers to look further afield. By late 1918 an RAMC doctor could report that 'Flying is not now confined to the public school boy, the cavalry officer, or the athlete. We take many of our pilots at present from the lower middle classes and some from the artisan class.'[155] Even so, at much the same time another doctor who had already spent eighteen months as the chief medical officer of various RFC and RAF training camps could write:

[O]ne would much sooner accept a well-educated nervous type as a pilot than one whose mental training has been very limited. For the nervous, pale-faced, introspective East End clerk with little or no experience of outdoor exercise and sport, whose habit of life almost compels him to think far too much of [i.e. about] himself, one would probably advise rejection; while for the university athlete, equally nervous but

trained to ignore himself and to control his feelings, trained
to act and think of and for others, of good physique and
broad in mental outlook, one would on the whole advise
acceptance.[156]

Here, a public school housemaster disguised in RAMC khaki has
plainly had the last word. Clean-limbed, clear-eyed and sporty
'varsity boys versus weedy working-class townees? No competition. And after all, he was probably right. The one thing that
upset this easy preference was the influx of pilots from the
Dominions – Canada, Australia, New Zealand and South Africa
– because they were more unreadable in class terms. They
tended overwhelmingly to be country boys, and mostly far
tougher and fitter even than Oxbridge men who rowed. Better
still, thanks to lives lived in the great open spaces, they often had
terrain-reading skills that seemed positively uncanny to their
British instructors and proved less likely than their British counterparts to get lost in the air.

   The belated introduction of the Special Medical Air Boards
ensured that the RFC's doctors began to catch up with the more
scientific approach of their Continental counterparts. However,
anyone looking through bibliographies of the medical problems
that early flying threw up will be struck by how few of the contemporary books are in English. Whether addressing aviation
accidents, ear-nose-and-throat conditions, altitude sickness or
the psychology of fliers, the majority of the texts are in French,
German and Italian with only the occasional British or American
book. It was not that Britain lacked scientists of J. S. Haldane's
calibre – or even first-rate doctors, come to that. As we know, the
German and French army high commands were at first equally
sceptical about an air war. But their scientists were clearly ahead
of the game, the Germans being particularly advanced in aviation medicine thanks to their supremacy in airship technology
(while nevertheless allowing at least some of their Zeppelin
crews to fly without oxygen).

At any rate the RFC did eventually adopt physiological and even rudimentary psychological tests for airmen. These included measurement of reaction times (using French-designed apparatus), visual acuity tests and sometimes pressure chamber tests to weed out those abnormally susceptible to altitude. Yet even here a doctor writing in a British journal after the war could say: 'On the Continent observations have been made upon the circulatory system in the air at different heights. I had hoped to carry out a series of similar observations myself as it does not follow that one would obtain the same results with British pilots.'[157] Evidently he felt Britons were physiologically different from Continentals.

Some aviation doctors formed their own rule-of-thumb notions of how to spot a potential aviator that may well have had a modicum of validity:

I have noticed that if a man had a good 'sense of projection' he made a good aeronautist ... This test seems to me to be almost decisive of a man's fitness for flying. By 'sense of projection' I mean that a man having looked at a small object [at arm's length] will afterwards be able quickly and accurately to touch it with the eyes closed.[158]

The real problem, of course, was that while it was theoretically possible by now to subject men to all sorts of physical tests to see if they were suitable for flying training, it was far more difficult to evaluate a man's psychology or character in a way that would yield reproducible scientific data. Thus in the latter half of 1918 an American doctor could write:

While at a medical conference at the central recruiting office in England for [RAF] aviators, at which there was an exhaustive discussion of physical tests, I was surprised to note how little stress was laid on the psychological element. It was admitted that even the most experienced examiner could

not predict how a flier would behave in action, or whether he
would cease to be useful after he had met with an accident,
or had had a narrow escape from death.[159]

This was hardly surprising, given that nearly a century later such
things are still to some extent unpredictable, despite batteries of
psychological tests and widely-held beliefs that the mechanics of
the mind are today far better understood. At the time, RFC and
RAF doctors had to rely on first impressions of each candidate
as a suitable 'character'. Their recorded assessments could then
be matched up with those of the men's first instructors – although
in many cases it is hard to see how the wretched candidate was
ever allowed to climb into an aircraft in the first place, even if he
had been to the right sort of school:

| Remarks of M.O. | Instructor's Remarks |
|---|---|
| 7. All there – guts | Good – plenty of guts |
| 19. Uptake slow | Good but silly |
| 24. Slow uptake, no sports, clerk | Average – slow learning |
| 40. Dull and windy | Poor – sent to heavier machines |
| 42. Mentality very poor | Hopeless |
| 50. Quick but bumptious & over-confident | Good but objectionable |
| 72. Little stamina, clerk | Average |
| 89. Civil Service clerk | Poor – slow |
| 107. No physique – windy | Poor, windy and sick |
| 139. Charterhouse School, but slow, heavy | Poor, very slow[160] |

'Windy' in this context meant timid and fearful, with unmistak-
able overtones of cowardice: the polar opposite of 'guts'.
Number 40 was probably not an ornament to the unlucky squadron (presumably bombers) to which he was posted.

It can be seen that predicting the sort of man who would make a good aviator in the RFC or RAF was, until late in the war, considerably a matter of personal prejudice on the part of the examiner, whether he was a doctor or a flying instructor. In the absence of more sophisticated medical tests this was not unreasonable, given that he would have formed his opinions by means of experience (in an instructor's case experience that had probably come very close to killing him on several occasions). By September 1918 it seemed that something of a consensus had been reached in RAF medical circles about the qualities that made a good combat pilot:

> The fighting scout is usually the enthusiastic youngster, keen on flying, full of what one might call 'the joy of life', possessing an average intelligence but knowing little or nothing of the details of his machine or engine; he has little or no imagination, no sense of responsibility, keen sense of humour, able to think and act quickly, and endowed to a high degree with the aforementioned quality, 'hands' [i.e. lightness of touch on the controls]. He very seldom takes his work seriously, but looks upon 'Hun-strafing' as a great game.[161]

A very British prescription, this, of the 'playing fields of Eton' variety. Apparently the requirement was for young men who were not very bright, pig-ignorant about the technicalities of their aircraft, and with a feckless enough sense of humour to view killing and being killed as just a game. Certainly this profile was very much at variance with the far better informed, professional and seriously accomplished airmen Robert Smith-Barry's Gosport system was even then trying to train.

★

By the end of the war active RAF units in France at last had their own medical officers rather than just a medical orderly, most of whom would have had a working knowledge of the particular

ailments to which airmen were prone. They might not have
been able to predict a newly posted man's aptitude for war flying
with any accuracy, but the attrition of Bloody April in 1917,
the temporary reign of the German massed-Jasta 'circuses' and
the ever-widening scope of air operations had made them practised judges of what today is known as Combat Stress Reaction.
W. E. Johns's first description of the fictional Biggles, quoted in
the Introduction, is that of a pilot showing all the symptoms
of 'battle fatigue' (although with artistic licence the often exuberant aerial adventures he went on to enjoy miraculously belie
this). Dr Birley gives a still bleaker description of a pilot at the
end of his combat usefulness:

> To keep himself going he smokes to excess, or may even
> come to rely on alcohol. If he meets an enemy formation on
> patrol he either turns tail or attacks recklessly, too tired to
> think about manoeuvring. In the last stage the noise of
> engines on the aerodrome distresses him; he cannot bear to
> see a machine take off or land, and he even hates to hear
> 'shop' talked. Sooner or later he must give in. The career as
> a war pilot of an individual who reaches this extreme stage is
> irrevocably finished.[162]

The tragedy was that aircrew shortages meant such diagnoses
were often ignored by station commanders desperate to keep
their machines in the air. In some ways it was even worse that so
many of these shattered men were sent back to Britain to act as
flying instructors.

It was generally agreed that observers in two-seaters suffered
more strain than pilots. Not surprisingly, any loss of confidence
in his pilot's skill greatly increased the observer's anxiety. This
could become extreme if, for instance, his usual pilot went off
on leave or was injured and he was assigned a greenhorn straight
out of flying school. Not only would he have no faith in the
man's flying ability until it was proved, but there was a lot to

learn by bitter experience about surviving in the air over the front, and the first few weeks were crucial. Any experienced observer would have found this learning period agonising. Furthermore, an observer had far more to do in the air than did his pilot. Not only had he to keep a constant lookout for enemy aircraft that could appear in a split second as if from nowhere, especially from the blind spot beneath the aircraft, and be prepared to use his gun at an instant's notice; he usually had to combine this with taking photographs or making pencil notes or drawings of enemy positions and movements he could see below. He might also have to tap out wireless messages in Morse. It became recognised on all sides that observers usually broke under the strain before pilots did, and to a more serious degree.

★

One of the most intractable physiological difficulties to beset aviators became apparent almost as soon as the earliest aeroplanes encountered mist or cloud. It was commonly known as 'pilot's vertigo' and medically as disorientation. That word (derived from the mediaeval 'orienting' of churches so as to face east) normally implied losing one's sense of direction in the usual two earthbound dimensions. It was the addition of a third dimension that led to pilot's vertigo. After some two million years' evolution as a bipedal animal, our genus *Homo* has acquired a pretty reliable sense of balance when dealing with abrupt changes of direction, especially at running speeds (while hunting or being hunted), even though this can easily be disturbed – as any child knows who spins around fast enough to induce giddiness. But until humans flew powered craft they did not have to deal with abrupt changes of direction in three dimensions, and at undreamt-of speeds. Suddenly, human physiology was found wanting. The appropriate circuitry had never evolved because it had never been needed.

Early aviators commonly became lost in the conventional sense of compass bearings. But for what was surely the first time in human history they also found themselves not always knowing which way was up and which down. It is difficult to convey to someone who has never flown a light aircraft in thick cloud how astonishingly easy it is for the body's sense of up and down to become completely fooled; and the longer this state of 'blind' flying lasts, the more disorientated a pilot can become. This is why a vital part of training is in instrument flying. Instruments are generally reliable; the fabled seat of one's pants less so. Without instruments virtually nobody manages to blind-fly dead level for very long. It may sound hard to believe but there are instances on record of an aircraft emerging from a thick bank of cloud *inverted*, without the pilot having realised he has gradually turned upside down. It would be a considerable shock to burst suddenly into brilliant sunshine to find rivers and fields overhead.

One of the very first instruments in aircraft was the 'slip bubble'. This was simply a sealed tube of liquid with either a bubble or a ball in it, much the same as a builder's level but slightly curved. It was essentially an athwartships spirit level. If the aircraft's wings were parallel to the horizon and its vertical axis in line with the earth's gravity, the ball would remain in the centre. But this primitive gadget could seriously mislead a pilot flying blind in a cloud if the aircraft was in a banked turn and centrifugal force counteracted gravity. Not only could this cause the ball to remain in the centre despite the aircraft being tilted, but because the pilot felt his weight increase the turn could also give him the illusion that that he was in a climb. Seeing the slip bubble apparently registering level flight, he might be tempted to push the stick forward to descend or to pull it back hoping to fly out of the cloud. Obviously this could easily lead to disaster or at the very least to acute disorientation, as happened to Cecil Lewis one day in 1916, slowly climbing up through 2,000 feet of thick cloud and at last emerging into sunlight:

> But what in heaven had happened to this cloud-bank? It wasn't level. It was tilted as steeply as the side of a house. The machine

was all right – airspeed constant, bubble central – and yet here were the clouds defying all natural laws! I suppose it took me a second to realize that *I* was tilted, bubble or no bubble; that I had been flying for the best part of fifteen minutes at an angle of thirty degrees to the horizon – *and had never noticed it!*[163]

It might be thought that, a century on and with all the sophisticated electronic instrumentation and gadgetry available to modern military and civil aviation, disorientation would no longer be a problem. Yet an article in the May 2013 issue of *Aerospace International* entitled 'Battling spatial disorientation' shows this to be wishful thinking. It begins with a description of an onboard video recording made in the cockpit of an RAF Tornado while its two-man crew practised anti-missile evasive manoeuvres high above the North Sea. They began by

going to full afterburner and rolling the aircraft into a 60° nose-down descent through thick cloud… with the navigator calmly counting down the altitude from 17,000 ft. It was not until the cockpit low altitude voice warner could be heard saying 'Pull up! Pull up!' that the crew grasped the immediacy of the danger they were in and managed to recover the aircraft only 350 ft above the sea by pulling a 7G manoeuvre. The video was sent around all squadrons to show the danger of spatial disorientation (SD) and how it can occur even during routine missions.

Bluntly put, a highly trained combat pilot and his navigator had come within an ace of flying their £9.4 million aircraft straight into the sea at supersonic speed, instruments or no instruments. In fact, spatial disorientation has recently been blamed for 20 per cent of all fatal mishaps in military aviation and has been named as a factor in many high-profile civil accidents.[164]

In the First World War most army doctors would probably have understood little enough about the sense of balance and how the vestibular system works. However, it was clear that many trainees as well as experienced pilots were being killed by losing all sense of their aircraft's attitude. Nor was this just a matter of flying into the ground. In many aircraft, including the Sopwith Pup, it was easy to stall or spin simply by not flying straight and level at the right airspeed, and neither slip-bubble nor compass was reliable enough to ensure safety in all circumstances. Once again Arthur Gould Lee describes it well:

> Ordinarily you keep on an even keel, both fore-and-aft and laterally, by reference to the horizon, to which you continuously and unconsciously adjust the controls. In a cloud there is no horizon, and you use the air speed indicator for fore-and-aft checks – increased speed means you're going down, and vice versa – and the bubble, like a carpenter's level, a joke as an instrument, for lateral angles. Wind on the side of the face means you're side-slipping. You keep straight by holding to the bearing on your compass, but this is another joke, for the slightest jerk of the rudder sends it spinning, and it needs a longish spell of smooth, straight flying to settle down again – and this you can't do in a cloud.[165]

Compasses were notoriously easy to 'topple' by even quite mild aerobatics, and after a dogfight surviving pilots often found themselves completely lost, especially if there was a wind and they had drifted during the battle. On a grey day without sun and with a uselessly whirling compass, a pilot might find himself heading further into enemy territory instead of homeward.

> It was at Tramecourt that I was sent my first NCO pilot, who I am sorry to say did not last very long, for apparently he got lost in the air and was last seen flying east into enemy country. We never heard of him again. No doubt this sounds incredible to the uninitiated, but it was astounding the number of new pilots who were lost in this way.[166]

This was presumably where certain Australians and Canadians had an advantage by allegedly being better able to 'read' directions from such things as rivers and by having a more developed memory for terrain than many of their British comrades.

From December 1917, under the aegis of the Special Medical Air Boards, cadets applying for commissions went for medical examination at the newly established RFC Central Hospital at Mount Vernon in Northwood, Middlesex, and standards became more demanding. Many of the tests were based on those already used by the French Air Force, such as d'Arsonval's chronometer for measuring reaction times. There were tests for heart and eyesight and co-ordination, as well as for balance and disorientation. Among the test equipment favoured by French aviation doctors was the Bárány chair. This was a device designed by the Hungarian physiologist Robert Bárány as part of his work on the balance mechanisms of the inner ear that had earned him a Nobel Prize in 1914. The blindfolded subject sat in the chair which was then spun. When it stopped the blindfold was removed and the subject asked to point at something in the room. Measurement could then be made of how wide of the mark his aim was.

There is evidence that the British never took such things quite as earnestly as did other nations even though the Bárány chair tests showed that Dr McWalter had been fumblingly along the right lines when he looked for a 'sense of projection' in prospective fliers. Still, such tests were being used by RFC doctors at least by the autumn of 1916, if in a somewhat perfunctory manner. When Billy Bishop, the future Canadian air ace who had hitherto been flying as an observer, applied to re-train as a pilot in September that year he recalled his physical examination as having been less than rigorous:

> After the doctor had listened to your heart and banged your lungs and persuaded you to say 'aah' and 'ninety-nine', you were put into a swivel chair, spun around, and suddenly

invited to spring to attention. If you did not fall flat on your face it was presumed that you were a healthy individual and fit to fly. You also did things like walking a chalk line with your eyes shut. That was about all there was to it.[167]

By contrast an article in *The Lancet* of 8th September 1917 makes it clear the American Army took such tests as the Bárány chair very seriously indeed, and that the standards of the medical examination undergone by prospective aviators in the United States were high, much more so than those of the equivalent British examination. (The Bárány chair is still used in research departments worldwide today.)

British would-be aviators were also quizzed about their personal habits, especially drinking and smoking, as well as their family histories. So also was any airman admitted to Mount Vernon as an in-patient. When in 1918 the establishment became the RAF Central Hospital, Dr H. Graeme Anderson noted that a patient 'was asked to give as complete account as he is able of his family: their ages, nationalities (particularly as to any Celtic or Hebrew blood), and habits…'[168] W.B. Yeats's Irish airman foreseeing his own death probably did well not to wind up in Mount Vernon. Yet despite the great step forward that the Central Hospital's more thorough testing represented, the official attitude towards its true value – as *The Lancet* ruefully admitted in September 1917 – was still the familiar one of 'We must wait and see. We don't yet have enough data.' It was an attitude that had served (and still serves) Britain long and well in its instinctive refusal to commit itself to anything much other than cautious fence-sitting, especially if it might cost money. Certainly in aviation medicine in the last two years of the First World War the British did sometimes give the impression they believed they were a race apart physiologically; that 'Continental' medical ideas were all very well for Continentals (not to mention Celts and Hebrews), but such things needed to be taken with a pinch of salt when testing British subjects.

★

Powered flight had revealed yet another phenomenon for which evolution had not equipped humans but which, as aircraft improved, pilots suddenly had to deal with. This was g-forces. What is believed to be the first recorded case of someone losing consciousness because of 'g' occurred in 1903 when the American-British inventor, Sir Hiram Maxim, was testing his 'Captive Flying Machine'. He had designed this as a ride for an amusement park in London's Earl's Court. It consisted of a central revolving pole with metal arms attached at right angles from which hung individual seats. As it sped up the seats were flung outwards under centrifugal force. Maxim himself dismissed it as nothing more than a 'glorified merry-go-round', but its derivatives survive to this day in amusement parks the world over. While trying out the Captive Flying Machine Dr A. P. Thurston blacked out under 6.87 g, which surely testified to the machine's sturdy construction as well as to Dr Thurston's. The Medical Research Council's 1920 report 'The Medical Problems of Flying' cited a test pilot in a Sopwith Triplane who, 'flying a 4.5 g banked turn, experienced "characteristic darkening of the sky which was preliminary to fainting"'.[169] The truth was that this sort of thing had long been familiar to combat pilots everywhere. 'I zoom up violently, pressure pushes me into my seat, my sight goes for a second...'[170] It was practically an everyday event in single-seat fighters.

Since the phenomenon was transient (even if it could momentarily incapacitate a pilot at a crucial juncture), no test had yet been devised that would reveal the exact moment of positive g at which a pilot's vision blacked out as the blood drained from his brain, or of negative g at which he 'redded' out. In Britain, Dr (then Colonel) Martin Flack already had his subjects blow up a column of mercury as a test of their heart and lungs' ability to deal with the lack of oxygen at high altitudes. Evidently he also saw this as a reliable indicator of the subject's susceptibility to g.

'It has been estimated that the centrifugal force of a vertical turn may amount to as much as four times that of gravity,' he observed, concluding that if the heart wasn't strong enough it could lead to 'anaemia of the brain and insensibility'. He noted that 'turning chairs' (i.e. Bárány chairs) were used in the USA to test every prospective pilot but that in Britain this had not been thought necessary because 'a heart that can support the height tests is found able to meet the demands of centrifugal force'.[171] This is odd because it suggests Dr Flack had completely mistaken the purpose of Bárány chairs. They were designed to test disorientation and vestibular illusion, not the 'g' effects of centrifugal force. To do that, the chairs would have had to tilt at the end of the arms of a centrifuge.

★

If today it seems that, overall and for much of the war, the principal combatants' air forces appeared to do surprisingly little to protect their own aircrew, it must have been partly because as the war progressed aircraft were recognised as a new weapon rather than as a mere vehicle for observers. The priority of weapons in a war is that they be deployed to inflict maximum discomfiture on the enemy, while the safety and well-being of those sent to deploy them are very much secondary considerations. As we have seen, even aircrew themselves were often reluctant to adopt protective measures.

Aircraft designers, too, could seem comfortably distanced from the consequences of their designs. To take an example at random: the radiator of the German Albatros D.III, the bane of the RFC in early 1917, was initially placed over the centre section immediately above the pilot's cockpit. If it was holed in flight the pilot could be suddenly drenched in boiling water. One would have thought this foreseeable, and in time the radiator was indeed moved off to starboard along the top wing. But then, it wasn't designers who flew combat missions. On the other hand military doctors undoubtedly became much more experienced at treating the conditions and injuries associated with flying, especially crash injuries. Even by early 1916 the *British Medical Journal* could draw up a short list of some of the commoner problems medics might need to deal with:

1. Head and neck injuries in crashes caused by violent deceleration when the pilot is strapped in.
2. Eye injuries from loose nuts or bolts blown back from the engine.
3. Frost-bite of the face at high altitudes.
4. Partial anaesthesia by petrol vapour.
5. Exhaust gases causing headache and drowsiness.
6. 'Aeresthenia': the suggested name for the inability of flying students to achieve hand-eye co-ordination.[172]

To these might have been added the permanently stiff and sore neck (to become known in the Second World War as 'weaver's neck') caused by constantly looking all around the sky for enemy aircraft. It was the chafing, rather than a wish to cut a sartorial dash, that led so many fighter pilots to wear silk scarves. Still, amid the urgent pressures of war stiff necks, frost-bite and the rest were thought of more as occupational hazards than as matters requiring remedy.

Added to which, certain types of injury recurred with certain designs of aircraft. A good deal depended on whether the crashing aircraft was of the 'tractor' type (with the engine in front) or the 'pusher' type with the engine behind and the aircrew in the boat-like nacelle that formed the aircraft's nose. Obviously this form offered the least protection. It was common for the occupants to survive the impact but immediately to be crushed by the hot engine tearing loose from its bearers behind them.

Fractures of the upper or lower jaw and nose were very frequent in crashes when the pilot's face hit the cockpit edge or the instrument board or – as so often – the butt-ends of the machine guns that protruded into the cockpit. Many of these injuries could have been avoided with a safety belt and shoulder harness combined, but as will be seen in the next chapter this would probably have been thought namby-pamby as well as carrying risks of its own. Following crash-landings, fractures of the talus (the ankle bone), very seldom seen in civilian life, became common enough in the air war to be thought of as aviators' fractures. Such injuries led to all sorts of new orthopaedic procedures at which the surgeons at Mount Vernon became increasingly skilled.

Terrible injuries could also be caused on the ground by men carelessly walking into turning propellers. Decapitation was not uncommon. Even swing-starting aero engines was hazardous, especially in the case of a backfire. Anybody brought up in the era when most motor mowers came with a starting handle and all cars still had one for emergency use was taught never to grip the handle with the thumb wrapped around it, but always with the thumb on top because otherwise a backfire could dislocate it. Similarly, the technique of how not to swing an aircraft propeller had to be learned, otherwise broken limbs or worse might easily follow.

The whole mysterious business of why so little was done to protect valuable aircrew better – and why it was the men themselves who so often resisted it – is the subject of the following chapter.

# CHAPTER 9

# PARACHUTES AND FATALISM

---

*Thursday, January 3rd [1918]*

I'm terribly depressed this evening. Ferrie has been killed. He led his patrol out this afternoon, had a scrap, came back leading the others, then as they were flying along quite normally in formation, his right wing suddenly folded back, then the other, and the wreck plunged vertically down. A bullet must have gone through a main spar during the fight.

The others went after him and steered close to him in vertical dives. They could see him struggling to get clear of his harness, then half standing up. They said it was horrible to watch him trying to decide whether to jump. He didn't, and the machine and he were smashed to nothingness.

I can't believe it. Little Ferrie, with his cheerful grin, one of the finest chaps in the squadron. God, imagine his last moments, seeing the ground rushing up at him, knowing he was a dead man, unable to move, unable to do anything but wait for it. A parachute could have saved him, there's no doubt about that. What the hell is wrong with those callous dolts at home that they won't give them to us?[173]

This, the penultimate of Lieutenant Arthur Gould Lee's daily letters home to his wife before he was posted back to England, manages to encapsulate three of the air war's defining parameters: the utter randomness of violent death, the apparent refusal of the authorities to save lives where they could, and ordinary human grief. Capt. R. L. M. Ferrie was a Canadian pilot who had been posted to 46 Squadron the previous June and had already survived seven months' combat flying. By the standards of the RFC's attrition rate he was a veteran. As a knowledgeable old hand he would be extremely valuable to any squadron, with its rapid turnover of inexperienced young pilots. It was men like Lee and Ferrie who provided enough continuity to keep morale up. A death as seemingly arbitrary and pointless as Ferrie's only further took the heart out of men already sick of the war.

So why were British aircrew not issued with parachutes until the closing weeks of the war, and then only for use with specific aircraft types that in the event were never used before the Armistice was declared? This is a question that has puzzled historians ever since. Perhaps the *locus classicus* of the debate is to be found in Appendix C of Lee's own book under the rhetorical title 'Why no parachutes?' This appendix was presumably written considerably later than the letters because his book was not published until 1968, by which time he had long retired from the RAF as an air vice-marshal and was well placed to forage through such archives as remained. He summarised the 'official' answers as follows: 1) the War Office of the day seemed to believe that if a pilot carried a parachute he might be tempted to use it too soon and abandon a valuable aircraft that he could otherwise have nursed home; and 2) it was maintained that no parachute reliable enough existed at the time.

Lee quickly disposes of both these supposed rationales. In the first instance he says his thorough searches through War Office files have failed to turn up any official document confirming the allegation; and in the second he points out that parachutes had long been in use for jumps from balloons, a common enough spectacle at pre-war fairs and air shows and generally accident-free. This was certainly true. A daring American named A. Leo Stevens had successfully jumped from a Curtiss aircraft as early as 1908 and another American had also jumped from an aircraft in 1912. Captain Edward Maitland had done the same in 1913 from 2,000 feet above a large crowd at a Hendon display. Also in 1913 a Breton named Jean Bourhis made several successful jumps from a Deperdussin monoplane piloted by a certain Lemoine, so there was no lack of precedent. Bourhis was using a parachute designed by Frédéric Bonnet that functioned well until he and Lemoine came to grief the following year when the opening parachute fouled the aircraft's rudder, tearing it off and ripping the chute. Bourhis fell and the aircraft crashed, but by a miracle both men lived. In any case, even a parachute that was less than a hundred per cent reliable still offered pilots a sporting chance of survival. Lee then goes on to recount the constant rebuffs officialdom had given a retired British engineer named Everard Calthrop who in 1913 had invented a parachute that was an improvement over the Spencer model that would be issued to observers in balloons at the beginning of the war. It should be pointed out that none of these parachutes so far mentioned was of the 'free fall' type. All required a static line that was fixed to the balloon basket or to the aircraft and pulled the canopy out of its pack as the jumper fell.

Calthrop was not a man who gave up easily. Born in 1857, he had a long and distinguished career as a railway designer and engineer. One of nature's inventors, he was a close friend of the Hon. Charles Rolls and was deeply upset by witnessing Rolls's death at the Bournemouth air meeting in 1910 referred to in Chapter 2, p.45. This led him to turn his inventive energies towards parachutes. He designed his first in 1913 and by 1915 had improved it and patented it as the 'Guardian Angel'. Like the Spencer type this was also issued to balloon observers, slung in bulky containers outside their wicker baskets. Though men were naturally reluctant to jump at all, the Guardian Angel undoubtedly saved very many of them, in some cases more than once. However, its use in aircraft was much more problematic, chiefly owing to considerations of weight. In October 1915 Mervyn O'Gorman wrote to the Director-General of Military

Aeronautics suggesting that Farnborough should test the Guardian Angel.

When O'Gorman's minuted suggestion reached Sir David Henderson's desk, that otherwise sympathetic aviator scrawled 'No, certainly not!' This official opposition evidently remained in force because in January 1917 a successful series of jumps from a B.E.2c using Calthrop's parachute took place at Orfordness but still failed to interest the Air Board. After the carnage of Bloody April that year and the subsequent chronic shortage of aircrew it might have seemed likely that a senior enough officer would be able to induce a change of attitude. At that point Hugh Trenchard himself suggested that the Guardian Angel tests should be continued over in France, but even this was turned down. General Charles Longcroft, who despite his seniority still flew missions in France, wrote that he and his pilots 'keenly desired' parachutes. He, too, was ignored. On the other hand an order by Trenchard for twenty black Calthrop parachutes for dropping spies over the lines by night was quickly approved and filled.

In short, there seemed to be an unbridgeable gulf between the fighting men in France and those in Whitehall too senior to fight, although even a flying man like Robert Smith-Barry turned out to have no use for parachutes. His Gosport training schedule was designed to instill a spirit of aggressive competence rather than passive survival. Nevertheless, according to Lee the issue of parachutes would have done wonders for the morale of pilots and observers over in France, especially in Bloody April, and his fellow aviators had made it clear they wanted them. The trouble was that their views seldom got beyond squadron level, possibly because commanding officers were nervous of acquiring a reputation for weakness or for not showing enough 'offensive spirit' (in the current Army cant). That year Calthrop's company began offering his parachute for sale in flying magazines. Even in 1917 it was perfectly normal for officers to buy their own supplementary kit, including pistols, from London retailers such as the Army & Navy Stores and Gamages, and it can be assumed that a good few pilots in France would have had fantasies about ordering a Guardian Angel from the stores' catalogues even though the prevailing squadron ethos made it clear they would never be able to use one.

Over in Germany, however, attitudes were finally shifting. On 1st April 1918 – coincidentally the very day the RFC became the RAF – a pilot from Jasta 56 hit the headlines for having parachuted safely to earth after baling out of his burning Albatros D.Va. By that summer group photographs of German pilots show many of them wearing the new Heinecke parachute harness. Then came the news that the top surviving German ace, Ernst Udet, had also saved his life by parachuting from his stricken aircraft and angry articles began appearing in the British press asking why, if the German air force were now being issued with parachutes, British pilots were not? In June 1918 the new RAF formed a Parachute Committee and as a result ordered 500 Guardian Angels from Calthrop's firm and 500 of a neater type of parachute that the pilot could wear called the Mears, but they came too late to be useful. After the war, summing up his years of campaigning, Calthrop wearily gave what he felt was the reason for the British authorities' foot-dragging: 'No one in high quarters had any time to devote to investigating the merits of an appliance whose purpose was so ridiculously irrelevant to war as the saving of life in the air.'[174] It was an understandably bitter diagnosis but it probably contained a degree of truth and makes a bizarre kind of sense when taken in conjunction with the ready fulfilment of Trenchard's order for the black parachutes. Dropping spies was a properly warlike activity; preventing deaths was not.

Overall, Lee's argument appears unassailable. Yet there are further points to consider, the first being that the British were by no means unique in their resistance to parachutes. It was surely not accidental that the Germans did not issue them until late in the war, while neither the French and Italian air forces nor the

American command did until afterwards. One underlying reason was that until at least 1916 when the design of aircraft and engines had progressed, the added weight of a parachute would have significantly affected an aircraft's performance. While increasing fuel consumption it would also have reduced the machine's potential ceiling and rate of climb, as well as making it that much more sluggish in combat.

> The basic struggle in aeroplane design was to secure maximum rate of climb and ceiling against the limitation of engine power, and the only solution was light wing loading. Every pound saved was vital. A parachute, with container and static line, weighed about 15% of the entire disposable load of armament, pilot, fuel and oil carried by the [Sopwith] Pup. Most pilots judged that a preferable life-saver was in expending that weight on another gun and more ammunition ... for with a single gun they had only 50 seconds' total firing before their ammunition was finished.[175]

It was all very well for Lee to write in another letter, 'Every pilot would sacrifice a little performance to have a chance of escape from break-ups and flamers,'[176] but it is clear that he was *not* speaking for every pilot. Squadron-Commander J. R. Boothby of the RNAS wrote (in a seemingly perverse spirit of self-sacrifice), 'We don't want to carry additional weight merely to save our lives.'[177] His was the authentic voice of a fighter pilot who knew life could depend on the tiniest margin of his aircraft's performance.

Apart from this there was the question of where to stow the parachute and how best to deploy it. One has only to look at a typical single-seater cockpit of the period to realise that there simply wasn't room for anything besides the pilot: a tiny wood-and-fabric-framed compartment with a flimsy seat. Once forward-firing guns became the norm, their padded ends protruded into the cockpit over the front coaming and still further restricted available space. It is also clear from contemporary photographs that aircrew of the period were generally skinny by today's standards. (In fact an early British book on flying had already noted the obvious: 'To be an aviator it is best to be small, compact, and wiry...'[178]) Writing of one of his fellow pilots Lee observed that he was a big man 'and has to practically use a shoehorn to work himself into the [Pup's] narrow cockpit'. Photographs show the French ace and national hero Georges Guynemer to have been, in Keats's phrase, 'spectre-thin', his putteed legs mere sticks. Indeed, it is very doubtful whether the average pilot today could fit into a Sopwith Pup or a SPAD S.VII, let alone when wearing a Sidcot suit. There was simply no extra room for a bulky parachute without altering the entire design of the cockpit.

Nevertheless, once aero engines had become powerful enough for the small additional weight to be ignored, a static line parachute could in theory have been fitted into or on top of the fuselage immediately behind the pilot, and in the event this was exactly what was done in 1918 with Calthrop's Guardian Angel (for example in the S.E.5a). Such comparatively minor structural alterations were obviously possible; it just needed the will. Space for the less bulky Mears type which the pilot wore on his back was created behind the pilot in the S.E.5a and the D.H.9 by removing his backrest and installing a light bulkhead a little further back, against which he could lean with the parachute forming an uncomfortable sort of cushion. In fact, in the early months of 1918 experiments were successfully carried out in equipping the S.E.5a, the Sopwith Snipe and Dolphin, the Bristol Fighter, the D.H.4, D.H.9 and D.H.9a with Calthrop parachutes, but all – thanks to official dilatoriness – too late to save any lives. One of the problems cited by opponents of parachutes was that both the Mears and the Guardian Angel were static types, which meant they had to be attached by a lengthy webbing strap to an anchor point on the aircraft. As Bourhis and Lemoine's experience in 1914 had shown, the opening parachute could snag on part of the aircraft as a man jumped. When jumping from a biplane with its fixed undercarriage and cat's cradle of wires and spars while still connected to it by a strap, there was always a chance that the pilot might become entangled and unable to free himself from the falling aircraft. In due course the Bristol Fighter's tailskid also proved notoriously capable of snagging parachutes. This was a valid point, and accidents of this sort did occur. Yet once again this objection could have been trumped by the simple fact that just because success might not be guaranteed every time it was no reason for not giving a valuable airman a fighting chance to save his life.

As regards Lee's assertion that he was unable to find any War Office document confirming the allegation that parachutes were to be officially discouraged, it is true that no such policy statement has yet come to light and quite possibly does not exist, if it ever did. What is usually quoted today is a sentence from a report that reads: 'It is the opinion of the [Air] Board that the presence of such an apparatus might impair the fighting spirit of pilots and cause them to abandon machines which might otherwise be capable of returning to base for repair.'[179]

This may well have represented the semi-official view and seems to have been endorsed in other air forces, notably by the French and the Americans. In the French Army in the early part of the war, when the old generals were still thinking snobbishly in terms of gentlemen cavalry, it is alleged they believed 'pilots of [common] origin would be tempted to abandon their aeroplane too easily if they could do so by parachute'.[180] (Ah, those craven lower orders!) And the commander of the American 1st Pursuit Group, Harold Hartney, claimed later that the subject of parachutes had several times been brought up and certain very senior officers had said that 'pilots could quite possibly lose their nerve in a hot fight and might perhaps jump prematurely, and there was to be no more discussion of the matter'.[181] It is hard to know whether these opinions were reached independently or were simply reflections of attitudes commonly held among the top brass of all sides. At any rate the French-American Raoul Lufbery died when he jumped out of his blazing machine at 2,500 feet and a parachute might well have saved this celebrated ace.

Hartney was a Canadian by birth who initially fought for the RFC in France before being sent back to Toronto in late 1917, promoted to major and given command of the (US) 27th Aero Squadron. He later became a US citizen. In his book he makes another claim that is even more revealing: that some pilots thought the idea of parachutes 'sissy'. Arthur Gould Lee does not mention this in his letters, simply leaving the clear impression that pilots were unanimous in wanting parachutes. It may be significant that apart from his quite extraordinary luck in surviving months of combat with scarcely even modest injury, Lee was unusual in that for most of the time he was the only married pilot in 46 Squadron, which he admits made him feel older (at twenty-two!) and more 'responsible' somehow, even if he knew he wasn't. As already noted he habitually wrote home to his wife each day, often more than once, so he must have been keenly aware of having another life and affections elsewhere, just as Billy Bishop was.

Yet this was by no means true for every airman. In books and memoirs of the period (many of them posthumous) there are frequent references to battle-weary young men who had given up all hope of surviving the war. As comparative veterans in their squadron they had seen too many others take off on a sortie and fail to return; had watched too many former friends fall across the sky trailing flame; had had too many undeserved escapes of their own to assign either sense or importance to their continued survival. There were many such airmen in all the combatant air forces, not least those Britons who had lived through the RFC's darkest days in spring 1917. Such combat veterans tended to be leached-out men with nervous tics, strange habits, fearful nightmares often audible even from the sheds, superstitions and lucky mascots without which they refused point-blank to leave the ground even under threat of court-martial. They had become a race apart, and knew it. They were often morose monomaniacs, thinking of little else but the air war. Fatalists, they were obsessed with identifying and further developing that elusive edge they apparently possessed that had enabled them to survive when so many others had not. They would go on until their luck ran out or a 'Blighty' wound cursed them with forcible repatriation. In the worst case their six-month tour would be ended by rotation to 'H.E.' or Home Establishment, a posting many of them dreaded as a kind of official emasculation. These were men who might take a revolver up with them, not so much for self-defence if they were forced down over enemy lines but to shoot themselves if faced by that bleak choice of jumping out of their blazing aircraft or staying in it to be roasted alive before being smashed to pulp.

Even if such macho and despairing types were in a minority in any squadron their outlook was contagious in that their ethos, together with the CO's bullishness about the squadron's reputation, would set the general tone. Everyone joined in with the nihilistic mess songs, just as everyone recognised that the squadron's honour was sacred. It now becomes a little easier to see why aircrew might have agreed that parachutes were 'sissy'. (*Who dreads to the dust returning? Who shrinks from the sable shore?*)

It is certainly not hard to imagine their reaction had a member of their squadron actually ordered his Guardian Angel from a London shop. It would have been quite impossible to live down, and he could never have worn it even had it been allowed. Who would have wanted to become the mocked outsider, the only person to do a show wearing a parachute? Had he any *idea* what other squadrons would say? 'Windy' would be the least hurtful nickname he could hope to acquire. He would be finished in that squadron, and his reputation would precede him wherever he went. For in the background would always be the obscure and unvoiced thought: if your parachute did actually save you it would somehow imply that your life was of more value than those others it might also have saved, thereby constituting a betrayal of the dead. (*Hurrah for the next man that dies!*)

★

Such are some of the difficulties with Lee's simplistic polarity: on the one hand airmen wanting parachutes and on the other the seemingly callous intransigence of the top brass. This is more or less how the argument has been positioned ever since. Yet the truth was certainly more complicated and shadowy than that, as can be seen from reactions to several other safety measures for airmen that were gradually introduced. A British doctor specialising in air accidents wrote in 1918: 'There is a natural disposition on the part of most pilots to feel they want to be free and unimpeded whilst flying. In the old days many used to scoff at goggles, safety helmets or belts; but at present most aviators realise the value of these things...'[182] This makes it clear that even by the end of the war not every pilot was wearing goggles, a helmet or even a belt. In fact there was considerable resistance to all three, just as there was to carrying oxygen. The young RFC ace Albert Ball VC reportedly never wore goggles or helmet. He used to claim that 'he liked to feel the wind in his hair.'[183]

One objection to goggles was that sometimes a speck of oil on a lens could be mistaken for an enemy aircraft, and many pilots flying rotary-engined machines refused to wear them because they so easily fogged up with the oil fumes being blown back. But in any case there was an instinctive conviction, at a time when visual acuity was vital, that eyesight was at its best when not mediated by glass. And this when it could be daily shown that goggles fitted with 'Triplex' shatterproof lenses were saving many an airman's eyesight. They were protection not only against fragments of shrapnel from 'archie', something blown back from the engine or a sudden gush of alcohol or mercury from an instrument hit by a bullet, but against the endemic conjunctivitis caused by staring into the slipstream.

As for safety helmets, they were principally worn by trainees. Once he had his 'wings' no airman worth his salt wanted to wear an absurd padded hat and go on looking like a 'Hun' at flying school. Aircrew preferred the normal leather flying helmet with ear flaps. Never mind that it offered no real protection other than to stop the ears freezing: it had mysteriously become traditional (and was to last essentially unchanged, but for the addition of space for earphones, right through the Second World War). The matter of safety belts, on the other hand, was hotly debated, and with rather better reasons. They were clearly vital in violent dogfight manoeuvres when an aircraft might spend time upside down. But they were were no less desirable for flying in ordinary bad weather, as the German Oberleutnant Haupt-Heydemarck discovered when flying in the Balkans in 1917:

> I was supposed to be testing a two-seater which had had a new engine installed, so I took the mechanic up with me. The machine ran into a downward gust and pitched violently nose-down. I just managed to get her under control again but I'd had enough and landed as quickly as I could. While I was taxying I called out to the chap behind me: 'Man alive, we were damn lucky!' But as I got no answer I looked round and to my astonishment the observer's seat was empty. The poor fellow had been thrown out from about a thousand metres up![184]

At other times seatbelts could be a liability. Landing accidents in biplanes on rough or improvised airfields were common. No single-engined aircraft of the day had brakes, and in a short field the only way of stopping quickly was to do a 'three-pointer'. This was hard to get right in a crosswind, especially if the aircraft was damaged, and virtually every pilot had at one time or another ended up with the machine pitched up on its nose or even upside down, leaving him dazed and hanging by the seatbelt. Since turning turtle often sent petrol cascading over the hot engine and a single spark from a dying magneto could set the whole thing ablaze, some pilots preferred to take their chances by not wearing a belt or by opening it before impact and hoping to be thrown clear. Many a mess echoed to impassioned arguments about the pros and cons of seatbelts, with both sides ready and able to cherry-pick cases to prove their point.

Once again, it was not a simple open and shut matter. Indeed, precisely the same arguments could be heard in any British pub in the 1970s about the impending seatbelt legislation for car drivers and front passengers. They could be heard in 1983 when the law was finally passed and still can be from those constitutionally opposed to it. As for crash helmets, ever since the neurosurgeon Hugh Cairns had operated on T. E. Lawrence (of Arabia) after Lawrence came off his Brough Superior motorcycle at speed in 1935, sustaining a fatal head injury, Cairns campaigned for all dispatch riders to wear crash helmets. This measure saved countless lives during the Second World War and afterwards. Yet when wearing a crash helmet finally became compulsory for all UK civilian motorcyclists in 1973 there was no lack of bikers protesting that it was sissy to wear them. What was worse, they claimed, crash helmets removed much of the open-air pleasure of riding a motorbike and, like seatbelts, could even *cause* death in certain circumstances.

So maybe there was nothing very strange about combat-toughened young airmen during the First World War preferring to rely on their own skill and luck rather than on protective devices that might have hampered them. Above all, there was always that vital component to take into account: a pure revelling in unimpeded *flying*. This was the sheer exhilaration of youths who had so recently been liberated by aircraft not only from life in the trenches but from a world that was everywhere still largely horse-drawn and pedestrian. Lee himself became lyrical about 'contour-chasing' in his Sopwith Pup in a moment of boyish exuberance when issues of safety were cast to the wind:

> I went down to the area towards Bailleul where it's pretty level and raced across the countryside ten feet up, lifting over trees and cottages and camps, then surging on at full throttle. Because I'd set out only to do a test I wasn't wearing my helmet or goggles nor, of course, flying gear, and it was fine to feel the rush of air past my temples and my hair waving madly in the slipstream swirling around the tiny windscreen. And, of course, without my helmet the noise of the engine was terrific. This is the most marvellous thrill you can get out of flying, scudding along close to the ground, the feeling of speed, and especially in so smooth and docile a machine as a Pup. Everything is spinning by at ninety miles an hour. The plane's shadow skims across the fields just below. You come to a road without trees or telegraph poles and you go down until your wheels almost touch. This flying at two feet is really intoxicating, seeing people dive for the ditch, troops scattering, lorries lurching across the road like drunks. Turning west towards Hazebrouck I dived on a couple of staff cars and one of them, an open tourer with red-tabbed officers, nearly went up a tree and finished in the ditch. I certainly put the gust up *that* lot. All good, clean fun, and it makes these staff wallahs realise there are dangers even in their kind of war.[185]

Such intense youthful pleasures aside, serious aviators had tended from the first to be on the conservative side. The dangers of war only intensified this, pardonably leading them to mistrust innovation and change or any deviation from the tried and familiar. This point was well made by Biggles himself in full mess-bore mode – or rather, by W. E. Johns writing from his own memory of 55 Squadron attitudes some fourteen years earlier:

> 'That's the trouble with this damn war; people are never satis-fied. Let us stick to Camels and S.E.s and the Boche can have their D.VIIs – damn all this chopping and changing about. I've heard a rumour about a new kite called a Salamander that carries a sheet of armour plate.* Why? I'll tell you. Some brass-hat's got hit in the pants and that's the result. What with sheet iron, oxygen to blow your guts out and electrically heated clothing to set fire to your kidneys, this war is going to bits.'[186]

And yet by August 1918 all German pilots had access not only to parachutes and oxygen equipment but to electrically heated flying suits as well (not to mention the armoured Junkers J.I), and German aviators can't have been utterly different from their British counterparts. However, they were the beneficiaries of an air force high command with much smaller manpower reserves to draw on and anxious to conserve its greatest asset: its aircrew. Such pragmatism presumably outweighed diehard British con-servatism and the prodigality of being able to rely on a vast Empire to supply unlimited numbers of airmen. At any rate it must surely have been someone like Biggles in the Air Ministry in 1947 who decided that Britain's proposed new jet V-bombers should be designed with ejector seats for the two pilots but none for the three-man crew in the compartment behind, who would merely have parachutes. And in due course, very much in the spirit of 1917, there was no lack of crewmembers to be heard saying that they never missed having bang seats; that on the con-trary, they were so engrossed in their various electronic tasks the possibility of an emergency never crossed their minds and anyway they were happy to settle for parachutes.

* Sopwith Salamander. *See* Chapter 4, p.106.

Even so, none of this is to deny Arthur Gould Lee's implied point that the powers-that-be could have issued parachutes to RFC aircrew well over a year earlier had they really wanted to. It is here that we come up against that imponderable mixture of official indifference and bureaucratic languor, leaving us unable to decide where the ultimate responsibility lies. It is a perennial question. In the Second World War the eminent British-born Princeton mathematician Freeman Dyson was assigned to the RAF's Operational Research Section where he made a disturbing discovery. About half the crews of American bombers shot down in daylight raids were escaping from their aircraft to become PoWs. From the older British night bombers, the Halifax and the Stirling, about 25 per cent escaped. From the RAF's newest bomber, the Lancaster, a mere 15 per cent of the crews survived. Dyson established that this was because its escape hatch was not only badly sited but too small for men wearing parachutes to squeeze through easily. An informant on a bomber squadron told him that the true fraction of survivors among shot-down crews was kept secret from the airmen even more strictly than were the true odds against their completing an operational tour. 'If the boys had found out how small was the fraction who succeeded in baling out after being hit, some of them might have been tempted to jump too soon.'[187] This was an exact reprise of the WWI 'official' argument against parachutes.

There ensued a *two-year* attempt to get Bomber Command first to acknowledge the problem and then to notify Avro to modify the Lancaster's escape hatch. Avro took months simply to design a larger hatch and build a prototype, and the war ended before it could be installed. It had clearly never been considered a priority. The 'entrenched inertia of the military establishment' had been matched by that of the aircraft's manufacturers. Dyson hazards that the inadequacy of the Lancaster's hatch 'probably cost the lives of several thousand boys'. The military's instinct, then as earlier, was that the priority in war is killing the enemy and not saving the lives of one's own combatants.

★

In finally addressing the question of why no parachutes were issued to British aircrew in the first air war, perhaps the most important thing of all is to remember that it is simply no longer possible to understand exactly how people thought a century ago. On 11th November 1914, towards the end of the First Battle of Ypres, the Prussian Guard launched a concerted attack on the British 1st Guards Brigade. In the ensuing Battle of Nonnebosschen the Germans were defeated, but at terrible cost to both sides. Out of eighty British officers and 4,500 men who went into battle, five officers and 478 other ranks were left standing at the end. Afterwards, when the C-in-C asked a surviving brigadier how his men had done, he reportedly replied: 'We had an uncommonly good shoot,'[188] as though he had spent a pleasant day on a grouse moor.

This is not a code we can hope to crack merely by invoking stiff upper lips or British understatement. We are as much at a loss to grasp it fully as the brigadier would have been to understand our present conventions of health and safety, let alone modern free-for-all sexual mores. As the opening of L. P. Hartley's novel *The Go-Between* has it: 'The past is a foreign country: they do things differently there.' This crux has to be appreciated when trying to make any sense of the First World War and is too often left out of the equation. Apparent inconsistencies of attitude about such things as parachutes and seatbelts now seem baffling, contradictory or simply downright perverse but were obviously quite differently weighted at the time. Indeed, no sooner had an agreement been signed in 1919 for the first commercial flights to start between London and Paris than Frederick Handley Page 'civilianised' one of his big O/400 bombers as a passenger aircraft by turning it into a simulacrum of a suburban parlour. There were curtains for the windows, flowers in vases on the window sills and a drawing-room clock up on a bracket near the ceiling. For the fourteen passengers there were two rows of cane chairs with floral cushions, but not a seatbelt anywhere. Presumably to be hurled about the cabin in an 'air pocket' was all part of the thrill of flying, and if anyone were hurt it wouldn't occur to them to sue.

To remind us of how hard it is for people to grasp the attitudes of even two or three decades ago, let alone a century, in 2012 Andrew O'Hagan interviewed the veteran broadcaster Dame Joan Bakewell about the BBC's former internal culture that underwrote the sexual abuses of celebrities like the late Jimmy Savile. She wisely observed: 'You can't recreate the mood of an era. You just can't get into the culture of what it was like, transfer our sensibilities backwards from today. It would be like asking Victorian factory owners to explain why they sent children up chimneys... What we now find unacceptable was just accepted then by many people.'[189] The same will of course be true in a hundred years' time, when people look back at this era, at a loss to understand our antediluvian codes of taboo and licence.

It should be added that certain prevailing attitudes in 1914–18 were determined by urgent priority. In Britain the overwhelming preoccupation of the government, the War Office and the public generally was with the way the land war was going, and its unprecedented slaughter of hundreds of thousands of men for no apparent gain or purpose. By comparison the air war's casualty figures were insignificant, and therefore irrelevant. What gave the air forces everywhere a claim to public attention beyond that of their military uses was the still-novel status of flying and of aircraft in general. A mysterious aura of futurism and romance undoubtedly attached to men who flew. The idea of pilots as knights of the air was very appealing. But just as they fought as individuals, so did they die. Entire streets of industrial towns were not left grieving by an airman's death as they often were by a wholesale massacre of infantry. In Britain the RFC, with its vociferous advocates in the House of Commons and the press, undoubtedly attracted an amount of public attention quite out

of proportion to the size of its fighting force. In the khaki fast-
ness of the War Office, however, the generals made bleak
logistical calculations. In their brisk daily triage the lives of those
few hundred airmen who might have been saved by parachutes
had no weight.

## CHAPTER 10

# HOME DEFENCE

———

Sundry references have already been made to Hugh Trenchard's strategy of using his air forces aggressively, with the implication that compared to the RFC flying daily over the German lines, the Luftstreitkräfte flew much more rarely over the British lines in France. However, it would be a big mistake to conclude from this that the German Air Force was reluctant to take its own fight to the enemy (and remembering that for much of the war it was fighting on several fronts simultaneously). In fact, German air strategy was every bit as forward-looking as Trenchard's and in many respects a good deal more so because it formed part of the concept of *total war*. The German Army had been reared on *Vom Kriege* (*On War*), the classic treatise by the Prussian military theorist Carl von Clausewitz. This makes clear that it is futile going to war other than with an absolute determination to win. Anything else is an irresponsible sacrifice of lives and *matériel*. A real war – as distinct from a campaign or a local skirmish – presupposes the involvement of the combatants' entire nations, civilians as well as military, for reasons of psychological as well as of material back-up. In this view an army in the field needs robust supply chains and hence the full support of the electorate and politicians back home.

It was in this spirit that from the turn of the century Germany had built up a highly competent U-boat fleet that was to prove most effective in blockading the merchant shipping that brought Britain its vital supplies, resulting in periodic shortages of raw materials and food throughout the war. It was fortunate that in

1901 the Royal Navy had founded a submarine service of its own that was to have a far-sighted champion in Admiral John Fisher, the First Sea Lord, at a time when it really needed one. In general, the Admiralty's attitude towards this new weapon was analogous to that of the British Army's towards aircraft a decade later. As the then-Third Sea Lord, Rear-Admiral Arthur Wilson VC, memorably put it, 'The submarine is an underhand form of warfare, unfair, and a damned un-English weapon.' It is not known what he thought a truly 'English' weapon might be: possibly a cricket bat. However, it is clear that the 'Christian gentleman' ideal of Dr Thomas Arnold's public school system was not an adequate weapon for tackling bounders who had been brought up on Clausewitz. Luckily, despite the attitudes of many gold-braided old sea dogs who had served their apprenticeships in the days of sail, the Admiralty's younger and more progressive element realised the new technology of submarines was not going to disappear merely because it was un-English. Consequently the Royal Navy's submarines were steadily developed in the shadow of its grander and far more visible fleet of destroyers and dreadnoughts – symbols of Britain's global maritime hegemony. The Royal Navy's submariners were to cover themselves in glory throughout the First World War, especially while maintaining their own economic blockade of Germany; but so were the German submariners as they steadily disrupted British shipping.

Once the war had started the clash of the Clausewitzian idea of total war versus some very idiosyncratic British ideas of morality could be seen in action. Yet from the first the German General Staff's position had never been a secret. In 1902 it had published a handbook for its officers, *Kriegsbrauche im Landkriege* (*The Waging of Land War*) in which it stated 'The conduct of war allows any belligerent state to employ any means to bring about the war aim,' and went on to make it clear that this might quite properly entail attacking civilian targets. On 16th December 1914 six German warships suddenly appeared off the coast of northeast England and shelled Scarborough and Hartlepool. They killed 147 outright, with many badly injured, besides causing much damage. Such an attack without warning on mainly civilian targets produced general outrage in Britain as well as anger directed at the Royal Navy's failure to prevent it. British citizens struggled to accept that total war meant exactly that. They might indeed have found this abhorrent; yet before long it became anybody's guess who was holding the moral high ground.

> In 1915 a tactic known as The Tethered Goat was introduced, whereby a British submarine would remain submerged beneath a trawler fleet, connected to one of the vessels by a covert telephone link. Trawlers were a favoured target of U-boats, if only as a means of obtaining fresh food whilst on patrol, and they would surface rather than waste a precious torpedo on such insignificant vessels and instead sink them with explosives or their deck guns. Once an enemy was spotted, the British submarine was informed and it would attempt to sink the surfaced U-boat. This worked on several occasions, but was obviously not a long-term strategy since the Germans soon got wise to this arguably underhand and morally dubious tactic.[190]

Even as the Royal Navy were staking out their tethered goats they were also deploying the first of the 'Q' ships: vessels disguised to look like innocent merchantmen that tempted a German submarine to surface in order to investigate its cargo and see if it was worth stealing. As soon as the U-boat appeared, hinged panels would drop open in the 'Q' ship's side to reveal heavy guns that opened fire on the submarine. The Royal Navy, like the Kaiserliche Marine, understood from the first that there were to be no holds barred in their sea war. The British were much too aware of their islands' dependency on overseas supplies to give any quarter. This 'Q' ship ruse was soon used by both sides, as it would be again in the Second World War.

Initially, at least, the first air war did not offer quite the same opportunities for ruse and trickery, and tactics were more open. Aerial bombing was one such measure. A fortnight after the shelling of the northeast ports, German aircraft dropped the first small bombs on British soil, hitting Dover and Sheerness, although with little damage. Three weeks later came the first raid by an airship that bombed Great Yarmouth and King's Lynn on 19th January 1915. Predictably, this caused further outrage in a Britain taken by surprise and there came the first squalls in what was to develop into a four-year deluge of press rhetoric about German 'frightfulness' invoking the bucolic peace of British towns and villages and, of course, the sanctity of unarmed civilians and especially of women and children. This was promptly matched in the German press by accusations of British '*Schrecklichkeit*'. Yet you didn't need to be Clausewitz to know that in war people have always used whatever weapon confers superiority. Only ever in duels of honour in Hyde Park or Heidelberg were two combatants solemnly handed identical weapons with which to fight while their seconds monitored fair play. Once Giulio Gavotti had dropped his little bombs over Libya in 1911 it was inevitable that sooner or later the same technique would be used again. Given that at the outbreak of war Germany was the unchallenged world leader in airship technology, it was obvious the Zeppelin would become a weapon in wartime if only because in 1915 no German aircraft yet had the range to fly as far as London with a bomb load and return to Belgium. The rhetoric of 'frightfulness' was something of a smokescreen to cover the British public's impotent fury that as yet there seemed to be no reliable means of countering the Zeppelin raids. There was also fear that H. G. Wells's dire predictions in his 1898 proto-SF novel *The War of the Worlds* might actually be coming true. There was something primordial in the dread of attack from the sky.

In fact, as early as February 1913 there had been reports of strange airships seen over Britain's east coast and on the 28th the *Whitby Gazette* ran a headline that read:

## WANTED: AN AIR MINISTER
## ENGLAND AT GERMANY'S MERCY

This laid out the respective positions of both future combatants eighteen months before the war began. Nobody could reasonably claim Britain hadn't been warned. The idea of the country being at anybody's mercy was shocking enough to emphasise how unprepared and inadequate its defences actually were: a common theme in public debate ever since Erskine Childers's enormously popular 'invasion' thriller *The Riddle of the Sands* was published in 1903. Winston Churchill later claimed that this single novel had led directly to the Admiralty's building three major naval bases in north-eastern Britain (Scapa Flow, Invergordon and Rosyth). But with the coming of airships and aircraft the Grand Fleet was suddenly no longer enough to protect the British Isles, just as the journalist Harold Wyatt had predicted when Blériot first flew the Channel in 1909. Winston Churchill, ever the politician, had tried to allay fears in a speech on 17th March 1914 in which he predicted that 'Any hostile aircraft, airships or aeroplanes which reached our coast during the coming year would be promptly attacked in superior force by a swarm of very formidable hornets.'[191] At the very least this absurd piece of bombast implied ignorance: Zeppelins could not only fly far higher than any aircraft Britain had in 1914, they could also carry out raids at night.

However, it was one thing for the German military to embrace the idea of total war and quite another for 'Kaiser Bill' (Wilhelm II) to agree to all that this implied. As Queen Victoria's eldest grandson he realised that bombing London would not only escalate hostilities to a new, unheard-of level, it would also risk killing his own cousins in Buckingham Palace. To pacify his generals he reluctantly agreed to bombing raids outside London. That first Zeppelin raid on King's Lynn and Great Yarmouth 'was greeted with wild acclaim in Germany, where "*Gott strafe England*" was already a national rallying cry, daubed on walls, fences and lamp-posts and recited by German schoolchildren in their daily morning assemblies'.[192] As always, once the principle of bombing had been established it became easy to continue, and Zeppelin raids were soon extended to London and continued for the next two years until airships at last became too vulnerable to fighter aircraft and the defences Britain could belatedly muster. They were superseded by big twin-engined Gotha bombers, whose first raid took place in May 1917.

The psychological effect on Britons of being bombed in their own country, and especially in their capital city, was immense. They were quite used to the idea of sending troops and warships overseas to outposts of the Empire in order to bring uppity natives into line; they were absolutely unprepared for this sort of treatment to be meted out to themselves on home ground. Worse still, for a long time they were powerless to stop it. In the first place every available RFC aircraft and anti-aircraft gun was needed in France; and in the second combat flying was in its adolescence at best while *night* combat flying was not even in its infancy. This sense of national impotence was probably an important contributory factor to the VC awarded to Flight-Sublieutenant Reginald Warneford, a young RNAS pilot stationed in Belgium. On 7th June 1915, flying his Morane-Saulnier Type L monoplane, he chased Zeppelin LZ.37 over Ostend and dropped bombs on it until it blew up. The explosion flipped his own aircraft upside down and stopped the engine. Warneford managed to land in German-held territory, work feverishly on the engine, fix a fuel leak with his cigarette holder, restart and take off again before he could be captured. Almost immediately King George V awarded him the Victoria Cross and he was acclaimed in Britain as a national hero. A mere ten days later Warneford was killed while flying an American journalist over Versailles in a new Farman F.27, a pusher biplane, apparently because of mid-air structural failure. Both men were thrown out and fell to their deaths.

Meanwhile the Zeppelins attacking Britain came at night – huge, stealthy and terrifying. 1916 saw the introduction of the 'R' types that were over 200 yards long. Silent newsreels could not record the menacing drone of their six immense Maybach engines, nor how they might fall quiet as they drifted almost unopposed above London as though picking out something choice at which to take careful aim. By now there were searchlights and anti-aircraft guns that put up a fine show of activity, although mostly with few results. The spectators milled excitedly in the streets, staring upwards. The airships' ability to hit a specific target with their bombs was practically nil, but in a way this made it worse for those below as it turned the raids into a kind of sinister lottery by high explosive. Silver blades slashed the dark sky, criss-crossing feverishly as though in a hectic fencing match. None drew blood, however; and generally the sparkling blooms of shells sent up by the gunners in Hyde Park, for all the visible effect they had, might have been a benign firework display. The blow to British self-esteem is not recorded on film, but it soon had immense political impact.

To be sure, the numbers of casualties caused by the German raids on London and elsewhere in the First World War were not remotely comparable with those in the Second. The entire year's campaign by German bombers between May 1917 and May 1918 killed 836 Britons up and down the country and injured 1,965: figures that for much of the war would have represented light casualties for a single day on the Western Front. (In World War II the Luftwaffe's raids on Coventry alone were to kill 1,236.) But the panic the bombing inspired was quite out of proportion to the number and size of the bombs dropped and the damage they caused. A spirit of 'Britain Can Take It' or 'Keep Calm and Carry On' was often notably absent. Small wonder, since not only were the British public completely unprepared but they could all too plainly see that 'the authorities' were as well. For a long time there were no organised and co-ordinated civil defence measures: no air raid warning sirens, no official bomb shelters. Policemen wearing sandwich boards with messages in red capitals reading POLICE NOTICE: TAKE COVER or, alternatively, ALL CLEAR would pedal through East End streets on their regulation bicycles, ringing their bells.

The difficulties involved in setting up adequate defences against aerial bombing raids in 1915 should not be underestimated. Even giving the public an early enough warning was problematic. Telephones were still comparatively rare and every call had to be hand-connected by operators pushing plugs into switchboards at the few exchanges. The most reliable form of quick communication was probably by telegraph. (There were of course no household radio sets.) Observers stationed on the North Foreland or the Essex coast might – if they were extremely lucky – succeed in raising someone at a local airfield or in London by telephone or by 'sending a wire' if they heard what they thought were a Zeppelin's engines overhead; but what then? In those days aircraft climbed with painful slowness. Zeppelins could easily out-climb any of them and go as high as 15,000 feet, way beyond any defender's capability. It might take a single-seater scout half an hour to reach a mere 8,000 feet even before it began looking for the intruder. True, the airships had a top speed of only about 60 mph; but within two years the big Gotha bombers that succeeded them could reach 21,000 feet and a speed of 87 mph, a difficult challenge for any interceptor even in 1917, especially at night and without oxygen.

Meanwhile the British government, worried as they already were by the war's dismally slow progress in France, became increasingly concerned about unrest at home. The anger caused by food shortages and bad working conditions, especially in the armaments factories, was increased by the panic induced by air raids. Particularly in London's East End, where the docks were an obvious target and there were no proper air raid shelters, this led to spectacular public funeral parades for the victims and also to strikes and rioting in the face of which the police were sometimes helpless. In fact, air raid casualties were often split along class lines since to the west and south of Holborn, and particularly in the West End, the numerous underground stations at least afforded a network of deep shelters. This inequity was exploited by union and strike leaders to reinforce their message that the whole conflict was a capitalist war, deliberately waged to enrich international bankers and arms manufacturers: one in which the British working class were mere cannon fodder in France and bomb fodder at home. The largely right-wing press countered with denunciations of official incompetence over civil defence and appeals to Britons' innate bulldog patriotism. Propagandists like Horatio Bottomley, the crooked proprietor of the jingoistic newspaper *John Bull*, foamed with virulence against the Germans. Similarly, the otherwise socialist journalist Robert Blatchford fulminated at book length about the enemy's 'Cult of Frightfulness':

> The plea that the German atrocities in this war were perpetrated against orders, were against the wishes of the Kaiser, the General Staff and the German people, and that they have been magnified by the Allies, is a 'terminological inexactitude'. For fifty years the gospel of Frightfulness has been preached in Germany; and the Germans, prone to violence, prone to hatred, rude in their language, coarse in their manners, have been apt pupils. So far from its being alien to the feeling of Germany or the tradition of the German Army, Frightfulness is part of the German code of war and is looked upon by soldiers and civilians alike as a useful and proper part of tactics and – business.[193]

Blatchford naturally had his counterparts in Germany. One of the *Hamburger Nachrichten*'s journalists wrote that 'England's shamelessness is not only abominable; it drives the blood to our heads and makes us desire and demand a hard punishment for this frivolous and huckstering people. Therefore we cannot rain bombs enough on England, nor can enough of her ships be destroyed.'[194] Protecting those ships was a priority for both the Royal Navy and its air service.

★

Throughout the war the RNAS (rather than the RFC) was charged with the air defence of Britain's coasts and in particular the Channel and the North Sea. It entered the war with six airships and 93 aircraft. Many of these aircraft were seaplanes deployed on constant patrol for German U-boats; but as we know, RNAS squadrons were also land-based in France and Belgium where they shared duties with the RFC. 'Seaplanes' in this context generally meant floatplanes: aircraft that take off and land on water using fixed floats or pontoons rather than flying boats whose fuselage is also a hull for landing directly on the water. Since most early aircraft were single-engined they were best suited to become floatplanes because they rode high enough on the water on their pontoons for the propeller and engine to be clear of spray (which was not always true of flying boats floating on their hulls). On the other hand the floats added weight and aerodynamic drag that still further reduced their already limited agility in the air. All aircraft design represents compromise, and the Kaiserliche Marine made it still harder for its own airmen following an order in March 1912 that all German naval aircraft had henceforth to be amphibians, with the added weight and drag of wheels.

The major problem for all seaplanes was that of navigation, which in those days was hard enough for aircraft flying over dry land. Over a featureless ocean out of sight of land or in restricted visibility it could be nightmarish, and scores of naval aircraft on both sides simply disappeared without trace. It would be difficult to exaggerate the bravery of a pilot and observer setting off alone on maritime patrol looking for enemy ships, aircraft and submarines over grey wastes of sea in flimsy wooden machines with open cockpits, a single engine, limited fuel, often no wireless and an unreliable compass; and all this in maritime areas where winds could change in a moment and sea mists gather out of nowhere. They flew day after day, all year round, often never seeing any shipping at all. It was possible for airmen to see not one single enemy vessel in 400 hours' risky flying; and yet the job had to be done. If forced down by engine failure and lucky enough to make a decent landing on the sea they would probably be unable to take off again even if they managed to clear a blocked fuel pipe, for it would surely have been well-nigh impossible as well as dangerous to swing the propeller to restart the engine when standing on a narrow, heaving float. If they were carrying a wicker basket of homing pigeons they could send off a message giving their position as well as they were able, fully aware that they might be condemned to drift for days without water or food until they chanced to be spotted by a passing vessel of whatever nationality. That was if they were lucky. If they made a bad landing on a rough sea and wrecked the aircraft they would more likely cling to a float until cold or fatigue overcame them.

If a patrolling seaplane did spot an enemy ship or surfaced submarine, it would have to resist engaging because the priority was to report the vessel's course and position. It was some time before seaplanes on North Sea patrol were equipped with wireless, able like their dry-land equivalents spotting for the artillery in France to tap out messages on a Morse key. The RNAS had developed the Sterling Spark transmitter, also widely used by the RFC, but it only became at all common in 1917. It was even longer before aircraft carried a receiver as well as a transmitter, enabling the sender to know whether his message had even got through successfully. All in all, the demands on a naval seaplane observer were prodigious. He had to navigate for hours on end across a featureless expanse solely by means of a chart, a compass, and dead reckoning, at any time expected to be able to give an accurate 'fix' of his position. (German pilots coined their own somewhat scornful word for being lost, *verfranzt*, which derived from their generic name for observers, Franz.) He had to understand his wireless set thoroughly as well as be fluent in Morse code. He needed to be a practised machine-gunner and also able to aim and drop any small under-wing bombs the aircraft was carrying. And finally, if forced down he would need to be a good practical seaman to increase his chances of survival.

In the first two years of the war most British and German naval patrol aircraft were sent out singly and without wireless. If they failed to return by dark they were generally given up for lost. Once wireless sets were installed they might at least get off a distress call. However, even assuming a vessel was near enough to receive the call and search for them, rescue was by no means guaranteed, especially at night. The observer's compartment carried a signal pistol and flare cartridges, but these were in limited supply. Besides, anyone who has travelled by boat on a moonless night will know the extreme difficulty of judging the distance of any light. Spotting an object as small as a Short or Rumpler floatplane bobbing on the sea in daylight would be hard enough, but infinitely harder at night and well-nigh impossible in rough or foggy conditions.

It is worth briefly mentioning the seaplane that travelled furthest in the First World War. This was a two-seater Friedrichshafen FF.33 that accompanied the German ship SMS *Wolf* and was predictably nicknamed *Wölfchen* or cub. The *Wolf* was a classic 'Q' ship. It was slow, with a fake funnel, and looked every inch an innocent merchantman. In fact it was quite heavily armed with guns and four torpedo tubes and also carried 460 mines. *Wolf* sailed from Kiel on 30th November 1916, returning on 24th February 1918. In just under fifteen months *Wolf* and the *Wölfchen* visited the Pacific, the Atlantic, the Indian Ocean and the South Seas. The seaplane would fly ahead and scout for likely victims, then drop a message in English threatening that the ship would be bombed unless it kept wireless silence and steamed to meet the *Wolf*. From choice such victims would be other merchant vessels carrying valuable cargoes that were then offloaded into the *Wolf*'s capacious holds. By then the British naval blockade of German ports was resulting in acute shortages of vital supplies such as rubber, brass, copper, zinc, molybdenum and even cocoa, and after a long intrepid voyage the *Wolf*'s victims enabled it to return to Kiel with considerable stocks of such things. It also had on board 467 prisoners of war, having sunk 37 ships around the world totalling 110,000 tons and mined harbours from Colombo to Australia. In that time the faithful *Wölfchen* had been dismantled and rebuilt several times, meanwhile demonstrating how valuable a seaplane could be when tactically deployed in war. It was an astonishing voyage – in fact, the longest by any warship in the First World War – and earned the Blue Max for its skipper, Commander Nerger.

As the *Wölfchen* so brilliantly demonstrated, the seaplanes of both sides could to some extent track shipping as well as monitoring troop and other movements in ports, but they were ill-equipped to give much useful notice of attacks by air. Naval stations on Britain's east coast did indeed keep a sharp watch and, if they spotted German airships or bombers heading towards the British coast, RNAS aircraft would be sent up to investigate. However, by the time enemy aircraft had reached the coast it was generally too late to do much about a raid on London – even if hastily scrambled scouts could have found them in time. Incredibly, despite two years of Zeppelin raids and mounting public outcry, as late as the summer of 1917 there was still no comprehensive plan for the systematic defence of the capital and the warning and protection of its citizens. Neither was there any guaranteed co-operation between the RNAS and the RFC, thanks to inter-service disdain.

Stuart Wortley gives a plausible description of what he found when he was posted back from France to Home Defence duties in July 1917. At that time the only competent aircraft available for the defence of London were several squadrons of the Bristol

F.2A, the Bristol Fighter or 'Brisfit'. This was an excellent combat machine, structurally strong and manoeuvrable, but dogged by engine problems. These were almost entirely the result of the chaos in planning and procurement that resulted from the War Office and the Admiralty each going its own way. The designated engine for the Brisfit was the Rolls-Royce Falcon III, but this was in very short supply because Rolls-Royce had failed to keep up with demand. Bristol was forced to resort to a lower-powered Hispano-Suiza engine, which crucially took the edge off the Brisfit's performance while desperate efforts were made to uprate the French-built motor. Meanwhile the War Office had on a whim ordered 3,000 units of Sunbeam's new Arab engine, despite the company warning them that not only was the design untested but the novel casting techniques required for its aluminium parts were equally untried. This ill-conceived order tied up the production capacity of two large factories at a critical juncture and, just as the company had feared, the castings proved too weak. Nevertheless a stubborn attempt was made to fit Brisfits with Arabs, which were a complete failure. Bristol's final despairing choice of Siddeley's Puma engine proved no better. Most Brisfits wound up with the Hispano-Suiza once it had had the bugs removed and the horsepower increased. The aircraft deployed for Home Defence in 1917 were those stationed around the capital in 'advanced training' squadrons, but by no means all were reliably powered. Advanced or not, these were still training squadrons rather than dedicated units of machines in peak condition manned by experienced pilots; but even the increasingly pressured Prime Minister, Lloyd George, was having a hard time prising such men away from the RFC in France to serve at home.

Wortley's own unit was No. 35 Training Squadron based at Northolt. This had six Brisfits whose condition, since they were used and abused by trainees, was not always good and it was rare for more than two to be airworthy at the same time. No doubt this was also true for the other Home Defence stations. On one

morning of high winds the klaxon sounded and Wortley and his
pilot were scrambled to patrol for two hours between Greenwich
and Chingford at 17,000 feet. In the excitement Wortley had
forgotten to put on his heavy flying jacket and all he had on over
his ordinary clothes was a mackintosh. He steadily froze as they
flew up and down London's north-east flank for ninety minutes
without seeing a single other aircraft, friend or foe. Then, just as
they were turning for home to thaw out, Wortley spotted a formation of Gothas over Harwich heading for the capital. It must
have been a bad moment. There they were, a lone Bristol Fighter
facing an oncoming cloud of the big twin-engined German
bombers. The temptation must have been great simply to
pretend they had seen nothing and turn for home.

The bombers droned on, unmoved by the white puffs of anti-
aircraft shells bursting harmlessly well above and below them.
Wortley noticed that a couple of the Gothas were straggling
slightly behind the rest and his pilot Douglas Hill decided to
attack them. There was nothing they could do about the rest.
Hill made the combat-approved manoeuvre of diving behind
and pulling up under the tail of one of them in its blind spot
before opening fire. After half a dozen rounds his gun jammed.
Meanwhile Wortley, who was not wearing a safety belt, had
trained his own gun on the Gotha's companion off to the right
and likewise opened fire, only to have his gun jam as well after a
few shots.

> I was about to try to clear the stoppage when a violent lurch
> jerked me off my feet. For a fraction of a second I was sus-
> pended in mid-air, and it was only by desperately clutching at
> the gun-mounting that I was able to save myself from falling
> overboard and to haul myself back into my seat. Douglas Hill
> had dived steeply away in order to try to clear his gun. But it
> was the Constantinesco gear that was at fault. It had not been
> properly replenished with oil, so there was not enough pres-
> sure in the tube to fire the trigger. In a training squadron it

is nobody's job in particular to attend to these details. Consequently they remain neglected...[195]

They abandoned the fight and landed at Eastchurch, which turned out to be just as well because a sergeant-rigger there found the main spar of their lower left-hand wing had been shot nearly through. Had they taken off again the wing would almost certainly have collapsed, killing them both. What neither of them had known but had just learned the hard way was that Gothas were armed with a gun to defend their 'blind spot', shooting down and backwards from a port underneath the fuselage.

The incident that had probably led to Wortley's squadron's recall from France was the daylight raid a month earlier when on 13th June a fleet of Gotha bombers had bombed Bermondsey and Poplar. A single 50 kg bomb hit Upper North Street School in the East India Dock Road, killing eighteen children and severely injuring another thirty. Between them that day the Gothas spent a total of an hour and a half over south-east England, killing 162 and injuring 432. Brisfits from 35 and 39 Training Squadrons harried them, but with little effect. Before the children's funeral at All Saints, Poplar on 20th June a long procession of horse-drawn hearses each carrying a little coffin and heaped with flowers was watched by massed crowds on the pavements. The occasion became a focus for public anger and led to an onslaught from the press demanding proper warnings of air raids and calling for reprisals on German towns and cities. Noel Pemberton Billing MP, whose book *Air War: How to Wage It* had been published the previous year and laid out a virtual blueprint for home defence against air attacks, gave a speech in the House of Commons. It was a characteristic PB harangue that began along 'What did I tell you?' lines and went on with such vehemence directed against the government for their laxity and bungling that he was eventually expelled from the chamber.

Hurried War Cabinet meetings decided that squadrons of fighters must be recalled from France and reprisal raids undertaken. When these conclusions were presented to Trenchard and Haig in France Trenchard refused to sacrifice any of his aircraft merely to defend London. His squadrons were for offensive use only. He was also against reprisal raids, saying that 'reprisals on open towns are repugnant to British ideas', while admitting 'we may be forced to adopt them'. He then showed that he, too, understood the implications of Clausewitz by adding 'It would be worse than useless to do so, however, unless we are determined that, once adopted, they will be carried through to the end.' General Haig was similarly against retaliatory raids because he could see it all escalating out of hand. This of course is the nature of all-out war but he, like most Britons, was still reluctant to face the implications. Above all, Trenchard and Haig were against reassigning any aircraft to defend Britain at this moment because they were planning a major ground offensive for July and needed every last machine in France. After furious Cabinet sessions their hand was eventually forced to the extent that, with extreme reluctance, they released 56 Squadron (Cecil Lewis's) to be posted to Bekesbourne in Kent, with 66 Squadron to go to Calais to patrol the Channel approaches, but only on condition that both squadrons were back in France in time for the July offensive.

In the meantime London's East Enders finally lost patience. This was mid-1917; they had effectively been left unprotected for well over two years. They took the law into their own hands and carried out reprisals of their own against people and shops with Germanic names, looting and smashing. There was spreading xenophobia to the extent that practically anyone with a foreign name or accent was unsafe and sometimes police and even soldiers refused to intervene as people were beaten up and their premises ransacked. At first light on 7th July 56 Squadron left Bekesbourne to fly back to France as promised. They had not fired a single shot at a German machine all the time they had been in England even though a flight of Gothas had carried out at least one major raid while they were stationed in Kent.

Given how good German intelligence was by now, it seems likely it was no accident that another daylight Gotha raid was launched against London on the very morning 56 Squadron left. By now a London Warning Centre was in operation and a Royal Navy lightship sighted the incoming bombers and told the Admiralty, which then alerted the RNAS at Chatham. Their fighters joined with some eighty others scrambled from the advanced training squadrons in the London area. Anti-aircraft batteries also sent up a barrage of shells to meet the Gothas. It is a measure of how new aviation still was, and how exciting any aircraft seemed, that far from taking cover Londoners would come out of their houses to watch daylight raids despite the lethal hail of shrapnel from the ack-ack guns that killed and injured many on the ground. Small boys would scurry through the streets looking for the most sought-after trophies of all, the artillery shells' brass nose-caps and copper driving bands. On this occasion some distinguished witnesses observed the twenty-five bombers as they flew across the capital, 'packed together like a flight of rooks':

> Among the spectators were members of the Air Board, watch-ing from the balconies of the Hotel Cecil [their headquarters], who were probably less excited than humiliated by this latest demonstration of German daring and British aerial impo-tence. *The Times* published a breathless report on the raid the next day. 'As a spectacle, the raid was the most thrilling that London has seen since the air attacks began. Every phase could be followed from points many miles away without the aid of glasses, and hundreds of thousands of people watched the approach of the squadron, the dropping of the bombs, the shelling of the German aeroplanes and the eventual retreat.'[196]

The Gothas dropped their bombs right across London causing many casualties. There were the familiar scenes of children with their legs blown off, lumps of hair and gristle plastered to brick walls, the screams of a disembowelled drayhorse that was messily put down with a fireman's axe. One of 63 Squadron's pilots, Lieutenant W.G. Salmon, was shot in the air, attempted an emergency landing at Joyce Green airfield near Dartford, but died in the crash. Several arrests were made among sightseers who rushed forward and looted his body and the wreckage of his aircraft for souvenirs. In the poorer districts of London itself the looting and rioting increased as news of the casualties spread. One of the witnesses was Sylvia, the Suffragist daughter of Emmeline Pankhurst. She described how the air was

> filled by the babble of voices and the noise of knocking and splintering wood. Men were lowering a piano through the window … A woman and her children raced off with an easy chair, rushing it along on its castors before them. 'I shall sit, and sit, and sit on this chair all day,' the mother yelled. 'I never had an armchair to sit in before.' 'Bread! Bread! Bread!' The shrieks rang out. Women and children rushed by, their arms and aprons laden with loaves. Looting continued with impunity for days … men unknown in the district, with hatchets on their shoulders, marched through Bethnal Green, Green Street and Roman Road to the very end. Wherever a shop had a German name over it, they stopped and hacked down the shutters and broke the glass. Then crowds of children rushed in and looted. When darkness fell and the police made no sign, men and women joined in the sack. Only when adjoining English shops began to be looted did the police stir themselves to intervene.[197]

Lloyd George later toured the bombed areas and his report to the War Cabinet led to two more squadrons being withdrawn from France against the wishes of Trenchard and Haig, whose Flanders offensive was now put back to 31st July. 46 Squadron, which flew Sopwith Pups, returned in a hurry to England to be based at Sutton's Farm in Essex.

Once again, German intelligence must have been well informed because five days later, on 22nd July, the so-called 'England Squadron' of Gotha bombers ignored London and instead attacked Harwich and Felixstowe at breakfast time, scoring a direct hit on an army barracks that killed eleven men. This time Home Defence got more than 120 aircraft into the air though only one managed to fire a shot. A single Gotha out of twenty-one was shot down, but that was by two Dunkirk-based Brisfits as it crossed the Belgian coast afterwards, homeward bound. The real damage done to the RFC and RNAS fighters must have been to morale as a result of being peppered by their own anti-aircraft batteries. These had merrily shelled nine British aircraft over the Thames Estuary that morning, damaging several, and they were still firing away at 9.45 a.m., by which time the twenty remaining Gothas were even then landing back at their bases on the outskirts of Ghent. Being 'archied' by their own guns must have been enraging for the British defenders, who had survived the madhouse of Flanders only to find the war not one whit saner in their own homeland. Only four months earlier Field Marshal Viscount Sir John French, whom Haig had replaced as Commander-in-Chief of the British Expeditionary Force and reassigned as Commander-in-Chief Home Forces, issued a bizarre edict. All anti-aircraft batteries except those along the coast were forbidden to fire. 'No aeroplanes or seaplanes, *even if recognized as hostile*, will be fired at either by day or night.'[198] That way the batteries' personnel could be sent off to France where they were more urgently needed. This order was only rescinded in early June. Presumably the bemused returning gunners then decided to play it safe and fire at absolutely any aircraft they spotted.

Another equally lunatic measure was that restricting wireless communications with the defending aircraft. Sir David Henderson, the Director-General of Military Aeronautics, had been constantly urging that wireless receivers should be installed in Home Defence aircraft so they could be directed from the ground. By 1917 scout aircraft were generally powerful enough for the small additional weight to be easily manageable, and it seemed like one of those ideas that could only be sensible. Nevertheless it was promptly scuppered by the Admiralty, who protested that the transmissions might interfere with the Fleet's own communications. Eventually two-way wireless equipment was installed in four aircraft whose pilots could communicate with operations centres in the Hotel Cecil and Wormwood Scrubs. The rest of the Home Defence squadrons had to rely on AA batteries laying out broad strips of white cloth on the ground in the form of arrows pointing towards any enemy aircraft they spotted. Thus was Great Britain prepared to defend itself and its citizens.

In desperation the War Cabinet at last appointed the energetic old Boer leader, Lieutenant-General Jan Christiaan Smuts, as Home Defence supremo, a task he undertook with considerable efficiency. Fresh from his campaigns in Africa and untainted by the old inter-service prejudices that were bedevilling so much of the air war effort, he at once ordered RFC and RNAS squadrons to work together under a unified command. Secondly, he called for a protective ring of anti-aircraft batteries and searchlights around London, three new squadrons of fighters plus a reserve force on permanent detachment, and a new air raid warning system for the capital. This called for a command centre in County Hall able to contact any of eighty fire stations all over London so they could sound warning of an impending raid. Such long overdue measures were just as well, since the end of September 1917 marked the introduction of Germany's R.VI Zeppelin-Staaken bombers. These were the biggest aircraft of the war: four-engined giants with a wingspan of 138 feet. To see one of those droning over London must have fulfilled anybody's worst fears that H. G. Wells's nightmarish visions in *The War in the Air* were about to come true.

*

By now it was clearer to everyone what Clausewitzian ideas of total war entailed. Both sides were sustaining civilian casualties.

Both sides were experiencing periodic shortages of food and fuel, although without a large empire on which to rely Germany – now embattled on several fronts – was undoubtedly suffering more. Its war machine was beginning to feel the pinch with ever-acuter shortages of vital materials like rubber and copper. In fact, the time was not far off when German coins would become worth more for the metal they were made of than their monetary value.

Maybe after all Clausewitz had simply produced a highly sophisticated version of the age-old adage that anything is fair in love and war. Even so, this maxim could still backfire badly, as it did on the Germans over the sinking of the Cunard liner RMS *Lusitania* and the executions of two British citizens, the nurse Edith Cavell and the merchant seaman Captain Charles Fryatt. It may be that Clausewitz or the German high command did not pay enough attention to some of the negative effects of total war that might sometimes hand a propaganda and morale advantage to an enemy. In May 1915 the *Lusitania* was torpedoed off Ireland by a U-boat while in-bound to Liverpool from New York, killing 1,198, many of them Americans. Although the Kriegsmarine had previously declared the waters around the British Isles as a war zone, and the German Embassy in New York had published a warning in New York newspapers urging passengers not to travel on the ship, the sinking was a disaster for Germany as well as for the victims because it materially increased the chances of bringing the United States into the war – as it proved two years later. There is a conspiracy theory that the British deliberately used the *Lusitania* as a 'tethered goat' in order to lure America into the war. The Germans claimed the ship was a legitimate naval target because it was carrying munitions. This was vehemently denied at the time as a typical German lie, although divers have recently found upwards of four million rounds of .303 rifle and machine-gun ammunition in the wreck. However the various truths intersect, and once the mourning and bluster had subsided, the overall result was a major propaganda coup for the Allies.

As for Edith Cavell, there is no question that she was guilty as charged, having abused her presumed neutrality as a nurse to help over 200 Allied soldiers escape from Germany; but shooting her was likewise a dreadful mistake. It was a gift to propagandists and proof of German 'frightfulness'. And if Captain Fryatt's name is today much less familiar than that of Edith Cavell, at the time his execution caused equal outrage although his case was even more equivocal, morally speaking. He was not a naval man but simply the civilian captain of a merchant vessel. From early 1915 he had run the gauntlet of U-boat attacks in the English Channel, finally attempting to ram U-33 which had surfaced to torpedo him. He might not have been in uniform but he was acting in compliance with an order from Winston Churchill, by then First Lord of the Admiralty. This included a clause further stating that any German crews captured by a merchantman could legitimately be shot if that was more convenient than taking them prisoner, and another declaring that any white flag of surrender was to be ignored.

The attempted ramming took place in March 1915 but it was not until June 1916 that Fryatt and his vessel were finally captured by German destroyers and escorted to Bruges. He was court-martialled as a guerrilla fighter for trying to sink U-33 and tried in the Town Hall in July, sentenced to death (a sentence personally confirmed by the Kaiser) and shot on the 27th. Then-Prime Minister Herbert Asquith's statement to the House of Commons four days later unequivocally called this 'murder', describing it as an 'atrocious crime against the laws of nations and the usages of war', which conveniently ignored the fact that under Churchill's draconian rules of engagement the wretched Fryatt could have been arrested back in Britain had he *not* tried to ram the U-boat. Given that he was also permitted to shoot any prisoners he took and ignore any white flag – that most immemorial of all 'usages of war' – his role could reasonably be described as very far from that of an ordinary merchant skipper. Great international condemnation followed his death, including an impassioned article in *The New York Times*. However, so insistent were the Germans that the sentence was justified that they reviewed it after the war was over and reconfirmed its legitimacy in 1919. Poor Charles Fryatt could never have guessed his own death's propaganda value to the Allies, nor that a century later London's commuters would still be passing his memorial tablet daily in Liverpool Street Station.

After the Zeppelin and Gotha raids there was never any serious doubt that the British would eventually carry out retaliatory raids on German cities with a clear conscience. However, Trenchard's plan had always been to achieve air superiority before bombing industrial targets and Germany's infrastructure. Superiority in terms of sheer numbers of Allied fighters was not achieved until the spring of 1918, at which point the Independent Air Force was formed under Trenchard's command. Designed expressly for the purpose of bombing German targets from eastern France by night and day, the IAF eventually comprised British, French, Italian and US units. Many of Handley Page's big twin-engined O/400 bombers were deployed, but the majority of the RFC's bombers were much smaller single-engined aircraft such as D.H.4s.

Long-range raids were carried out on cities like Mainz, Stuttgart, Coblenz, Mannheim, Trier and Metz, as well as on targets such as railways and factories. (It was on one such sortie that W. E. Johns and his observer were shot down.) The Entente's air forces might theoretically have been in the ascendancy but it was still an extremely hazardous enterprise for the aircrews, with round trips of up to 200 miles and 'archie' defences and German fighters still highly active and competent. Post-raid aerial photos showed many of the targets badly damaged; less visible was the inevitable toll of limbless children and disembowelled horses. Nor did the photos reveal the tally of roast or smashed airmen, nor those captured to spend long months in ever-worsening conditions in prison camps as Germany's food shortages grew more acute.

An American writer and columnist, Irvin S. Cobb, wrote an article for the *Saturday Evening Post* in 1918 describing a visit he had made in the spring of that year to Night Bombing Squadron No. 100. This was now an IAF outfit flying F.E.2bs and based at Ochey, near Nancy: far enough south and east in France to be within reach of some important German targets. One day a biplane landed near him and out of it climbed two very young British aviators. When Cobb asked what they were doing, the following conversation ensued:

'Well, you see, we were a bit thirsty – Bert and I – and we heard you had very good beer at the French Officers' Club here. So we just ran over for half an hour or so to get a drop of drink and then toddle along back again. Not a bad idea, what?' The speaker wore the twin crowns of a captain on the shoulder straps of his overcoat. His age I should have put at twenty-one and his complexion was that of a very new, very healthy cherub. 'Anything happening at the Squadron since I was over that way?' I enquired. 'Quiet enough to be a bore – weather hasn't suited for our sort these last few evenings,' stated the taller boy. 'We got fed up on doin' nothing at all, so night before last a squad started across the border to give Fritzie a taste of life. But just after we started the Squadron Commander decided the weather was too thickish and he signed us back – all but the Young-un here, who claims he didn't see the flare and kept on goin' all by his little self.' 'It seemed a rotten shame, really it did, to waste the whole eve-nin'.' This was the Young-un, he of the pink cheeks, speaking. 'So I just jogged across the jolly old Rhine until I came to a town, and I dropped my pills there and came back. Nice quiet trip it was – lonely, rather, and not a bit excitin'.'[199]

If this suggests Bertie Wooster more than Biggles it is because of the upper-class Edwardian drawl that was already becoming the linguistic hallmark of the newly formed RAF. Out of hunting

field jargon, public school cant and aviation slang was created a
verbal tradition proper for a gentleman's breezy relationship
with sudden death. This was *style*: an affectation that was to
persist, most famously in the Second World War when cries of
'Tally ho!' and languid talk of wizard prangs and pieces of cake
became indelibly associated with the Battle of Britain and the
boys of Fighter and Bomber Command. Under the pressure of
attrition rates far greater than those suffered by airmen in the
previous war, this argot then reached its zenith as the studied
nonchalance of the dashingly doomed. By then, too, the awful
lessons of the nation's complete vulnerability to bombing raids
in the earlier war had been learned, and a well-organised and
effective early warning system was at last in place as a vital part
of Britain's home defence.

*

Even so, an idea had taken hold that was to dominate strategic
– and particularly air force – thinking for decades to come,
above all in Britain and the United States. This was that
bombing was the way forward, despite evidence from the First
World War that for all the localised panic the air raids had at
first caused, civilian morale overall had been very little injured
by it – had maybe even been strengthened, especially once it
could be seen that the air force was putting up a serious
defence. Moreover, what appeared from aerial photographs to
be grievous damage inflicted on an enemy's factories and infrastructure often turned out to cause no very great reduction in
industrial output.

Yet between the wars the idea that strategic bombing was the
key to winning future conflict took hold strongly in various air
forces. In 1932, in the wake of Japan's indiscriminate bombing
of Shanghai which killed thousands, the Geneva Disarmament
Conference tried vainly to outlaw aerial attacks on vulnerable
citizens, Clausewitz or no Clausewitz. Britain's then-Prime
Minister, Stanley Baldwin, said resignedly that the man in the

street had to realise 'there is no power on earth that can protect him from being bombed… the bomber will always get through'.[200] And so it was to prove. All the same, the ensuing world war provided no evidence that, with the sole exception of America's use of nuclear bombs against Japan in 1945, strategic bombing, area bombing or 'precision' bombing was ever the critical factor in the war's outcome. Even massive damage to Germany's Ruhr industries by the RAF and the USAAF did less to disrupt Hitler's war machine than did an increasing lack of raw materials from outside Germany. Neither did the setting on fire of entire cities bring about a mass uprising of citizens willing to sue for peace. Yet the idea of bombing's supremacy persisted in the military mind, and after the Second World War it became enshrined as an eternal truth that has to some extent dominated strategic thinking ever since, above all in the United States. Aerial bombing by drones in the Middle East has yielded its daily 'collateral damage' of limbless children and disembowelled donkeys and nothing remotely approaching a victory has yet been achieved, and nor can it be. Quite the reverse. As the first air raids a hundred years ago demonstrated, attacks that leave dismembered children strewn among rubble are more likely to strengthen a people's resolve than to weaken it.

Yet that first air war did establish one military principle that has endured unchallenged: that of the vital importance of air superiority in general. By the end of 1918, with sheer weight of numbers, the Entente had at last achieved aerial dominance over the battlefields of Europe. The critical advantage this conferred was noted by all sides and was to be confirmed many times in the Second World War as, indeed, ever since. As one senior RAF officer recently remarked, 'The Gulf War of 1991 was a sharp reminder of what can happen to even a large and well-equipped army [i.e. Saddam Hussein's retreating from Kuwait] when caught in open ground by an opponent enjoying total air supremacy.'[201] That was decisive; whereas the shattering bombardment of 'Shock and Awe' in the second Gulf War of 2003 was not. Baghdad fell, but it brought the Coalition forces no overall victory in the war. Back in 1918 a few wise heads on all sides might have predicted that.

## CHAPTER 11

# BALKANS AND MESOPOTAMIA

———— ◆ ————

Pilots and observers have consistently maintained the ever-changing fortunes of the day and in the war zone our dead have been always beyond the enemy's lines or far out at sea. Our far-flung squadrons have flown over home waters and foreign seas, the Western and Italian battle line, Rhineland, the Mountains of Macedonia, Gallipoli, Palestine, the Plains of Arabia, Sinai and Darfur...

King George V to all RAF squadrons after the Armistice

'OUR FAR-FLUNG SQUADRONS ... battle-line...' Kipling's 'Recessional' was evidently echoing in the unconscious of whoever drafted the King's message. The poet's anxious prayer to the 'Lord of our far-flung battle-line' embodied the worry that without His blessing Britain's global empire represented vainglorious overstretch. 'Far-called, our navies melt away...' It was inevitable that the war in Europe should have had tentacles reaching overseas into the Balkans, Middle East and Africa since the major combatants – Britain, France, Germany, Russia, Austria-Hungary and Italy – all had empires or spheres of interest and influence far beyond the main European fronts. As usually happens in wars, well before the end men in suits were cooking up post-bellum deals, scheming how various frontiers might be redrawn and what colour the new maps should be. Among the more notorious of these deals was the secret Sykes–Picot agreement in which one Briton and one Frenchman decided how the entire Middle East should be carved up. The fallout from those arbitrary lines drawn across a map in crayon on a May day in 1916 has now persisted for a century and may yet become literal.

The political geography of the Middle East was considerably determined by the twin fading dynasties of Ottoman Turkey and Qajar Persia. The protracted struggle for the Ottoman Empire's former possessions had already been a background factor of the Crimean War in the mid-nineteenth century. In 1914 Turkey sided with Germany and the Central Powers, which left the Entente – chiefly Britain, France and Russia – with regional wars on its hands, Britain fighting the Turco-German forces from the Balkans to Sinai and Palestine and on through Mesopotamia. It was above all vital for Britain to maintain its lifeline with the Empire via the sea route that included the Suez Canal and Aden, an important coaling station. But in view of the Royal Navy's gradual switch from coal to oil at this time (the new *Queen Elizabeth*-class battleships were oil burners), it was equally vital to secure the Anglo-Persian Oil Company's oilfields in Mesopotamia, and especially its huge refinery at Abadan in what is now Iran. In order to drive the Turks out of Palestine and elsewhere, Britain entered into an alliance with Sherif Hussein bin Ali of Mecca, who was leading an Arab nationalist movement that also wanted the Turks out of the Middle East. The British army officer under General Allenby's command working with Sherif Hussein to free the Hejaz (the western coast of Arabia) was T. E. Lawrence, who gave this assessment of the Arabs' campaign:

Of religious fanaticism there was little trace. The Sherif refused in round terms to give a religious twist to his rebellion. His fighting creed was nationality. The tribes knew that the Turks were Moslems who thought that the Germans were probably true friends of Islam. They knew that the British were Christians, and that the British were their allies. In the circumstances, their religion would not have been of much help to them, and they had put it aside. 'Christian fights

Christian, so why should not Mohammedan do the same? What we want is a Government which speaks our own language of Arabic and will let us live in peace. Also, we hate those Turks.'[202]

The armies involved in the Middle East conflict were naturally accompanied by air support which, especially in desert landscapes with little cover, was useful for observing troop movements and bombing supply lines. As far as maintaining an air presence went, the British had an advantage over the Germans for purely logistical reasons. The merchant fleet, escorted by the Royal Navy, could reliably supply Britain's protectorate, Egypt, via Alexandria and Port Said, whereas the Germans had to bring their aircraft, spares and equipment overland from Germany on the long and difficult haul down through the Balkans and Turkey.

Some RFC and RNAS squadrons were even further-flung than King George's message-drafter knew, for they were also present in a minor way in East Africa and India. In India a few squadrons were based almost exclusively on the North-West Frontier in what today is Pakistan, dealing with the 'troublesome tribesmen' in Waziristan who were part of Britain's continuing imperial headache, albeit one that was independent of the Great War. In Africa, though, the Kaiser's colonial presence was fought with varying success in both German South-West Africa (Namibia) and German East Africa (today's Tanzania).

Probably the most famous air action in the latter was the destruction of the German light cruiser *Königsberg* in 1915 after it had hidden some ten miles inland in the complex delta of the Rufiji river, temporarily immobilised by engine failure. The *Königsberg* had long been a menace to British shipping in the Indian Ocean and the Admiralty viewed her elimination as a priority. Royal Navy warships arrived off the Rufiji delta but failed to find the German vessel because its crew had camouflaged the ship with foliage cut from the surrounding forest. It was a clear case for aerial reconnaissance. A local pilot was hired, together with his privately owned Curtiss F. seaplane, but this did not survive many missions. Two G.III Caudrons and two Henri Farman F.27s were sent down from Dar-es-Salaam (the F.27 was essentially a 'Rumpty' with a bigger engine and without its 'horns': the curved skids on the undercarriage) but nor were these up to the task. The Navy then deployed two RNAS Sopwith 'Folders': Type 807 biplanes with folding wings for shipboard storage. However, their Gnome Monosoupape (single valve) rotary engines proved too weak in the hot climate even as their airframes came unglued in the tropical damp. Three of Short's 'Folders' were then deployed that, while also suffering in the heat and unable to climb above 600 feet, did manage some useful photo-reconnaissance work and finally pinpointed the *Königsberg*'s position. Two shallow-draught monitors were sent whose guns fatally crippled the German ship, thereby removing a major threat to Allied traffic in the Indian Ocean.

However, the *Königsberg*'s menace did not end there because most of its crew went to join an extraordinary guerrilla force led by a true genius in the art of bush warfare. This was General Paul Emil von Lettow-Vorbeck who was the officer in charge of all military forces in German East Africa. Between 1914 and 1918, living off the land and with a mere 14,000 men – German and local African – he managed to tie down and harry 300,000 Allied troops, remaining uncaptured at the time of the Armistice. It is pleasant to record that 'The Lion of Africa' survived until 1964. He was the only German commander ever to invade British imperial territory in the First World War, and his four years of improvised bush tactics mark him as probably the greatest-ever exponent of this form of warfare.

It was against Lettow-Vorbeck and in support of General Smuts that 26 Squadron flew reconnaissance missions in their B.E.2cs and 'Rumptys' (by that time the sort of antiquated aircraft most easily spared from the Western Front). But theirs was a tiny contingent and the task proved hopeless since little could be observed in thick bush from the air. Apart from that the

African climate proved too much for fragile wooden aircraft designed for northern Europe, susceptible to wood-boring pests and warping as well as to weakened adhesives. No airman is much comforted by the thought of termites in his airframe and still less by the possibility that at any moment it might come unglued in the air. Thirty years later in the Second World War this same problem had to be addressed when the wood-framed de Havilland Mosquito was deployed in the Far East. By then new formaldehyde-based adhesives had been devised that seemed mostly to work; occasional airframe failures were attributed to sloppy assembly in de Havilland's factories at Hatfield and Leavesden.

King George's reference to Darfur in his message was significant for the way in which it related to the wider picture of the British campaign in the Middle East. Since the turn of the century the Sudanese sultanate of Darfur (the land of the Fur people) had effectively been independent under its ruler, Ali Dinar. From its geographical position of sharing frontiers with Italian-administered Libya and the French-administered district of Chad (then part of French West Africa), Dinar felt himself drawn into the wider conflict, being already estranged from Sudan's British administration ever since Kitchener had ordered the mass killing of wounded Mahdists after the Battle of Omdurman in 1899. Instinctively, the Sultan sided with Libya's politico-religious Senussi tribe, who were waging their own anti-colonial war against the Italian occupation. He believed Turkish and German propaganda that promised the creation of an Islamic state in North Africa after the war was over and the Italians, the French and the British had all been driven out.

Ali Dinar's rebelliousness led to British intervention in 1916, motivated half by needing to keep the peace in Sudan and half by macro-political considerations. Four B.E.2cs flew observation and reconnaissance missions over remote Darfur territory as well as dropping propaganda leaflets on the town of Al Fashir, Dinar's stronghold. After fierce ground battles between the

British Army and Dinar's men Lieutenant John Slessor in his B.E.2c bombed the Fur troops retreating to Al Fashir, during which he was hit in the thigh by a bullet. Shortly afterwards all four aircraft and Lieutenant Slessor himself were withdrawn to Egypt for repair and the Darfur campaign ended with Ali Dinar's death in November 1916. Many years later John Slessor was to become Air Marshal Sir John and finally a hawkish Cold War Chief of the Air Staff in the early 1950s.

It is shaming to see how quickly Europeans betrayed their promises to the Middle-Eastern allies they had so assiduously cultivated during the First World War. The Libyans' faith in Turco-German visions of an Islamic state in North Africa was shattered when the Italians not only stayed on after 1918 but began importing Sicilians en masse to displace local Arabs and turn the country's sole fertile coastal strip into 'the garden of Italy'. The Arabs' faith in British promises of a pan-Arab state from Aleppo to Aden was likewise destroyed once it was clear the Sykes–Picot agreement had secretly broken the promises even before they were made. The hopes of young nationalistic Egyptians were similarly dashed when the British stayed on in their protectorate after the war with a military occupation of the Canal Zone that included a considerable RAF presence. And the Ottomans' faith in the Germans likewise came to naught. To this day the malign ghost of these and other betrayals haunts Middle East peace talks as an unbidden but ever-present delegate.

★

On the other side of the Mediterranean fighting had become general ever since the abortive British and French Gallipoli campaign that began in April 1915 at the western end of the Dardanelles – the narrow strait separating Europe from Asia. It was across this bottleneck that German lines of supply to the Middle East had to run. They came south-eastwards through the Austro-Hungarian Empire, through Bulgaria (which had finally sided with the Central Powers in September 1915) and thence through Turkey. Both the British and the French badly underestimated the fighting abilities of the Turkish troops defending the Dardanelles. This was curious, considering that before the war the Turkish army had been reorganised by the Germans, their navy by the British, and their air force by the French. It is hard to see how these military advisers could have overlooked the Turkish forces' combined competence on their own terrain. Nevertheless they did; and after a campaign that cost the French and the British and their Anzac divisions dear, the Entente armies withdrew to Egypt and Salonika in January 1916 to lick their wounds.

Among the survivors was the 22-year-old W. E. Johns, who had taken part in the Gallipoli fiasco as Private Johns of the Norfolk Yeomanry. He was well aware how lucky he was to have survived since he had left half his regiment behind in mass graves. Many had been killed in action but the great majority had died of dysentery, malaria or simply of exposure in the lethal late autumn blizzards. Once in Alexandria Johns was deployed for the next six months to various outposts of the Suez Canal defences, often in remote desert locations that he could not have guessed would prove extremely useful to him in twenty years' time as the setting for several of his Biggles stories. In September 1916 he was transferred from the Norfolk Yeomanry to the Machine Gun Corps, sent back to England on a brief leave and promptly dispatched once again by troopship, this time to Salonika.

This Greek seaport, more properly Thessaloniki, was some fifty very rough miles due south of Lake Doiran on the border between Macedonia and Bulgaria. In late 1915 the French general Maurice Sarrail had led a joint French and British force in an attempt to go to the aid of Serbia using the rail link that ran past this lake, but he left it too late. Bulgaria had just thrown in its lot with the Central Powers and its troops cut the railway line that Sarrail and his men were relying on and he had to turn round and withdraw south to Salonika. The port promptly became the main base for Entente troops in the so-called

Macedonian theatre. In true Balkan style Greece's political position was equivocal since the country was split between royalists
who, like King Constantine, favoured the Germans, and those
who sided with the revolutionary Prime Minister, Eleftherios
Venizelos, who favoured the Entente. It was not until June 1917
that Constantine abdicated after a coup supported by General
Sarrail, to be succeeded by his son Alexander who endorsed the
Prime Minister, and Greece as a whole (now often referred to as
'Venizelan' Greece) finally came down firmly on the side of the
Entente powers.

That was in the future, however. Greece was still on the edge
of civil war when in mid-1916 General Sarrail tried again to
advance beyond the Macedonian frontier, meeting the German
Eleventh Army from the west and the Bulgarians from the east.
In support of this effort the RFC's 17 Squadron was sent to
Salonika in July. It came fresh from flying in Sinai, the Western
Desert and Arabia and for a short while was the only RFC unit in
Macedonia. The squadron comprised twelve B.E.2cs and three
Bristol Scouts (both pre-war designs) plus two D.H.2s, the resil-
ient little single-seat fighter that was even then helping to end
the 'Fokker Scourge' over Flanders and France. Soon 47
Squadron was also sent to swell the RFC's presence on the
Macedonian front.

By the time Johns arrived at the front with the Machine Gun
Corps in October 1916 the British trenches ran through formidable country from Lake Doiran ('that fever-ridden sewer' as he
later called it) south-westwards along the Macedonian border. It
was the tactical stalemate of that terrible winter that confirmed
Johns's views about politicians and the military, as well as of war
in general. He wrote later of the 'lies and lies, and still more lies
that made it impossible for men to stay at home without appearing contemptible cravens':

I helped to shovel eighteen hundred of them into pits (without the blankets for which their next-of-kin were probably

charged) including sixty-seven of my own machine gun
squadron of seventy-five, in front of Horseshoe Hill in Greek
Macedonia. We were sent to take the hill without big guns.
Oh yes, they sent guns out to us, but when they got to Salonika
there wasn't any tackle big enough to lift them out of the
ships. At least, that's what we were told. Later, when we took
the hill and the guns afterwards appeared, there wasn't any
tackle powerful enough to haul them up the hill. So back we
came again.[203]

By early 1917 there was an increasing German presence in the
air over the Macedonian front, and in February they humiliatingly bombed the headquarters of the British XII Corps in
Salonika, the Yanesh Hotel. An eyewitness lamented that the
Entente's air defences were no match for the German machines
and that all they could do was get into the air to avoid being
bombed on the ground. It would have taken them twenty
minutes to climb to meet the Germans, by which time the
attackers would be landing back at their base at Drama. This
can't have been good for morale, particularly with such a wide
variety of potential witnesses of the raid, Salonika having
become the port where all the Entente's troops and supplies
for their Balkan armies were landed. At any one time the town
was a polyglot jumble of British, French, Italian, Russian,
Serbian, Venizelist-Greek, Indian, Algerian, Annamese and
Senegalese troops.

During this year Lance-Corporal Johns, like so many thousands of others, finally went down with malaria and was
hospitalised in Salonika. During his long recuperation he
decided he had had his fill of the infantry. He applied for a
transfer to the RFC, obtained his discharge from the Machine
Gun Corps and in September 1917 was commissioned as a 2nd
lieutenant in the RFC and sent home to be taught to fly. 'I was
learning something about war,' he wrote later. 'It seemed to me
that there was no point in dying standing up in squalor if one

could do so sitting down in clean air.'[204] It was an impeccably Bigglesian sentiment.

★

The importance of Salonika and the Macedonian front to the Entente meant that such air activity as there was became increasingly well organised. The Germans' *Fliegerabteilung* (Air Force Detachment) 30 was attached to the Bulgarian and Turkish armies, with an important base outside the Greek town of Drama, some forty miles north-east of a British airfield on the island of Thasos, itself along the coast to the east of Salonika. At that time Drama was not yet part of Venizelan Greece and the German machines regularly made reconnaissance flights from it over Salonika. However, the British had set up a chain of wireless-equipped observation posts along the front and any enemy aircraft crossing the line were reported to Salonika and Thasos, from where scouts were scrambled to meet the Germans.

Although aircraft on both sides were regularly shot down, there must have been something about the terrain and general conditions that reawakened a spirit of comradeship among the opposing airmen. The countryside which they daily overflew in their small biplanes was extremely daunting, and they knew that if they suffered engine failure or were shot down and injured rather than killed their chances of rescue were slender indeed among the thickly wooded mountains, ravines and coastal marshes, none of which offered a road or landing place for miles. At least in France with its open fields there was the chance of either rescue or capture, unless one fell in no-man's-land and the aircraft became an artillery target. The weather, too, was unpredictable in this area between the Aegean and the mountainous interior. Storms blew up within minutes, accompanied by violent winds and down-draughts such as the one mentioned in Chapter 9 that caused a German observer, unnoticed by his pilot, to be flung out of his cockpit over these same mountains. At any rate both sides regularly dropped message bags with

streamers on each other's airfields with notification of an aircrew's fate, and even with invitations. On one occasion a British
pilot dropped a note that read:

> As we have met so often in the air and peppered one another,
> we should also be very pleased to make the personal acquain-
> tance of the German airmen of Drama. We therefore make
> the following proposition. Give us your word of honour that
> you will not take us prisoners, and we will land a motor boat
> on the eastern shore of Lake Takhino to meet you.[205]

'Unfortunately,' the German pilot who recounted this added,

> we had bad experiences with that sort of fraternisation not
> long before on the Russian front, and so an order was issued
> forbidding us to go in for anything of that kind – and I'm still
> heartily sorry about it for I should have been ever so pleased
> to shake hands with those Tommies.

Their refusal was understandable given the reference to the
Russian front, long since a byword among German airmen for
duplicity and barbarities of every kind. Not only was there a
short film doing the rounds of captured men being crucified,
but wounded aircrew were frequently butchered, then stripped
and robbed of everything including all documents, so identification of the naked and dismembered corpses was often
impossible.[206]

In Macedonia, on the other hand, opposing airmen often
did their best to preserve the niceties. When Lieutenant Leslie-
Moore from the RNAS squadron at Thasos was shot down he
was brought to Drama and welcomed in the Staffel's mess, as
was normal. After a celebratory dinner his captors shame-
facedly apologised for only being able to offer him tea since
coffee had become virtually unobtainable. Leslie-Moore said
this was no problem if he might be allowed to pencil a note to

his commanding officer that the Germans could drop over Thasos. This read:

> Dear Major,
> I have just dined with the German Flying Corps. They have been very kind to me. I am going up to Philippopolis [Plovdiv] tomorrow. The Germans have asked me to ask you to throw them over some coffee on Drama which they want in [the] mess here. Good luck to all, A. Leslie-Moore.[207]

It was a shame that when a British pilot obliged, the German diarist noted regretfully that 'they could not catch the streamer he dropped because a strong wind carried it away into the mountains. But we were gratefully convinced that it contained the coffee we desired. I can only hope that it did not agree with the dishonourable finder,' a remark that probably reflected a degree of disenchantment with the locals, whether Greek, Turkish or Bulgarian. The Germans generally found their allies amiable enough, but language and cultural barriers often proved insurmountable and there was a complete lack of the rigorous Prussian army-style honesty and efficiency they were used to.

But as W. E. Johns had discovered in both Gallipoli and Macedonia, the real problem everybody faced in the Balkans was not bullets so much as microbes. Typhus felled thousands, malaria tens of thousands. One British Army officer later wrote: 'When we went to Macedonia, we knew it was a fever country. But no-one was able to realise the full extent of the deadliness of – for example – the Struma plain. Our people sank under the malaria like grass-blades under a scythe. One infantry battalion dwindled from its strength of 1,000 to one officer and nineteen men.'[208]

An incident tangential to the Macedonian front but still worth mentioning on account of its fame was the attempt by a German airship in the autumn of 1917 to take medical stores and other badly needed supplies from Bulgaria to East Africa (where the RFC's 26 Squadron's B.E.2cs and Farmans were flying patrols against General von Lettow-Vorbeck's guerrillas). It was a feat that merely confirmed Germany's supremacy in airship technology. The heavily laden Zeppelin L.59 took off from Yambol in Bulgaria, crossed the Mediterranean, flew obliquely across Egypt and down through Sudan to the confluence of the Blue and White Niles south of Khartoum. It was little more than halfway to its destination when it was recalled by wireless on account of a false rumour that the German garrison in East Africa had been evacuated and abandoned. Captain Bockholt simply turned the L.59 around in mid-air and headed back to Yambol, where in due course he landed uneventfully, having been in the air for ninety-six hours and flown 4,200 miles. It was an epic flight.

*

The Italian Front also offered airmen the challenge of forbidding terrain, and this at first without adequate maps. The Austrian maps of the Julian Alps, in particular, proved useless for military purposes, being too small-scale. In late September 1917 the German General Staff urgently needed to relieve the pressure on the Austro-Hungarian troops in Trieste, but couldn't advance its own divisions without reliable large-scale maps. German squadrons were called in to make a complete photographic survey of the region on both sides of the lines. This involved flying fifty miles each way over impassable mountains, itself a nerve-racking enterprise with the prospect of surviving a crash-landing small and of being rescued smaller still.

After the catastrophic Italian defeat at Caporetto in November 1917, the RFC rushed three Camel squadrons and two squadrons of R.E.8s to the Italian front. Air activity over the front became constant but by now, as in Macedonia, the Germans and Austro-Hungarians found themselves badly outnumbered, especially as the Italian fighter forces were becoming seasoned and effective. Even so, Austro-Hungarian aircraft still managed to bomb Padua, Treviso, Mestre and Venice in December, causing the usual terror and destruction. In fact the air war over the north of Italy had from the first been predominantly one of bombing. It will be recalled from Chapter 3 that the Italian military visionary Giulio Douhet had elaborated his ideas of air warfare well before the war, and he continued his warnings via the press. On 12th December 1914 he wrote in a Turin newspaper:

> To be safe from enemy infantry it is sufficient merely to be behind the battlefront; but from an enemy who dominates the air there is no safety except for moles. Everything that is to the rear and keeps an army alive lies exposed and threatened: supply convoys, trains, railway stations, powder magazines, workshops, arsenals, everything.[209]

Today this might seem like stating the obvious, but in 1914 the military on all sides needed to be reminded of their vulnerability to air attack. Immediately after Italy's May 1915 declaration of war on Austria-Hungary, until so recently its prewar ally, Austro-Hungarian airmen vengefully bombed Venice and Ancona, following up with a further raid on Venice in October. The Italians retaliated by bombing Austrian railways and aerodromes with their impressive tri-motored Caproni heavy day-bombers. Douhet had inspired Gianni Caproni to design this big machine and then ordered by him to go into production with it, an order Douhet had no authority to give and for which he was imprisoned. He was later pardoned thanks to the intervention of the poet, patriot and national hero Gabriele d'Annunzio, who had long been a friend and champion of Caproni's. Whatever else might be said about d'Annunzio's egomania, affectations and philanderings, there was no doubting his outstanding physical courage. Despite having lost an eye and been rendered nearly blind in an air crash in 1916 he was not only given the command of a squadron of Caproni's bombers but flew with them on raids, such as one in August 1917 when, at the age of fifty-four, he led a fleet of thirty-six aircraft to bomb Pola in the south of the Istrian peninsula. So far all the Italian Army's smaller scout and observation aircraft had been imported from France; but by the end of the war Italy had developed a lively and efficient aviation industry of its own that Mussolini went on to foster with great enthusiasm. In Italy, at least, aviation and Fascism had begun to be close bedfellows, as Mussolini's biographer Guido Mattioli would observe.

For their part the Austro-Hungarians kept up their own bombing campaign, which in its way was as impressive as the Italians' effort since they were mostly flying single-engined aircraft on long sorties. Even though by the end of the war Austro-Hungarian air raids on northern Italy – including several on Venice and at least one on Milan – had killed upwards of 400 civilians, and Italian air raids had probably killed a similar number of Austro-Hungarians (the exact number is not known), the most decisive effects of the air war in that European theatre probably came from what the combatants learned for future use in terms of organising an aero industry and the military deployment of aircraft generally.

This was certainly true where recognising the potential of fighter aircraft was concerned. The top Italian ace, Francesco Baracca, fell in flames in June 1918 with a total of thirty-four victories. An inspirational figure, he flew French machines exclusively, mainly Nieuports and SPADs, painted with his personal emblem of a prancing horse: the *cavallino rampante*. Many years after his death, when Baracca was an enshrined national hero, his mother presented a copy of this emblem to Enzo Ferrari who adopted it as his company logo and on whose cars it can be seen to this day.

★

However, the theatre of war outside France and Belgium that had the gravest long-term consequences was that of Palestine and Mesopotamia. It is easy enough to see now why the Turco-German attempt to gain the Suez Canal, hold Palestine and Baghdad and retain the Turkish grip on Mesopotamia was doomed. Their lines of supply from the north were far too long, too shaky and critically affected by adverse weather in the winter months, with terrible roads and the incomplete rail link easily washed out or undermined. The steam trains hauling the goods could also not rely on supplies of coal, wood or even water along this increasingly desert route. It was some 900 miles by rail and road from Constantinople [Istanbul] down through Palestine to Beersheba, their base for the Canal campaign. Added to that, in the northeast Russian troops began crossing the Ottoman border from around the Caspian, marching south to harass the Turks holding Baghdad. Yet in the early months of 1916, following the humiliating rout of the Entente forces in Gallipoli and the Dardanelles, it is understandable that the Germans and Turks fancied their chances of success.

The Germans began their Suez campaign in early 1915 and soon acquired an aerial presence with fourteen two-seater Rumpler C.1s, 'tropicalised' for desert use as best they could be with enlarged radiators. They were facing the British Canal defence forces, some of whom (like W. E. Johns) had been withdrawn there after the retreat from Gallipoli, and others who were fresh reinforcements. Compared to the Germans, reliant on their creaking rail-and-road link, the British were well supplied. They were already laying a railway with a twelve-inch cast-iron water pipe running beside it from Ismailia across Sinai up towards Palestine, and had reached Bir Qatia. Meanwhile, Colonel Kress von Kressenstein had moved his men and two observation aircraft to El Arish, only about ninety miles from the Canal, and carried out a brilliant lightning raid on Bir Qatia, taking prisoner twenty officers and 1,200 men. The Turks had been counting on the Libyan Senussi to divide the British effort by attacking Egypt from the west at the same time, but the attack never took place and Bir Qatia was as near as the Turco-German forces ever came to menacing the Suez Canal directly. From now on, their story turned into one of steady northward retreat. Nevertheless, one of their Rumplers did achieve an astonishing morale-boosting coup by flying the 600-mile round trip from El Arish to Cairo, where the crew bombed the railway station and took various aerial photos, including one of the Pyramids at Giza.

Despite the setback at Bir Qatia, the British went on building the railway across Sinai at the rate of over 700 yards a day and reached El Arish just before Christmas 1916. They were soon in Khan Yunes and threatening Gaza, at which point the German forces must have realised they would do well if they could hold on to Palestine. They regularly sent observation machines back over the long haul to Suez, taking photographs of the British supply chain and doing what they could to harry the troops. By now the military on both sides were learning the techniques of desert survival, including camel riding, and were well aware of the logistical problems involved in desert warfare, the primary one being, of course, water. Any deployment had to be planned with reference to known wells. Aircraft presented problems of their own, including the need for large supplies of petrol and oil as well as spare parts. The airframes were drying out, the wood warping and cracking, while the sand in the air abraded propellers, stripped the dope from the wings' leading edges and blasted windscreens opaque. Both sides managed to maintain a very high level of intelligence using spies and double agents often landed by air and robed à la Lawrence of Arabia, sneaking hither and yon through the desert on various clandestine escapades. This was to become the setting for one of W. E. Johns's most exciting early novels, *Biggles Flies East* (1935), which has Biggles based first in Al Qantarah in the Canal Zone but flying for a German Staffel as a double agent. The narrative is full of the details of a desert campaign that Johns would have gleaned first-hand during his seven months in Egypt in 1916, spiced up with facts about flying in such unforgiving country that he briefly experienced in 1924 when he was in the RAF and spent time in both Iraq and Waziristan on India's North-West Frontier.

Meanwhile, 700 miles to the northeast in Iraq, one of the most humiliating defeats in British military history was imminent as

Major-General Charles Townshend's contingent of largely Indian troops was bottled up in the town of Kut al Amara by the Turkish Army's XVIII Corps. Kut was a hundred miles south of Ottoman-held Baghdad, and the defenders had been trapped there since December 1915. In the following four months various attempts to relieve them had failed in a series of battles the British Army had lost. In April 1916 30 Squadron RFC carried out daily drops of food and ammunition over Kut, possibly the earliest example of supply by air. At the time 30 Squadron contained an Australian 'half-flight' that had been recalled from India to help in Mesopotamia, but it is hard to see what on earth the wretched airmen could have been expected to do with the aircraft they were given. They had two ancient Maurice Farman 'Rumptys' and an even more veteran Maurice Farman 'Longhorn': the hideous pusher-engined contraption with enormous upward-curving wooden skids in front of its wheels to which a forward elevator was attached. What anybody was hoping such ludicrous museum pieces might achieve in a Middle Eastern battle zone is beyond conjecture. They not only had an absolute top speed of 50 mph in an area where desert winds frequently blew a good deal faster, but the machines' antique wing design lost most of its lift in the hot air, to the extent that above certain temperatures neither type could even take off, let alone fly missions.

The Turkish besiegers were not much better supplied and were uncertain of being able to defend Baghdad at all costs. At this point Turkish Fokker E.III monoplanes arrived and began to bomb Kut. A German Staffel also arrived in Baghdad. One German pilot, Hans Schüz, shot down three RFC machines over Kut in short order and brought to an end the British supply drops. This, together with the Turks' daily bombing of the town, led to a collapse of morale among Major-General Townshend's mainly Indian troops. He finally surrendered the garrison and his men to the Turkish commander, having failed to negotiate an abject cash deal for their release using T. E. Lawrence as an intermediary. It was a resounding triumph for the Turco-German forces, and the Germans in Baghdad treated it as being on a par with their victory in the Dardanelles. However, the rejoicing was short-lived because it was here that the Germans' own lines of supply began to break down badly. Aircraft and spares were not getting through on the long haul from Constantinople and, thrown back on its own resourcefulness, the Staffel in Baghdad was forced to become inventive.

After petrol, one of the biggest necessities for maintaining aircraft in the desert was a supply of propellers. At that time these were all made of wood that was laminated, glued and pressed before being accurately carved into the final complex shape. In the extreme desert heat the glue softened, the wood dried out and the laminations began to open up. The German airmen in Baghdad were reduced to making their own propellers from scratch even though they lacked the proper equipment. Improvisation was the order of the day, and they scoured the workshops of Baghdad for anything they could use. They even built an entire aircraft that they later claimed flew remarkably well. Some also taught themselves to distil petrol and to make bombs out of cast-iron pipes.

Their Turkish allies were now being threatened from the other direction by Russian forces advancing down through Persia. Soon the Staffel in Baghdad was reduced to a ratty handful of old aircraft plus a single new one that had managed to get through. It was a copy of a British R.E. type, and the RFC airmen stationed behind the British lines noted this with glee. One day they dropped a parcel of spare R.E. parts on the Staffel's base with a note that read: 'We congratulate the newly arrived bird upon its success. Herewith a few spare parts which, no doubt, will soon be required.' This was only one of a series of jocular notes dropped by the airmen of both sides, echoing those in Macedonia that betokened mutual esteem and a joint recognition of the dangers and hardships that operations in such extreme landscapes offered. Hans Schüz, who ended the war with ten victories after flying an Albatros D.III in the retreat through Palestine, observed:

> The limit was reached one day when the English airmen pro-
> posed that we should all land at some neutral spot to meet
> over a cup of tea and exchange newspapers and gramophone
> records. However, we were unable to see eye to eye with them
> in this conception of warfare. Those who know the English
> are aware that, in spite of events like this, they would always
> fight in the air with the greatest determination and keenness.
> No doubt our machine guns and bombs provided them with
> plentiful antidotes to boredom.[210]

It was a repeat of the RFC's proposal for a get-together in Macedonia, the sort of gesture soldiers tend to make only when they suspect they have the upper hand. Thereafter the decline in conditions for their German opponents in Iraq accelerated. The Staffel's few remaining aircraft managed to photograph evidence that the British Army was preparing for an attack on Baghdad in the shape of new encampments beside the Tigris and increased steamer traffic on the river. Unfortunately, the heat tended to melt the chemicals on the photographic plates, which were anyway in short supply, and the results of these flights were not always commensurate with the risks. Captain Schüz's retrospective narrative began to show signs of sheer frustration:

> One request for more aeroplanes and the necessaries of war
> followed on another; but it was a long way to Constantinople.
> In vain did the handful of Germans endeavour to accelerate
> the arrival of supplies. All such demands were rendered
> nugatory by that peculiarity of the Turkish temperament
> about which we have already complained. If it should be
> Allah's will that we should be victorious, then victory shall be
> ours, even without new aeroplanes; but if Allah hath ordained
> otherwise, then nothing can help us. Kismet! All is fate![211]

By the time the British finally attacked towards Baghdad in December 1916 the remaining German aircraft were barely airworthy. Their wings were warped, instruments were missing from the cockpits and the wheels no longer had tyres, the rubber having perished. The aircraft had to take off and land on wheels whose rims were bound with wired-on rags. (It would not be long before rubber was in such short supply back home in Germany that training aircraft were shod with wooden wheels.) Baghdad at last fell to the British and after a hectic retreat the Turkish army reassembled in Mosul only sixty or seventy miles from the Turkish border. Captain Schüz went back to Germany to demand fresh supplies in person and returned in April 1917 with nine new scouts:

> In order to confound the English by the unexpected appearance of a new type, I covered the 300-odd miles from the railhead of the Baghdad line to the front in one day. But even this rapidity was of no use. On the same day an English machine appeared at a great height and dropped a tin of cigarettes with the following message: 'The British airmen send their compliments to Captain S. and are pleased to welcome him back to Mesopotamia. We shall be happy to offer him a warm reception in the air. We enclose a tin of English cigarettes and will send him a Baghdad melon when they are in season. *Au revoir.* Our compliments to the other German airmen. The Royal Flying Corps.' The English secret service had again done a brilliant piece of work.[212]

For the next sixteen months the Germans and the Turks were steadily pushed back as British and Indian troops moved northwards, having already taken Gaza and Beersheba on the way to Jerusalem. They were supported by RFC squadrons under their GOC Palestine, General Sefton Brancker, the man who in 1914 had flown a B.E.2c hands-off from Farnborough to Netheravon. (Brancker was to survive the war only to die in the crash of the

R.101 airship in 1930. He was last heard from via a spirit medium in a séance, describing himself as 'rather busy'.)

In December 1917 General Allenby secured Jerusalem after several battles. The following September he finally defeated the Ottoman army at the Battle of Megiddo and was free to march into Damascus. After making heroic efforts in the air, the remaining German Staffeln retreated to Aleppo and thence flew northwards in stages across Turkey to Samsun on the Black Sea. By then they knew the war was lost and their efforts in the blazing sands of the Middle East had been in vain. News was coming in from Germany of increasing unrest and mutiny there as, inspired by the Russian Revolution and utter disenchantment with the men who had led the country to ruin and defeat, Communists and anarchists fomented social unrest. It must have been a bitter moment for the airmen on the shores of the Black Sea, looking back on the hundreds of hours they had spent in the air, wobbling in the thermals above the endless camel-coloured landscapes of rock and sand and dried-up wadis beneath which they had left so many of their former comrades. Retrospectively, the desert must have seemed to them as Mount Everest does today: a locus of pointless travail. At the same time they were no doubt looking forward with a mixture of relief and apprehension to being back in a changed Germany they might scarcely even recognise as their homeland.

They certainly had no monopoly of bitterness. Prince Feisal, Lawrence and his victorious Sherifian forces were in Damascus when Allenby arrived and had already announced a provisional Arab government. Lawrence had to translate for the Prince as Allenby informed him that this might not be recognised. Seventeen months later, shortly after he had proclaimed the independent Kingdom of Syria, Feisal was abruptly told that this was null and void and Damascus was to be handed over to the French. Sykes–Picot had triumphed. By then Lawrence was back in Britain on leave, sick with forebodings of the betrayal he knew was in store for his Arab comrades.

★

That story had a curious sequel. In 1920, and with some difficulty after the wholesale demobilisations that followed the war,
W. E. Johns had managed to get himself reinstated on the RAF's
active list. With the recently established rank of Flying Officer he
was posted to the deskbound job of an Inspector of Recruiting
in London. The new downsizing RAF was keen to reinvent itself
with fresh volunteers, and F/O Johns was under strict instructions not to enlist former officers of the RFC, RNAS or RAF. He
was based in offices in Covent Garden and was deeply affected
by the pathetic sight of jobless ex-servicemen living rough in the
city. One day a former pilot from 110 Squadron, who had been
in Landshut POW camp in Germany with him, walked into the
office, having survived a week of sleeping in the crypt of St
Martin-in-the-Fields with a single penny bun to eat each day.
Forbidden to wangle him a job, Johns could only give the man
some of his own cash and send him away. The anger and disgust
he felt at the way neglect was being lavished on these men who
had risked their lives for their country came out in a story
he later wrote about an ex-RFC pilot who decided to live a
postwar life of crime in order to give the proceeds to needy ex-
servicemen. So much for Lloyd George's ringing promise of 'a
land fit for heroes to live in'. Johns's mistrust and contempt for
politicians became yet more deeply ingrained.

One day in August 1922 a potential recruit walked in to whom
Johns took an instant dislike. He was thin, pale-faced and
somehow arrogant. He gave his name as Ross but failed to
provide a birth certificate so Johns sent him away to get the nec-
essary documents and meanwhile contacted Somerset House.
This check confirmed that the man's identity was false, so when
Ross returned Johns quite rightly rejected him. He came back
within an hour in the company of a messenger from the Air
Ministry bearing an order for Ross's enlistment. Reluctantly,
Johns sent him upstairs for the obligatory medical inspection,

but one look at the scars on Ross's back was enough for the doctor to turn the man down on medical grounds. He was all too plainly not of the calibre needed for the rejuvenated RAF, since apart from anything else he was already thirty-four. This time the Air Ministry sent its own doctor to the Covent Garden depot to sign Ross's medical form. Furious at this high-handed treatment, Johns complained to his own CO who simply told him that he had just rejected Lawrence of Arabia, so he might as well shut up if he wished to keep his job. There was nothing anybody could do. The Chief of Air Staff, Sir Hugh Trenchard himself, had facilitated the whole process of smuggling Lawrence into the RAF disguised as Aircraftsman Ross, and that was that.[213]

Johns never forgot this lesson in military realpolitik. Together with his wartime experiences it no doubt accounted for the deep scepticism of his later editorials in *Popular Flying* and elsewhere when commenting on official pronouncements by service chiefs and politicians. In some ways his belligerent advocacy for a properly prepared British air response to Germany's rearmament in the 1930s had something in common with Noel Pemberton Billings's denunciations and warnings in the House of Commons during the First World War. Though vastly different in character, both ex-pilots were unafraid of men in gold braid and had admirably clear vision and opinions when it came to understanding air power and its consequences.

CHAPTER 12

# POSTSCRIPT

———

A T THE END of a book about the beginnings of the Royal
Flying Corps and the Royal Air Force a century ago it is
impossible to prevent a valedictory note from sidling in. After
1918 a little over two decades of comparative decline would pass
before the hastily expanded RAF reached its illustrious peak
during the Second World War. There followed a further thirty-
odd years when it remained the most charismatic of the nation's
three services in terms of public awareness and fascination. It
was also at its military zenith in size, importance and the power
it could wield – not to mention its annual budget. Its heyday
arguably ran from the Battle of Britain in 1940 to the moment
in 1969 when Royal Navy submarines took over the duty of
delivering the UK's nuclear deterrent in the Cold War, thereby
rendering Britain's remaining V-bomber force of Vulcans and
Victors redundant as vehicles for Britain's nuclear retaliation.
Between those years the RAF achieved its pinnacle in terms of
global reach, with squadrons stationed somewhere on every
continent and Transport Command flights in the air twenty-four
hours a day ferrying supplies and personnel to and from Britain's
military outposts all over the world.

After 1969 the RAF's story, like that of its sister services (and
especially the Fleet Air Arm), became one of gradual shrinkage
and 'rationalisation'. Although various fighter and other squadrons were still stationed abroad in Germany and elsewhere, and
although a new generation of fast jets had vastly increased firepower up to and including the delivery of nuclear weapons, it

was difficult to overlook that Britain was struggling to afford them, just as it became progressively less clear exactly why it should. Missiles had already taken the place of aircraft in any likely scenario for nuclear war; and even though the USAF's B-52s went on raining down conventional bombs on people's heads in Indo-China for another couple of years, to onlookers it seemed an oddly dated and crude sort of warfare and, given that war's final outcome, ineffective. In Britain, at any rate, there was no ignoring that the twin constraints of diminishing budgets and a less obvious role for its many aircraft were foreshadowing a much reduced future for the RAF.

This process of shrinkage accelerated after the formal death of the Soviet Union on Christmas Day 1991 and has inexorably continued until within today's RAF there are pessimists who unattributably (and sotto voce) foresee the effective end of the service that has done so much to shape British – and world – history over the last hundred years. They believe the RAF today is experiencing what the cavalry went through in the First World War: a sense of its own impending obsolescence, much bolstered by a widespread lack of confidence in ever again getting serious government investment and support. The traditions, the trophies, the mess songs, the memories: all are gradually fading from view as the names of those men to whom they once meant everything appear on the Obituaries page of their squadron association's newsletter. (*Hurrah for the next man that dies!*) Even the jaunty slang and studied understatement have been displaced by a grim defence-industry babble riddled with acronyms and transatlantic business jargon. Of course (they concede) the RAF will survive in a nominal sense as a rump force 'flying' drones, together with some military transports, a handful of AEW&C (airborne early warning and control) aircraft, the odd tanker, a few squadrons of fourth- and fifth-generation fast jets plus a scattering of helicopters. But it will never go back to being what it so gloriously was for those three decades at its apogee: an international byword for flair and competence. Having once displaced horses, the pilot is now himself being elbowed out by aerial robots as his service ineluctably heads for a 'fully pilotless offensive capability' – a change that will be welcomed in the corridors of Whitehall with champagne and cheers because of the massive savings, especially in personnel and pensions. Ironically, it is almost exactly what a former Minister of Aviation, Duncan Sandys, envisioned in his notorious cost-cutting White Paper of 1957, except at that time it was missiles rather than drones he was hoping would make aircraft redundant.

This depressed argument is of course hotly repudiated by many defence experts who regard both the RAF and the pilot as irreplaceable. However, it does hinge on the undeniable fact that neither Britain nor its military any longer have the international political clout they once had. Any likely future call upon Britain's armed forces will come from the treaty obligations the UK has with NATO – itself something of a Cold War fossil – and other allies, rather than from a call to arms as a truly independent instrument of Westminster's will. Gone for ever are the days of Britain picking its own fight and off its own bat sending the RAF to dominate the airspace above a foreign battlefield. The world is no longer like that, and Britain certainly isn't. There remains intact the one sacred obligation that falls to any Prime Minister: that of ensuring the defence of Britain's shores. Yet even this sacred obligation comes with built-in leeway. As Sir Humphrey Appleby acutely pointed out in *Yes, Prime Minister*, 'The purpose of our defence policy is to make people *believe* Britain is defended.'

There is an irony in observing how history repeats itself. Once the first air war had been won Britain complacently allowed its aviation industry to decline, believing that the 'war to end all wars' removed any immediate urgency for developing more advanced aircraft. In effect, the hideous sacrifice of the Great War was rendered in vain from the moment Hitler's re-arming of Germany began to infringe the clauses of the Versailles Treaty unopposed. In 2015, with its depleted armed forces and public opposition to war, Britain is once again showing many of the same ostrich-like signs: a blind faith in international treaties as if no-one ever broke them; an entirely understandable loathing of war as if that had ever prevented one; and a near-mystical belief that if the worst ever did happen Britain would once again muddle through as on the last two occasions when the nation was bombed and threatened.

*Plus ça change*, and all that; but one definite advantage of today's unmanned drones and vastly expensive modern technology is that at least there can never again be the wholesale wastage of aircrew in both training and battle that in the first air war seemed to be accepted without question by the military hierarchy. It shocks and baffles us still, viewing that crackling bonfire of young men a hundred years ago. Had their lives really no value? The answer in the actuarial sense is no, they hadn't. No parent or wife was ever going to sue the government for negligence, stupidity or other culpability. It was wartime: the state could expend lives with impunity. No-one would ever be held personally responsible, still less in a legal or financial sense. If a teenager was sent into combat in an aircraft he was quite unqualified to fly and failed to return, his empty chair in the mess that night would by official decree be filled with his equally unqualified successor. If a drunken, burnt-out instructor crashed and killed his eighteen-year-old student it was either God's will, the luck of the draw or hard cheese: you took your pick. The era of citizens' rights still lay far in the future.

Perhaps nothing better exemplifies the hundred-year gulf between that first air war and today's Britain than this change in attitude. Wars are no longer popular. Prime ministers who nowadays blithely commit their armed forces to military adventurings abroad more from an abject desire to appease an ally than out of a primary duty to defend the realm risk paying for it at the ballot box. It is difficult enough even to write about war for readers who have no military experience and have known only a peace that has so far stretched uneasily for seventy years. It is still harder to do so at a time when (if the *Daily Mail* is to be believed) prevailing social attitudes can be so anti-military that sometimes servicemen and -women hardly dare wear their uniforms in public for fear of abuse and even violence. It is a contrast so immense with the Britain this writer grew up in, where an RAF uniform was a good deal more revered than an archbishop's mitre, that it transcends any private emotional response and simply becomes a historical phenomenon.

Nor is there an easy way of speaking about the gallantry and suffering that took place on such an epic scale a century ago. As always, the currently alive are fully taken up with their own mortal problems. In addition there is the dead weight to overcome of war's misrepresentation by newspapers, film and TV companies that are inevitably driven more by the quest for sales and ratings than for factual accuracy. Once war has been turned into entertainment, once nursery toys are sent into imaginary combat and PC game warriors take on the Red Baron from their armchairs, the men who actually did the fighting must die afresh. Those who were converted in an instant to rags of flesh and char on and above the fields of France and Flanders vanish behind the ritual humbug of 'The Glorious Dead' every bit as comprehensively as the men slain at Waterloo, who were piled into barges and brought home to be dug into the fields of Lincolnshire as fertiliser. No cenotaphs for *them*. Only those who have actually fought fully understand the nature of this deal; the rest of us can have no idea. Like everybody else, the war dead live on as individuals only to those who knew them personally. And when these, too, are gone they die the second death of Thomas Hardy's poem 'The To-Be-Forgotten' and vanish into blank oblivion, as shall we all. In his 1936 memoir *Sagittarius Rising* the RFC pilot Cecil Lewis made a point of remembering his dead comrades. Of the friend who was blown to pieces in the air that day by a British artillery shell he wrote: 'Pip is dead, twenty years dead, and I can still hear the lark over the guns, the flop and shuffle of our rubber-soled flying-boots on the dusty road; I can remember, set it down, that here on this page it may remain a moment longer than his brief mortality. For what? To make an epitaph, a little literary tombstone, for a young forgotten man.'[214] When that was written Pip was not forgotten; he became so at the moment Lewis himself died in 1997.

Little the airmen of the first air war achieved seems reflected in any discernible political reality today, except perhaps for their having established aviation as a vital dimension of modern warfare. Yet their more benign legacy survives indelibly in the aircraft we fly about the world in and whose safety we take for granted. In effect they were all unwitting test pilots, which is why so many were marked for death as they climbed up among the wires and spars into their tiny bare cockpits and called to the mechanic to swing the propeller.

# CHRONOLOGY OF THE FIRST AIR WAR

1903   The Wright brothers' first powered and manned flight.

1908   Sam Cody makes the first powered aircraft flight in Britain at Farnborough.

1909   Louis Blériot flies the Channel.

1910   Hon. Charles Stuart Rolls becomes the first person in Britain to die while flying a powered aircraft.

1911   Italian army airmen in Libya are the first to drop bombs from an aircraft.

1912   French army airmen bomb Moroccan rebels.

The British Army forms the Royal Flying Corps strictly for aerial observation. The Central Flying School is established for instructors. The Royal Navy forms the Royal Naval Air Service and inherits the Army's Balloon Corps. The Royal Aircraft Factory at Farnborough becomes the official British aviation research establishment under its superintendent, Mervyn O'Gorman.

1913   *February*: German airships are seen over Whitby.

*August*: Sam Cody is killed at Farnborough.

**1914**  *July 28–August 4*: the First World War breaks out incrementally. Britain declares war on Germany on August 4.

*August 13*: Britain's four RFC squadrons of largely obsolete aircraft fly in stages to France, one crashing at Netheravon and killing both aircrew.

*August 22*: The first RFC aircraft to be shot down, an Avro 504, succumbs to ground fire from German infantry.

All the combatants' air forces are beginning to employ aircraft for observation.

*September*: Observation and reconnaissance by RFC aircraft prove invaluable to Allied commanders on the ground in the Battle of Mons and the Battle of the Marne, where the German advance into France is halted.

Aircrew on all sides are using pistols and rifles to shoot at each other in the air as the war on the ground becomes increasingly static and literally entrenched. Various experiments are made in mounting machine guns in aircraft for the observer's use.

*October*: A French Voisin shoots down a German Aviatik: the first successful downing of one aircraft by another.

*October–November*: First Battle of Ypres. An Allied Pyrrhic victory in which the regular British Army is decimated, emphasising the need for rapid recruitment.

*December 16*: German warships shell Scarborough and Hartlepool.

*December 24 & 25*: Two German aircraft drop the first bombs on British soil near Dover and Sheerness. Opposed only by inaccurate anti-aircraft fire, they escape.

**1915**  *January*: Zeppelins bomb Great Yarmouth and King's Lynn.

The European battlefront has more or less stabilised and now stretches from the Channel to Switzerland.

Most aircraft over the battlefields in France and Belgium are still two-seat observation machines but single-seat 'scouts' are being designed purely as fighters.

*January–February*: Ottoman and German forces attack the Suez Canal at the start of a long Middle-Eastern campaign in which aircraft play a major role in reconnaissance.

*February*: British and French troops respond to a Russian request to help weaken a Turkish attack in the Caucasus. The naval campaign begins.

*April*: The Gallipoli campaign also gets under way on land.

First Zeppelin air raids on London.

*April 1*: The French airman Roland Garros in a Morane-Saulnier 'Parasol' monoplane becomes the first pilot in history to shoot down another aircraft using a fixed machine gun firing through the arc of his own propeller, but the synchronisation gear still needs development.

*April 22*: Second Battle of Ypres begins, during which Germans use poison gas for the first time. Heavy British casualties.

*May*: British Cunard passenger liner RMS *Lusitania* is sunk by a German U-boat, causing outrage on both sides of the Atlantic.

The British Army's growing shortage of artillery shells causes the 'Shell Crisis' whose repercussions will help bring down the Asquith government in 1916.

Italy joins the war on the side of the Entente (Allies).

*July 11*: The German light cruiser SMS *Königsberg* is destroyed in German East Africa as the result of aerial reconnaissance by RNAS aircraft.

*July 18*: The French pilot Adolphe Pégoud shoots down his sixth German aircraft and is awarded 'ace' status, becoming the first-ever air ace.

*July 25*: Captain Lanoe Hawker shoots down three German aircraft in one day, earning the Victoria Cross.

A turning point is reached in the history of aerial warfare. Having learned from a crashed Parasol's secrets, Anthony Fokker designs his own superior synchronisation system and installs it in his new E.I *Eindecker* (monoplane). Thus begins the so-called 'Fokker Scourge' that lasts roughly six months when Allied aircraft, lacking synchronised machine guns, are regularly outclassed in the air. The RFC's B.E.2c observation aircraft prove particularly easy meat and increasingly need to be escorted by F.E.2s and Vickers 'Gunbuses' to have much hope of survival.

By the autumn Max Immelmann and Oswald Boelcke, both flying the new monoplanes, have become the first German aces.

*October 12*: Edith Cavell is executed by a German firing squad for spying, causing widespread condemnation of German 'frightfulness'.

*December*: French and British forces abandon the Dardanelles/Gallipoli campaign with heavy losses and retreat to Egypt and Salonika.

Lanoe Hawker VC becomes the first British ace with seven victories, achieved by means of a single-shot rifle.

**1916** *January*: Max Immelmann and Oswald Boelcke are both awarded the Blue Max.

*March*: Noel Pemberton Billing MP's maiden speech in Westminster mocks the RFC's inadequate aircraft and its inept administration.

The 'Fokker Scourge' is effectively ended by the Nieuport 'Bébé' plus the D.H.2 and F.E.8.

*April*: Romania enters the war on the side of the Entente.

*April*: In Mesopotamia the RFC carries out daily drops of food and supplies to besieged British and Indian troops in Kut-al-Amara, Iraq.

*April 29*: Major-General Charles Townshend humiliatingly surrenders Kut and 13,000 Allied troops are taken prisoner by Ottoman forces.

*May*: The RFC in France takes delivery of the first Sopwith 1½ Strutters with Sopwith-Kauper synchronised machine guns.

*June*: Sopwith's prototype triplane fighter is sent to France for evaluation.

RFC squadrons participate in the Macedonian campaign.

*June 1*: At the Battle of Jutland Admiral Jellicoe's fleet comes off second best to the Germans' in terms of ships lost and damaged.

*June 18*: Max Immelmann is killed when his aircraft disintegrates in a dogfight.

*July 27*: Captain Charles Fryatt is executed in Bruges by a German firing squad for trying to ram a U-boat with his merchant vessel, a propaganda disaster for the Germans.

*July–November*: The Somme offensive reveals crucial limitations in the RFC's observation and photo-reconnaissance capabilities.

Simultaneously, German aircraft encounter the same problems over Verdun.

*August*: The Sopwith Pup is delivered to the RNAS in small numbers. The RFC's large order of Pups is delayed and delivered only in early 1917, by which time the newest German fighters are superior.

*October 8*: The creation of the Luftstreitkräfte, the near-independent German air force, from the army's *Fliegertruppen*.

*October 28*: Oswald Boelcke is killed as the result of a collision during a dogfight.

*November 23*: Lanoe Hawker VC is shot down and killed by Manfred von Richthofen.

*November 28*: The first bombing raid on London by German aircraft (as opposed to airships).

*December*: Robert Smith-Barry is posted as CO of No. 1 Reserve Squadron at Gosport to institute a radical new training regime for RFC instructors and aircrew.

**1917**   *January*: Manfred von Richthofen is awarded the Blue Max for his eighteen victories.

*February*: RNAS Sopwith Triplanes appear in numbers and are soon seen to be superior to the German Albatros. Fokker hastily aborts his current fighter design to convert it into a triplane.

The German Navy steps up its U-boat campaign with orders to sink on sight all Allied shipping and any neutral ships heading for British ports.

*April*: This month is forever known to the British as 'Bloody April': the RFC's lowest point when German air superiority is decisively re-established by the Albatros D.III, the skills of individual aces like the 'Red Baron' Manfred von Richthofen and his younger brother Lothar, and the Jasta fighter groups planned by the late Oswald Boelcke.

*April 6*: The United States declares war on Germany, but RFC and French expectations of vast reinforcements of

American aircraft are dashed when it turns out they don't exist. To the end of the war American pilots are almost entirely reliant on French and British aircraft.

*May*: The first raid on London by twin-engined Gotha bombers, the start of a series of raids that will at last lead to the organisation of a proper system of home defence.

*July*: The Smuts Report 'Home Defence Against Air Raids' calls for RFC and RNAS squadrons to have a single command and London to have better anti-aircraft defences, a proper air-raid warning system and three squadrons of fighters permanently on call.

*September*: The Germans introduce the giant four-engined Zeppelin-Staaken biplane bombers in raids on London.

Manfred von Richthofen tests the prototype Fokker Triplane and hundreds more are ordered.

*November*: The Constantinesco synchronising gear belatedly becomes standard for all British aircraft fitted with forward-firing machine guns, well over two years after Fokker's system was pioneered for German fighters.

The Third Battle of Ypres ends with Canadian troops' capture of Passchendaele.

British tanks are used in a devastating massed attack at Cambrai.

The catastrophic defeat of Italian forces by German and Austro-Hungarian forces at Caporetto.

*December*: General Allenby takes Jerusalem.

**1918**    *March*: Following the Bolshevik Revolution, Russia and Germany sign the Treaty of Brest-Litovsk and are no longer at war.

*April 1*: Formation of the Royal Air Force by amalgamation of the RFC and RNAS.

*April 21*: Death of Manfred von Richthofen, the war's greatest ace, with eighty victories.

*June*: Formation of the allied Independent Air Force for the long-distance bombing of Rhineland targets.

*August*: General Haig's attacks begin the Battle of Amiens.

In the Balkans/Macedonia, the Allies break through from Salonika.

*September*: General Allenby occupies Damascus, but Prince Feisal, T. E. Lawrence and the victorious Sherifian forces are already in possession of the city and have announced a provisional Arab government in accordance with British promises, later reneged. Bulgaria capitulates.

*November 9*: Kaiser Wilhelm II ('Kaiser Bill') abdicates.

*November 11*: The Armistice signed between the Allies and Germany ends the war in Europe.

1919   *August*: The first scheduled commercial airline flights between London and Paris begin.

1922   *August*: T. E. Lawrence ('of Arabia') joins the RAF as Aircraftsman Ross.

# NOTE ON THE CLASSIFICATION OF AIRCRAFT TYPES

For the type and marque numbers of British aircraft I have used the format favoured by J. M. Bruce in his authoritative *British Aeroplanes 1914–1918*. Thus the Airco (de Havilland) 4 appears as the D.H.4, the Royal Aircraft Factory's Blériot Experimental 2c as the B.E.2c.

The original Superintendent of the Royal Aircraft Factory, Mervyn O'Gorman, devised his own system for classifying the designs produced at Farnborough. The earliest nomenclature he used was based on pre-war foreign aircraft types, which at least made it clear that at that time Britain was not yet in the forefront of powered flight. It also showed that *any* design at the time could be considered experimental. According to this system 'F.E.' stood for Farman Experimental, after the 'pusher' type favoured by France's Farman brothers, Maurice and Henri, which placed the engine behind the pilot. Thus any aircraft from Farnborough designated 'F.E.' would be a pusher type. Similarly, 'tractor' aircraft with the engine at the front would duly become 'B.E.' for Blériot Experimental, after the monoplane that had first flown the Channel. Any 'canard' types with the tail mounted at the front, such as the Wright brothers' 'Flyer' or Santos Dumont's aeroplane, would be named after Santos as 'S.E.'. However, these early canard aircraft soon vanished from the skies and thereafter 'S.E.' came to stand for Scout Experimental. Eventually Farnborough would also come up with other denominations including 'R.E.' for Reconnaissance Experimental.

The German system of classification also used prefix letters to denote an aircraft's type and function. B machines were unarmed observation aircraft; C machines were two-seaters for reconnaissance and escort duties with the observer/gunner in the rear seat; D were single-seat multi-winged scouts/fighters; E were single-seat monoplane fighters; G denoted bombers; and so on. The numerals used were Roman. Examples of the German style would therefore be Rumpler C.IV or Albatros D.III.

French aircraft, like most British aircraft from private companies, simply had their own type number, letter or name in any combination according to each manufacturer's whim or system. Thus from the way they were styled it is impossible to guess the roles filled by the Hanriot HD.3, the Nieuport 28 or the Sopwith 3.F.2. Hippo.

In addition, most aircraft that saw service naturally acquired nicknames, whether derogatory, affectionate or just whimsical. This was true in every air force and has remained so ever since. Sopwith's Biplane F.1 became known as the Camel from its earliest prototype days on account of the 'hump' caused by the breeches of its twin Vickers guns. Martinsyde's G.102 was known to all in the RFC as the Elephant, probably because for a single-seat fighter it was an unusually large machine. On all sides there was no lack of aircraft with even less flattering names such as 'Killer', 'Flaming Coffin', 'Spinning Doom' or 'Corkscrew', partly in acknowledgement of an aircraft's known tendency but also perhaps as a superstitious way of taming it by making light of it. 'Flying Coffin' (*Fliegender Sarg, bara volante*, etc.) has been a popular nickname for countless aircraft from WWI onwards. To both the Luftwaffe and the German press in the 1960s Lockheed's F-104G Starfighter was known as the 'Widowmaker', whereas the Canadians knew it more wittily as the 'Lawn Dart'. The more the danger increases, the blacker aircrew humour becomes.

# GLOSSARY

——— ✦ ———

*Some of the commoner RFC slang phrases and technical aviation terms included*:

**ack-ack:**    anti-aircraft gunfire. This was how 'AA' was pronounced in the British army signaller's phonetic alphabet (*see also* ack toc, ack emma, pip emma, Toc H)

**ack emma**:    army usage for a.m. Also RFC usage for air mechanic

**ack toc:**    <u>a</u>bsolutely <u>t</u>urtle (as in: the aircraft turned ack toc)

**alphabet, phonetic:**    the RFC used the army's alphabet, which ran: Ack, Beer, Charlie, Don, Edward, Freddie, Gee, Harry, Ink, Johnnie, King, London, Emma, Nuts, Oranges, Pip, Queen, Robert, Esses, Toc, Uncle, Vic, William, X-ray, Yorker, Zebra

**archie:**    RFC slang for hostile anti-aircraft fire, supposedly derived from a pilot who, on being shot at, shouted out 'Archibald – certainly not!': the refrain from a popular music hall song by George Robey

**art. obs.:**    artillery observation

**Blighty:**    Britain. To 'cop a blighty' was to sustain a wound bad enough to earn repatriation but unlikely to be fatal

**Boche:**    dismissive (French) slang term for any German

**Bradshawing:**    Navigation in the air by following railway lines

**bus:**    RFC slang for aircraft

**chocks:**    big wooden wedges put under an aircraft's wheels to stop it rolling

**CFS:**    Central Flying School

**CO:**    Commanding Officer *or* Conscientious Objector (conchie)

**Comic Cuts:**    the RFC's sarcastic nickname for the army's official weekly newssheet, generally considered to be full of 'hot air'

**contour-chasing:**    very low flying, hedge-hopping

**crate:**    RFC slang for aircraft (the German air force used the same word, *Kiste*)

**dud:**    anything useless or unserviceable or, in the case of a bomb or shell, that failed to explode. Dud weather was weather too bad for flying

**EA:**    Enemy Aircraft

**eggs:**    bombs

**effel:**    wind sock (from FL: 'French letter' or condom)

**Emil:**    German generic slang for a pilot

**fizz:**    champagne, as in a 'fizz lunch/dinner' meaning celebratory

**Franz:**    German generic slang for a observer/navigator

**GOC:**    General Officer Commanding

**gone west:**    dead

**gong:**    a medal

**HA:**    Hostile Aircraft

**Harry Tate:**    RFC rhyming slang for the R.E.8 aircraft. Harry Tate was a popular music hall comedian, the Harry Tate a less popular aircraft

**hate:**    a 'hate' was a bout of enemy shelling, as in 'the usual evening hate'

**HE:**    Home Establishment (i.e. Britain) *or* High Explosive

| | |
|---|---|
| **HD:** | Home Defence |
| **hot air:** | a politer alternative to 'balls', it could mean anything of dubious truth. It might include any official pronouncement, a chaplain's (or padre's) sermon, a commanding officer's pep talk or an airman's boasts about his combat or amatory prowess |
| **Hun:** | *either* any German *or* a British trainee pilot. Usually more dismissively jocular than seriously derogatory |
| **IdFlieg:** | Inspektorat der Fliegertruppen: the German Army's aviation administration arm until the 'Fliegertruppen' became the 'Luftstreitkräfte' in October 1916 and IdFlieg disappeared. Its place was taken by the Kogenluft, *q.v.* |
| **Jagdgeschwader:** | a group of Jastas assembled for a particular task, much like a 'wing' in the RFC/RAF |
| **Jasta:** | Jagdstaffel, a German fighter squadron |
| **Kofl:** | German abbreviation for Kommandeur der Flieger, a rank analogous to that of Hugh Trenchard as Officer Commanding the RFC in France |
| **Kogenluft:** | German abbreviation for Kommandierender General der |
| **Luftstreitkräfte:** | (Commanding General of the Air Forces), to whose office all claims of combat victories were sent, together with witness reports, corroborative evidence etc. |
| **MO:** | Medical Officer |
| **nacelle:** | the boat-like housing containing the cockpit(s) in a 'pusher' aircraft. Nowadays the term is used for the external aerodynamic pods on aircraft that house engines, fuel, radar equipment etc. |
| **pancake:** | either a noun or verb usually describing a |

|  | stalled aircraft dropping more or less flat to the ground or water from a few feet up |
|---|---|
| **PBI**: | Poor Bloody Infantry: how RFC airmen thought of their earthbound colleagues |
| **pills**: | bombs |
| **pip emma**: | army usage for p.m. |
| **planes**: | an aircraft's wings |
| **Quirk**: | the B.E.2c |
| **radial engine**: | a stationary engine whose cylinders are arranged in a circle about its revolving crankshaft |
| **RAMC**: | Royal Army Medical Corps |
| **Rumpty, Rumpity or Rumpety**: | the Maurice Farman M.F.11 |
| **rotary engine**: | one that revolves about its fixed crankshaft |
| **sheds**: | 'the sheds' was the usual name for an airfield's hangars |
| **show**: | 'a show' was a sortie or mission, as in 'a dawn show' or 'a good/bad show'. Clearly derived from the theatre or music hall |
| **split-arse turn**: | usually any very abrupt turn whose centrifugal force is likely to separate a pilot's nether cheeks, but sometimes applied to a particular kind of turn resembling a reversed Immelmann |
| **Staffel**: | the German equivalent of a squadron |
| **stunt**: | an aerobatic evolution |
| **Toc H**: | TH, standing for Talbot House in the army's phonetic alphabet. A Christian club and rest house for soldiers founded in 1915 in Poperinghe, Belgium |
| *verfranzt*: | German pilot's slang for 'lost', implying it was the observer's fault |
| **Very pistol**: | often misspelt as 'Véry' (the inventor was American, not French): a pistol for sending up signal flares of various colours |

**volplane**: a controlled downward glide with the engine shut off

**wash out**: either a noun or a verb meaning cancellation, as it might be on account of bad weather

**windy**: unduly nervous behaviour, with distinct over- tones of cowardliness

# ACKNOWLEDGMENTS

———

To this book's dedicatee Chris Royle I owe not merely friendship but many a flight from White Waltham airfield in his shared Piper Cherokee, an invitation to speak to the club there, and the subsequent opportunity to pick the brains of his many friends, some of whom learned to fly 'hands-on' back in the days when the nearest thing to a modern electronic flight simulator was a Link Trainer. Their combined wealth of experience has been of the greatest value in helping me grasp the finer points of aerodynamics. This is true also of my Canadian ex-test pilot friend Richard Bentham and my retired US Navy pilot correspondent Edward Roberts.

I am most grateful to Stephen Slater for the opportunity to examine his beautiful flying B.E.2c replica at Sywell and for permission to use his picture of it, and to Matthew Boddington for spending so much time graciously answering my questions about the aircraft. To Tony Purton I owe my introduction to the Farnborough Air Sciences Trust, as well as to FAST Museum's David Wilson who gave us an enthralling day, including flying the simulator attached to their magnificent replica of Sam Cody's British Army Aeroplane No. 1: a challenging experience I would recommend to anyone, and particularly to pilots accustomed to biddable modern aircraft. I should also like to thank sundry informants at the Shuttleworth Collection at Old Warden airfield as well as at the RAF Museum, Hendon and the IWM Museum at Duxford.

In addition, warm thanks are due the following for the various kinds of help and advice they have so generously given me: John

Farley, Pat Malone, Ian Marshall, Lindsay Peacock, Brian Rivas, Chris Roberts, Richard Robson, Russell Savory.

My long-time friend and editor Neil Belton, my even longer-time friend and agent Andrew Hewson and his colleague Edward Wilson all merit deep gratitude for their constant support over the years.

My sister Jane Stephens and my brother-in-law Michael have been endlessly generous with their hospitality, and I am particularly grateful to Jane for her sane and knowledgeable company on visits to Brooklands Museum and for her introduction to me of Chris Roberts, an expert on the development of airborne wireless at the Brooklands Experimental Establishment during WWI.

Tribute is once more due to the Royal Air Force Historical Society and its Chairman, Air Vice-Marshal Nigel Baldwin. The Society's *Journal* is not only required reading for anyone interested in British military aviation in all its aspects but constitutes an ever-expanding scholarly source.

Yet again I would like to thank Brian Riddle, the Librarian of the National Aerospace Library, Farnborough, for his help. His encyclopaedic knowledge and painstaking assistance have been invaluable to me, just as they benefit all who use this magnificent resource.

The Bibliography shows the works to which I am indebted. Special mention should be made of two particular books on which I have leaned heavily: Ellis and Williams' biography of W. E. Johns and Neil Hanson's beautifully researched *First Blitz*. This is by far the best book I know about German air raids on Britain in the First World War and should be the starting point for anyone wishing to investigate the subject. I would also like to acknowledge various dedicated online forums, in particular The Aerodrome (www.theaerodrome.com), Cross and Cockade International (www.crossandcockade.com) and the Great War in The Air Forum (www.greatwaraviation.com). The late Dan-San Abbott's scholarly contributions, especially to The Aerodrome, are deeply missed.

Lastly, the writing of this book – as well as that of its two pre-decessors – has been indelibly marked by the constant help and friendship offered me in Austria by Carmen Bausek, Helene Belndorfer and Fritz Koller, Christian and Beatrix Horicky, Fritz Kroath, Walter and Waltraud Schobermayr, and Elke and Robert Schuster. Thanks to their tireless support computer and other practical problems have melted away, as have a great many happy hours (and Euros) in Weissl's restaurant and Mayr's café.

In place of the authorial ritual of admitting that even Homer nods I shall simply cite the principle of TUDA: The Usual Disclaimers Apply.

# BIBLIOGRAPHY

Alder, J. Elrick, 'Some Notes on the Medical Aspect of Aviation', in Hamel, Gustav & Turner, Charles C., *Flying* (London, 1914)

Anderson, H. G. *et al.*, *The Medical and Surgical Aspects of Aviation* (London, 1919)

Barker, Ralph, *The Royal Flying Corps in World War I* (Robinson, 2002)

Barnett, Correlli, *The Collapse of British Power* (Alan Sutton, 1984)

Beckett, Ian & Simpson, Keith, eds, *A Nation in Arms* (Manchester, 1985)

Berriman, A. E., 'Parke's Dive', *Flight*, 31st August 1912

Birley, J. L., 'The Principles of Medical Science as Applied to Military Aviation', *The Lancet*, 29 May 1920

Birley, J. L., 'War Flying at High Altitudes', *The Lancet*, 5th June 1920

Bishop, William A., *Winged Warfare* (Crécy, 2002)

Bishop, William A., *Winged Peace* (Viking Press, New York, 1944)

Blatchford, Robert, *General von Sneak* (Hodder & Stoughton, 1918)

Bruce, J. M., *British Aeroplanes 1914–1918* (Putnam, 1957)

Burge, Major C. Gordon, ed., *The Annals of 100 Squadron* (facsimile reprint, Bivouac, 1975)

Cameron, Ian, *Wings of the Morning* (Hodder & Stoughton, 1962)

*Chronicles of 55 Squadron, The* (Naval & Military Press/IWM, n.d.)

Clark, Alan, *Aces High* (Cassell, 1999)

Coe, H. C., 'The Flying Temperament', *The Military Surgeon*, vol. XLIII, 1918

Cooper, Malcolm, *The Birth of Independent Air Power* (London, 1986)

Dangerfield, George, *The Strange Death of Liberal England* (London, 1935, & Granada, 1983)

Davis, Mick, *Airco* (Crowood, 2001)

DeGroot, Gerard J., *Blighty* (Longman, 1996)

de Havilland, Geoffrey, *Sky Fever* (Airlife, 1999)

Douhet, Giulio, *Le Profizie di Cassandra* (Genova, 1931)

Duiven, Rick & Abbott, Dan-San, *Schlachtflieger!* (Schiffer Military History, 2006)

Dyson, Freeman, *Disturbing the Universe* (Pan, 1981)

Ellis P. B. & Williams P., *By Jove, Biggles!* (London, 1981)

Fokker, Anthony & Gould, Bruce, *Flying Dutchman* (London, 1931)

Franks, Norman, *Sharks Among Minnows* (Grub Street, 2001)

Gibbs, N. H., *History of the Second World War*, Vol. 1 (HMSO, 1976)

Gibson, T. M., 'The genesis of medical selection tests for aircrew in the United Kingdom', *RAF Historical Society Journal*, no. 43

Gilchrist, Norman S., 'An Analysis of Causes of Breakdown in Flying', *British Medical Journal*, 12th October 1918

Green, N. D. C., 'The Fight Against G', *RAF Historical Society Journal* 43

Grider, John MacGavock, *War Birds* (Texas A & M, 1988)

Grinnell-Milne, D. W., *Wind in the Wires* (London, 1933)

Hadley, Dunstan, *Only Seconds to Live* (Airlife UK, 1997)

Halliday, Hugh, *Valour Reconsidered: Inquiries into the Victoria Cross* (Toronto, 2006)

Hallmann, Willi, *Ballone und Luftschiffe im Wandel der Zeit* (Heel, 2002)

Hamel, Gustav & Turner, Charles C., *Flying* (London, 1914)

Hanson, Neil, *First Blitz* (London, 2008)

Hartney, Harold Evans, *Up and At 'Em* (London, 1940)

Haupt-Heydemarck, Georg Wilhelm, *War Flying in Macedonia* (London, 1935)

Henshaw, Trevor, *The Sky their Battlefield* (Grub Street, 1995)

Hine, Air Chief Marshal Sir Patrick, *RAF Historical Society Journal*, no. 57 (2014)

Hughes-Hallett, L., *The Pike* (Fourth Estate, 2013)

Hyde, Andrew P., *The First Blitz* (Leo Cooper, 2002)

Imperial War Museum, *Naval Eight: A History of No. 8 Squadron RNAS* (London, 1931)

Jefford, Wing Commander C. G., *Observers and Navigators* (Airlife, 2001)

Johns, W. E., *Popular Flying*, various articles, 1932–8

Johns, W. E., *The Modern Boy*, London, 1931

Johns, W. E., *The Camels are Coming* (London, 1932; Red Fox, 1993)

Jones, H., *The War in the Air, Vol. III* (OUP, 1931)

Kilduff, Peter, *Black Fokker Leader* (Grub Street, 2009)

Kilduff, Peter, *Billy Bishop VC* (Grub Street, 2014)

Kulikov, Victor, *Russian Aces of World War I* (Osprey, 2013)

Lawrence, T. E., *Seven Pillars of Wisdom* (London, 1935)

Lee, Arthur Gould, *No Parachute* (Arrow, 1969)

Lee, Arthur Gould, *Open Cockpit* (Grub Street, 2012)

Lewis, Cecil, *Sagittarius Rising* (Frontline Books, 2009)

Mackay, Richard, *The Royal Naval Submarine Service 1901–18* (www. fylde.demon.co.uk/submarines.htm)

Maclennan, Roderick Ward, *The Ideals and Training of a Flying Officer* (Crécy, 2009)

McAllister, Hayden, ed., *Flying Stories* (London, 1982)

Mattioli, Guido, *Mussolini aviatore e la sua opera per l'aviazione* (Rome, 1939)

Morris, A., *Bloody April* (London, 1967)

Mückler, Jörg, *Aus der Chronik der Jagdstaffel 32 (Deutsche Luftkriegsgeschichte 1914-18)* (VDM, 2001)

Murphy, Justin D., *Weapons and Warfare, Military Aircraft, Origins to 1918* (abc-clio.com, 2005)

Nahum, Andrew, *The Rotary Aero Engine* (London, HMSO, 1987)

Neumann, Georg Paul, ed., *The German Air Force in the Great War* (London, 1920)

'Night-Hawk M.C' [W. J. Harvey], *Rovers of the Night Sky* (London, 1919, Naval & Military Press reprint *n.d.*)

Nordhoff, Charles & Hall, James, *Falcons of France* (Bantam, 1966)

Penrose, Harald, *British Aviation: The Great War & Armistice 1915–1919* (Putnam, 1969)

Pisano, D.A., Dietz, T.J., Gernstein, J.M., & Schneide, K.S., *Legend, Memory and the Great War in the Air* (Smithsonian, Washington, 1992)

Previc, F. H. & Ercoline, W. R., *Spatial Disorientation in Aviation* (American Institute of Aeronautics & Astronautics, vol. 203, 2004)

Revell, Alex, www.billybishop.net/bishopP.html

Reynolds, Quentin, *They Fought for the Sky* (Pan, 1960)

Rippon, T. S. & Manuel, E. G., 'Report on the Essential Characteristics of Successful and Unsuccessful Aviators', *The Lancet*, 28 September 1918

Sassoon, Siegfried, *Collected Poems* (Faber, 1947)

Seibert, E. G., 'The Effects of High Altitudes upon the Efficiency of Aviators', *The Military Surgeon*, vol. 42, 1918

Shute, Nevil, *Slide Rule* (House of Stratus, 2000)

Silbey, David, *The British Working Class and Enthusiasm for War, 1914–1916* (Frank Cass, 2012)

Stamm, L. E., 'Medical Aspects of Aviation', *The Aeronautical Journal*, vol. XXIII, Jan. 1919

Stark, Rudolf, *Wings of War* (London, 1933)

Stoney, Barbara, *Twentieth Century Maverick* (Bank House, 2004)

Strange, Louis A., *Recollections of an Airman* (Greenhill Books, 1989)

*The Times' History of the War* (vol. vii, London, 1916)

Treadwell, Terry C., *German and Austro-Hungarian Aircraft Manufacturers 1908-1918* (Amberley, 2010)

Turnill, Reginald & Reed, Arthur, *Farnborough: The Story of RAE* (Hale 1980)

Veale, S. E., *Guide to Flying* (London, 1942)

War Office, *Statistics of the Military Effort of the British Empire in the Great War* (HMSO, 1922)

Westerman, Percy F., *Winning his Wings* (Blackie, 1919)

Woodman, Harry, *Early Aircraft Armament* (Arms & Armour Press, 1989)

Wortley, Rothesay Stuart, *Letters from a Flying Officer* (Alan Sutton, 1982)

Wyllie, H., Imperial War Museum, document 84/5/1

Yeates, V. M., *Winged Victory* (Grub Street, 2010)

# ENDNOTES

———

## Introduction

1   Source: Henshaw, Trevor: *The Sky their Battlefield*
2   For these statistics see Pisano *et al.*, *Legend, Memory and the Great War*, p.75
3   Johns W. E. *Popular Flying*, June 1936
4   Johns W. E., 'The White Fokker', *The Camels are Coming*. The paragraph quoted here differs very slightly (but interestingly) from the original version that appeared in the April 1932 number of *Popular Flying* under Johns's pen-name, William Earle.
5   Ellis P. B. & Williams P., *By Jove, Biggles!*, p.178
6   Hyde, Andrew P., *The First Blitz*, p.16
7   Clark, Alan, *Aces High*, p.14

## Chapter 1

8   Dangerfield, George, *The Strange Death of Liberal England*, pp.249–50.
9   *ibid*, p.226
10  Turnill, Reginald & Reed, Arthur, *Farnborough: The Story of RAE*, p.41
11  Grinnell-Milne, D. W., *Wind in the Wires*, quoted in Bruce, J. M., *British Aeroplanes 1914–1918*, p.378
12  Stoney, Barbara, *Twentieth Century Maverick*, p.57
13  *ibid*, p.230
14  Clark, Alan, *Aces High*, pp.113–14
15  Murphy, Justin D., *Weapons and Warfare, Military Aircraft, Origins to 1918*, pp.90–1

16  Hanson, Neil, *First Blitz*, p.232
17  Stoney, *Twentieth Century Maverick*, p.109
18  Murphy, *Weapons and Warfare*, p.91
19  Malcolm Cooper gives 22,000 aircraft and 300,000 personnel for 1918, but by then the RAF was expanding rapidly and the date of the statistics is significant. See Cooper, Malcolm, *The Birth of Independent Air Power*, p.xv

## Chapter 2

20  Strange, Louis A., *Recollections of an Airman*, pp.21–2 (with some editorial shortening)
21  Shute, Nevil, *Slide Rule*, pp.35–6
22  Turnill & Reed, *Farnborough*, p.31
23  Fokker, Anthony & Gould, Bruce, *Flying Dutchman*, p.49
24  See Berriman, A. E., 'Parke's Dive', *Flight*, 31st August 1912, pp.787–789
25  Hadley, Dunstan, *Only Seconds to Live*, p.67
26  Lewis, Cecil, *Sagittarius Rising*, p.41
27  See Barnett, Correlli, *The Collapse of British Power*, p.86
28  Johnstone, E. G., in *Naval Eight: A History of No. 8 Squadron RNAS*, pp.115–16
29  See www.3squadron.org.au/subpages/RE8.htm
30  Statistics from Henshaw, Trevor: *The Sky their Battlefield*, p.576
31  Quoted in Kilduff, Peter, *Black Fokker Leader*, p.72
32  Yeates, V. M., *Winged Victory*, p.25
33  Bruce, *British Aeroplanes 1914–1918*, p.574
34  See John Thompson of Northern Aeroplane Workshops www.bbc.co.uk/bradford/content/articles/2008/05/09/sopwith_camel_batley_feature.shtml

## Chapter 3

35  Quoted in Hughes-Hallett, L., *The Pike*, p.380
36  Published in the September 1909 issue of the periodical *The Nineteenth Century and After*
37  Veale, S. E., *Guide to Flying*, p.3
38  Quoted in Turnill & Reed, *Farnborough*, p.40

39   Neumann, Georg Paul, *The German Air Force in the Great War*,
     p.54
40   See Kulikov, Victor, *Russian Aces of World War I*, p.8
41   Strange, *Recollections of an Airman*, p.218
42   See en.wikipedia.org/wiki/Fieseler_Fi_156.
43   Strange, *op. cit.*, pp.112–14 (lightly edited)
44   Woodman, Harry, *Early Aircraft Armament*, p.171
45   Lee, Arthur Gould, *No Parachute*, p.123
46   Quoted in Reynolds, Quentin, *They Fought for the Sky*, p.18

**Chapter 4**

47   Compston, R. J. O., in *Naval Eight*, pp.95–6
48   Lewis, *Sagittarius Rising*, pp.140-1
49   See Barnett, Correlli, *The Collapse of British Power*, p.112
50   Lee, *No Parachute*, p.84
51   Lewis, *op. cit.*, p.96
52   Lewis, *ibid*, p.114
53   Neumann, *The German Air Force in the Great War*, p.195
54   Lee, Gould, Arthur, *Open Cockpit*, p.168
55   *ibid*, p.169
56   Johns, W. E., *The Modern Boy*, 5th December 1931
57   Wortley, Rothesay Stuart, diary entry for 25th January 1915,
     *Letters from a Flying Officer*, p.46
58   Neumann, *The German Air Force*, p.243
59   Cameron, Ian, *Wings of the Morning*, p.150
60   'Night-Hawk M.C' [W. J. Harvey], *Rovers of the Night Sky*,
     pp.17–18
61   Jones, H., *The War in the Air, Vol. III* p.42; quoted in Kilduff,
     Peter, *Billy Bishop VC*, p.51
62   Ellis P. B. & Williams P., *By Jove, Biggles!*, pp.70–1
63   *ibid.* (quoting Johns, W. E., in *Popular Flying*, May 1932)
64   Ellis & Williams, *op. cit.*, p.69 (quoting Johns in *Popular Flying*,
     May 1935)
65   Lee, *Open Cockpit*, p.38
66   Draper, Major C., in *Naval Eight*, p.62. The dead pilot's name
     was C. R. Walworth, the date of his death 18th February 1918.

## Chapter 5

67    Quoted in Pisano *et al.*, *Legend, Memory and the Great War in the Air*, p.79
68    Hanson, *First Blitz*, p.58
69    Quoted in Nahum, Andrew, *The Rotary Aero Engine*, p.22
70    Fokker & Gould, *Flying Dutchman*, p.62
71    Yeates, *Winged Victory*, p.84
72    Lee, *Open Cockpit*, pp.23–4
73    Ellis & Williams, *By Jove, Biggles!*, p.34
74    War Office, *Statistics of the Military Effort of the British Empire in the Great War*
75    Clark, *Aces High*, p.77
76    Rippon, T. S. & Manuel, E. G., 'Report on the Essential Characteristics of Successful and Unsuccessful Aviators', *The Lancet*, 28th September 1918.
77    Wortley, *Letters from a Flying Officer*, p.165
78    Ellis & Williams, *By Jove, Biggles!*, p.34
79    Lee, Arthur Gould, *No Parachute*, p.23
80    Grider, John MacGavock, *War Birds*, pp.51 *et seq.*
81    Bruce, *British Aeroplanes*, p.191
82    Ellis & Williams, *By Jove, Biggles!*, p.40
83    Quoted in Barker, Ralph, *The Royal Flying Corps in World War I*, p.27
84    Quoted in Penrose, Harald, *British Aviation. The Great War & Armistice*, p.213
85    Maclennan, Roderick Ward, *The Ideals and Training of a Flying Officer*, p.12
86    *ibid*, p.77
87    *ibid*, p.93
88    Yeates, *Winged Victory*, p.273
89    De Havilland, Geoffrey, *Sky Fever*, p.65
90    Strange, *Recollections of an Airman*, p.158

## Chapter 6

91    Lee, *Open Cockpit*, pp.57–8
92    Stark, Rudolf, *Wings of War*, p.78
93    Mattioli, Guido, *Mussolini aviatore e la sua opera per l'aviazione*, p.22

94    Sassoon, Siegfried, 'The Child at the Window', *Collected Poems*
95    Wortley, *Letters from a Flying Officer*, p.83
96    Oberleutnant Dyckhoff, in Neumann, *German Air Force*, p.423
97    Lewis, *Sagittarius Rising*, p.137
98    Nordhoff, Charles & Hall, James, *Falcons of France*, p.85
99    Yeates, *Winged Victory*, p.330
100   Anderson, H. G. *et al.*, *The Medical and Surgical Aspects of Aviation*, p.24
101   Johns, W. E., 'The Last Show' in *The Camels Are Coming*, p.191
102   Rippon, T. S. & Manuel, E. G., 'Report on the Essential Characteristics of Successful and Unsuccessful Aviators', *The Lancet*, 28th September 1918.
103   Strange, *Recollections of an Airman*, p.169
104   Bishop, William A., *Winged Warfare*, p.146
105   *ibid*, p.150
106   Reynolds, Quentin, *They Fought for the Sky*, p.176
107   Bishop, *Winged Warfare*, p.38
108   Lewis, *Sagittarius Rising*, pp.231–2
109   Stark, *Wings of War*, pp.54–5
110   Quoted in *Naval Eight*, p.32
111   Strange, *Recollections of an Airman*, p.86
112   Westerman, Percy F., *Winning his Wings*, pp.90–1
113   Lee, *No Parachute*, p.197
114   Nordhoff & Hall, *Falcons of France*, p.215
115   Stark, *Wings of War*, pp.108–9
116   Wortley, *Letters from a Flying Officer*, p.118
117   Johns, W. E., *Popular Flying*, May 1932
118   Lee, *No Parachute*, p.208

**Chapter 7**

119   Compston, R. J. O., in *Naval Eight*, p.83
120   Wortley, *Letters from a Flying Officer*, p.153
121   See www.ncbi.nlm.nih.gov/pubmed/18309913
122   Franks, Norman, *Sharks among Minnows*, p.41
123   Bishop, *Winged Warfare*, p.116
124   Kilduff, *Billy Bishop VC*, p.71
125   Reynolds, *They Fought for the Sky*, p.81
126   Mackenzie, C. R., in *Naval Eight*, p.197

127　quoted in Kilduff, *op. cit.*, p.133
128　Hanson, *First Blitz*, p.58
129　Morris, A., *Bloody April*, p.15
130　Franks, *Sharks among Minnows*, p.113
131　Kilduff, *Black Fokker Leader*, p.8
132　Quoted in McAllister, Hayden, ed., *Flying Stories*
133　Kilduff, *Black Fokker Leader*, p.21
134　Halliday, Hugh, *Valour Reconsidered: Inquiries into the Victoria Cross*, p.145
135　Bishop, *Winged Warfare*, pp.221–2
136　Alex Revell, www.billybishop.net/bishopP.html
137　Kilduff, *Billy Bishop VC*


## Chapter 8

138　Lee, *Open Cockpit*, p.59
139　Neumann, *The German Air Force in the Great War*, p.125
140　Alder, J. Elrick, 'Some Notes on the Medical Aspect of Aviation', in Hamel, Gustav & Turner, Charles C., *Flying*, p.336
141　Quoted in Seibert, E. G., 'The Effects of High Altitudes upon the Efficiency of Aviators', *The Military Surgeon*, vol. 42, p.145
142　Birley, J. L., 'War Flying at High Altitudes', *The Lancet*, 5th June 1920.
143　*ibid.*
144　*The Chronicles of 55 Squadron*, pp.29–30
145　*British Medical Journal*, 27th April 1918, p.487
146　Neumann, *The German Air Force in the Great War*, pp.141–2
147　*ibid.* pp.163–4
148　The March 1917 issue of *Flying* advertised Sidcot suits for eight guineas from Robinson & Cleaver Ltd in Regent Street with the slogan 'Keeps you warm at 20,000 feet up'.
149　Wyllie, H., Imperial War Museum, 84/5/1, entry of 30th March 1916
150　Anderson *et al.*, *The Medical and Surgical Aspects of Aviation*, pp.199–200
151　Wortley, *Letters from a Flying Officer*, p.189
152　Gibson, T. M., 'The genesis of medical selection tests for aircrew in the United Kingdom', *RAF Historical Society Journal*, No. 43, p.11

153  Silbey, David, *The British Working Class and Enthusiasm for War, 1914–1916*, p.44

154  Beckett, I, 'The Territorial Force', in Beckett, Ian & Simpson, Keith, eds, *A Nation in Arms*, as quoted in DeGroot, Gerard J., *Blighty* (Longman, 1996), p.43

155  Rippon & Manuel, 'Report on the Essential Characteristics of Successful and Unsuccessful Aviators', *The Lancet*, 28th September 1918

156  Gilchrist, Norman S., 'An Analysis of Causes of Breakdown in Flying', *British Medical Journal*, 12th October 1918, pp.401–3

157  Stamm, L. E., 'Medical Aspects of Aviation', *The Aeronautical Journal*, Vol. XXIII, Jan. 1919

158  McWalter, J. C., letter to *British Medical Journal*, 7th November 1917

159  Coe, H. C., 'The Flying Temperament', editorial in *The Military Surgeon*, Vol. XLIII (1918).

160  Stamm, 'Medical Aspects'

161  Rippon & Manuel, 'Report on the Essential Characteristics'

162  Birley, J. L., 'The Principles of Medical Science as Applied to Military Aviation', *The Lancet*, 29th May 1920

163  Lewis, *Sagittarius Rising*, p.149

164  See Previc, F. H. & Ercoline, W. R., *Spatial Disorientation in Aviation*

165  Lee, *Open Cockpit*, p.130.

166  Draper, Major C., in *Naval Eight*, p.56

167  Bishop, W., *Winged Peace*, p.38

168  Anderson *et al.*, *The Medical and Surgical Aspects of Aviation*, p.110

169  See Green, N. D. C., 'The Fight Against G', *RAF Historical Society Journal*, no. 43, pp.67–8

170  Lee, *Open Cockpit*, p.142.

171  Stamm, 'Medical Aspects'

172  See 'Injuries and Diseases of Aviation', *British Medical Journal*, 11th March 1916, p.389

**Chapter 9**

173  Lee, *No Parachute*, pp.293–4

174  *ibid*, p.312

175  Penrose, *British Aviation*, p.271

176 *ibid.*, p.57

177 *ibid.*, p.308

178 Hamel, Gustav & Turner, Charles C., *Flying*, p.310

179 Barker, Ralph, *The Royal Flying Corps in World War I* (Robinson, 2002), p.313

180 'Vedrine' (posting 24), www.theaerodrome.com/forum/other-wwi-aviation/54948–parachutes-3.html

181 Hartney, Harold Evans, *Up and At 'Em*, quoted in the above forum, posting no. 19

182 Anderson *et al.*, *The Medical and Surgical Aspects of Aviation*, p.176

183 Reynolds, *They Fought for the Sky*, p.171

184 Haupt-Heydemarck, Georg Wilhelm, *War Flying in Macedonia*, p.131

185 Lee, *No Parachute*, p.95

186 Johns, W. E., 'The Last Show', *The Camels are Coming*

187 Dyson, Freeman, *Disturbing the Universe*, p.27

188 Quoted in Wortley, *Letters from a Flying Officer*, p.35

189 *London Review of Books*, 8th November 2012

## Chapter 10

190 Mackay, Richard, *The Royal Naval Submarine Service 1901–18*

191 Quoted in *The Times' History of the War*, Vol. vii, ch. cviii, p.1

192 Hanson, *First Blitz*, p.22

193 Blatchford, Robert, *General von Sneak*, p.53

194 *The Times' History of the War*, Vol. vii, p.19

195 Wortley, *Letters from a Flying Officer*, p.115

196 Hanson, *First Blitz*, p.122

197 Quoted in Hanson, *First Blitz*, pp.134–5

198 Quoted in Hanson, *First Blitz*, p.59

199 Burge, Major C. Gordon, ed., *The Annals of 100 Squadron*, p.20

200 Quoted in Gibbs, N. H., *History of the Second World War*, Vol. 1, pp.553–4

201 Hine, Air Chief Marshal Sir Patrick, *RAF Historical Society Journal*, No. 57 (2014), p.151

## Chapter 11

202  Lawrence, T. E., *Seven Pillars of Wisdom*, p.101
203  Johns, W. E., *Popular Flying*, October 1935, quoted in Ellis & Williams, p.29
204  Johns, W. E., *Popular Flying*, October 1938, quoted in *ibid*, p.32
205  Haupt-Heydemarck, *War Flying in Macedonia*, pp.53–4
206  See Kulikov, *Russian Aces of World War I*, p.46
207  Haupt-Heydemarck, *War Flying in Macedonia*, p.57
208  Quoted in *ibid.*, p.170
209  *La Gazetta del Popolo*, 12th December 1914 (reprinted in Giulio Douhet, *Le Profizie di Cassandra*, p.244)
210  Neumann, *The German Air Force in the Great War*, pp.260–1
211  *ibid.*, p.261
212  *ibid.*, p.263
213  This author is particularly indebted to Ellis & Williams's biography of W. E. Johns for the details of this episode.
214  Cecil Lewis, *Sagittarius Rising*, p.113

# LIST OF ILLUSTRATIONS

1. Royal Aircraft Factory Engine B.E.2c 100HP © SSPL / Getty Images
2. Replica B.E.2c © Stephen Slater
3. Maurice Farman MF.11 'Shorthorn' © Topfoto
4. Fokker E-III © Hulton Archive / Getty Images
5. Anton 'Anthony' Fokker (1890–1939), Dutch aviation pioneer and aircraft manufacturer © Imperial War Museum / Robert Hunt Library / Mary Evans Picture Library
6. Adolphe Pégoud, LC-DIG-ggbain-14327, Library of Congress Prints and Photographs Division
7. Death of Adolphe Pégoud, www.earlyaeroplanes.com
8. Sopwith 1 ½ Strutter taking off from gun turret platform © Robert Hunt Library / Windmill books / UIG via Getty images
9. Max Immelmann (1890–1916) and Oswald Boelcke (1891–1916), together regarded as the founders of the German technique of air combat © The Granger Collection / TopFoto
10. French airman Captain George Guynemer (1894–1917) © TopFoto
11. Recruitment poster © The National Army Museum / Mary Evans Picture Library
12. Women's Participation in War © TopFoto
13. A downed German aircraft near Verdun. France, 1916 © Photo12 / UIG / Getty Images
14. A dead British pilot lies on the ground next © General Photographic Agency / Getty Images
15. A falling German airman © Mary Evans Picture Library
16. A RNAS Sopwith Pup, N5186 © The Royal Aeronautical Society (National Aerospace Library) / Mary Evans Picture Library

# INDEX

British aircraft types are indexed under aircraft, British (types of).
Foreign aircraft are indexed under relevant country